IMAGES
of America

CERRO GORDO

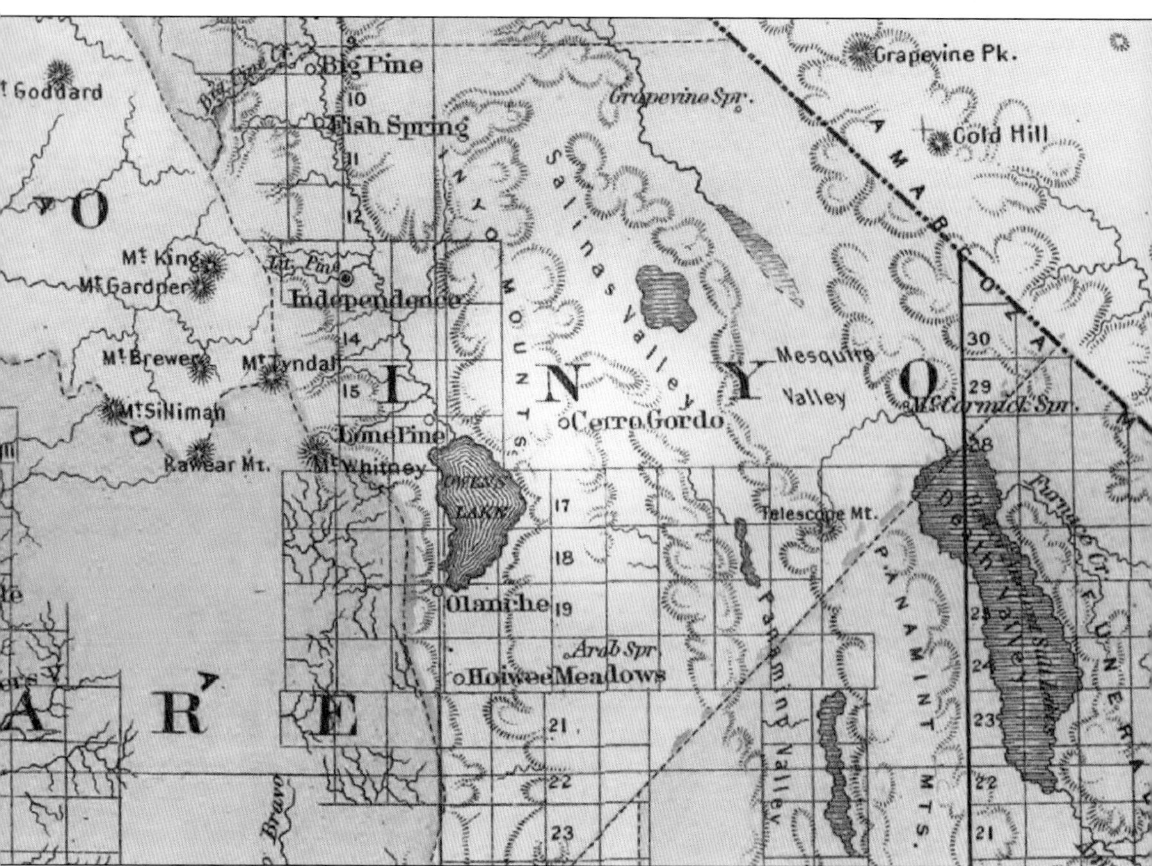

Cerro Gordo is seen in this 1876 railroad map of California prepared by G.W. & C.B. Colton & Co. of New York. The ghost town is located high in the Inyo Mountains of eastern California, between Owens Valley and Death Valley. The town, which went through several boom and bust cycles, is now privately owned and one of California's most authentic ghost towns. It is accessible today via an eight-mile dirt road (high-clearance vehicles recommended) that climbs into the Inyo Mountains east of Keeler. (Library of Congress Geography and Map Division.)

On the Cover: Three men pose outside a wooden office building near the Leschen tram at Cerro Gordo around 1915. During this period, Cerro Gordo underwent a revival as a major source of zinc ore 40 years after it was a rowdy western mining town and a major producer of silver and lead. (L.D. Gordon Collection.)

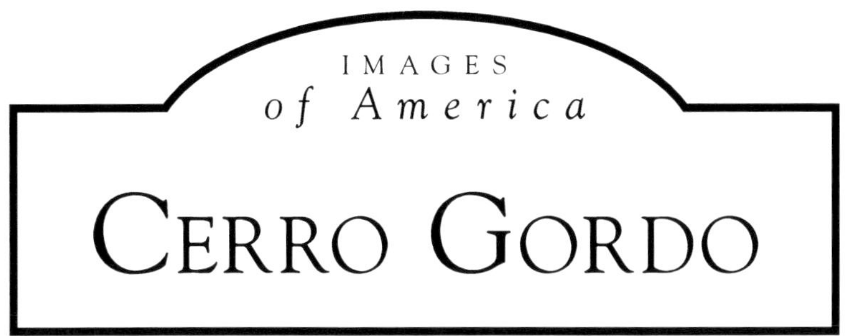

Cecile Page Vargo and Roger W. Vargo

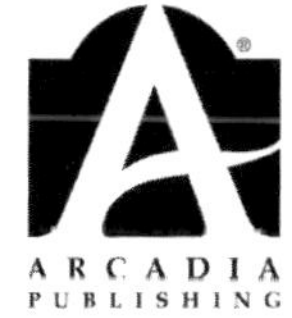

ISBN 978-0-7385-9520-7

Published by Arcadia Publishing
Charleston, South Carolina

Printed in the United States of America

Library of Congress Control Number: 2012933977

For all general information, please contact Arcadia Publishing:
Telephone 843-853-2070
Fax 843-853-0044
E-mail sales@arcadiapublishing.com
For customer service and orders:
Toll-Free 1-888-313-2665

Visit us on the Internet at www.arcadiapublishing.com

This book is dedicated in memory of Cerro Gordo owners Jody Stewart and Mike Patterson, and to Robert C. Likes, who wrote the histories.

Contents

ACKNOWLEDGMENTS

Without the vast photographic collection of Doug Gordon, this book would not be possible. We extend our thanks to him for giving us permission to use his grandfather's archives, and for hours spent in his little apartment here in Southern California trying to make sense of it all. Special thanks go to the late Jody Stewart and Mike Patterson, who kept the dream of Cerro Gordo alive with their restoration efforts and histories tall and true of the little silver-mining town that helped build Los Angeles. Mike Patterson's friendship and open-arms policy with his town after Jody's death allowed us to live the dream with him, and live the histories. Mary Grimsley and Jack Freer graciously filled in the pieces with pictures we did not already have in our collection. Also, we will never forget the late Robert C. Likes and his daughter, Phyllis Likes Fludine, who shared his photographs and histories and always reminded us to "Get 'er done!"

We would be remiss not to acknowledge Arcadia Publishing editors John Poultney and Amy Perryman. John Poultney saw the potential for this book and tucked it away in his files until the time was right for it and Amy Perryman took over and held our hands through the process nearly five years after our original proposal.

Introduction

The discovery of gold in the western foothills of the great Sierra Nevadas brought brave souls across the vast North American continent over remote and rugged deserts and mountain ranges in search of California's golden dream. Death Valley, Owens Valley, and the Panamint, Inyo, and Eastern Sierra mountain ranges were home to Native American tribes who learned to coexist with the harsh environment and live off the sparse land by eating game, insects, reptiles, and available vegetation. Early parties of Spaniards and American pathfinders passed through before the 49'ers, leaving little evidence of their presence except an occasional glyph in a rock and a faint trail.

William Lewis Manly and the Jayhawkers were amongst the fortune seekers setting out in 1849. As their dramatic story of loss of life and survival in the barren valley of death unfolded, legends of gold, lost gunsights, and silver were told. By the 1850s, prospectors lured by these tales began exploring the foothills and valley floors between Owens Lake and the Panamints. A decade later, the mining camp of Darwin and the Coso Mining District were formed. The Inyo Mountains reflecting in Owens Lake remained virtually unexplored.

By 1867, newspapers in Virginia City, Nevada, were reporting Mexican miners in the mountains between Owens Valley and Panamint Valley. An article in the May 14, 1867, edition of the *Virginia City Territorial* touts stories of a Mexican named Bernarda Arambula who came in from Kearsarge country and a place called Cerro Gordo 40 miles east of Camp Independence. The specimens of ore and silver bullion that he brought with him to Nevada's Comstock Lode sparked interest in the activity going on in the Inyo Mountains.

James Delavan, Lone Pine District, Inyo County, signed a letter reported to the *Territorial Enterprise* on November 12, 1867. According to him, Pablo Flores and two other Mexicans wandered into the Inyo Mountains in March of the same year and discovered rich silver and lead mines. Flores's companions were sent back to Virginia City for more supplies, but did not return when he expected them to. Out of provisions, Flores headed to Virginia City himself. There he found no evidence that his companions had ever arrived, and assumed they had been killed by Indians somewhere along the way. The stories he told about his mineral discoveries sparked an immigration of Mexican miners to the Inyos, and the camp of Cerro Gordo, the "Fat Hill" rich with silver, was born. The rugged mountain peak above the mines was notched in the shape of a gunsight, but no one ever paid any attention until the 21st century, when the Cerro Gordo Mines were a faded ghost.

In Camp Independence, a sutler by the name of Victor Beaudry saw his opportunity to cash in on the mines. His general store in the primitive mining camp of Cerro Gordo provided much-needed supplies to the Mexican miners, without them having to travel nearly non-existent trails up and down the 4,000-foot elevation drop to Owens Valley. Eventually, the miners would turn over a share of their mines in return for unpaid bills.

Two years later, in May 1868, Mortimer Belshaw of San Francisco got wind of the silver strike in the Inyo Mountains and hopped on the next stagecoach to the Owens River with his friend,

Abner B. Elder. Together they hiked around the mountain, pockmarked with individual mines and the Mexican *vasos* that smelted the ore. The lead the miners tossed aside showed promise and within no time, Belshaw acquired one-third interest in the richest galena lead ore.

Together, Belshaw and Beaudry gained control of the Cerro Gordo mines. A toll road was built to bring equipment up the precipitous grade and sophisticated smelters were built to extract silver and lead from the galena. A French Canadian by the name of Remi Nadeau brought freight teams with supplies up the Yellow Grade and carried 83-pound silver and lead bars back down, across the desert to Los Angeles, and on to the port of San Pedro. There, the bars were loaded on the steamship *Orizaba* to San Francisco.

Meanwhile, Cerro Gordo boomed with miners, bad men, bad women, and a few families. The sleepy pueblo seven days to the south thrived with the trade of ore and supplies to the camp. By 1872, the *Los Angeles News* reported that, "To this city, the Owens River trade is invaluable. What Los Angeles now is, is mainly due to it. It is the silver cord that binds our present existence."

As the years ensued, legal battles and failing prices of silver made it unprofitable to seriously continue mining. In the first decade of the 20th century, Thomas Boland arrived on the scene, refusing to let go of the dream. The population of Cerro Gordo, kept alive by the mining efforts, dwindled, with as few as five men employed at one point. The Great Western Ore and Reduction Company acquired the mines in 1905, and Keeler, by the shores of Owens Lake, became the teaming center of Owens Valley. Sixty head of animals carried ore-laden wagons over the old Belshaw toll road once again. Later attempts to replace mules and wagons with modern technology failed, thanks to the steepness of the grade. Four Metals Company acquired Great Western Ore and put in the Montgomery tramway with more success, but by that time, the ore body was depleted.

In 1910, Louis D. Gordon, of Round Mountain, Nevada, fame, recognized the value of carbonate zinc ore, which had previously been tossed aside. Under his direction, the improved Leschen aerial tramway was built and Cerro Gordo boomed for the last time. The modern age arrived with Gordon in the form of electricity and an icehouse. Existing buildings were spruced up and a few new ones were built, but the town survived primarily as a company town, with little evidence of the "man for breakfast days" of the 1870s.

A few other companies tried their hand at mining Cerro Gordo's riches on and off until World War II, when all mining was stopped unless it was necessary for the war effort. The "Fat Hill" was left in the hands of caretakers, who watched over the dilapidated town and hoped it would rise again. This book tells the story in images provided by pioneer and modern families with interests in the little silver-mining town, from the early days of discovery through the boom years and on to its present status as a thriving ghost town.

One

A Mining Town is Born

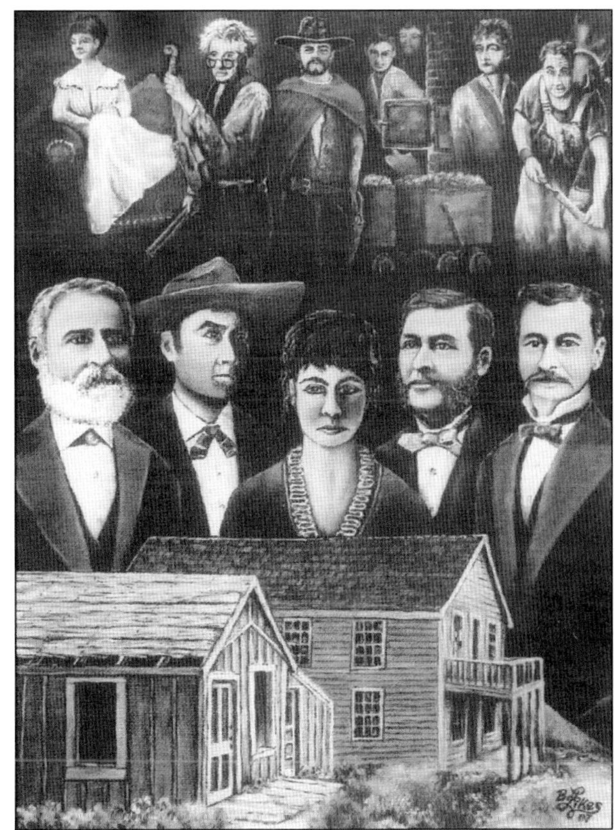

Author and artist Robert C. Likes depicted the key characters of Cerro Gordo in this painting. At the bottom, the Billy Crapo house (left) and the American Hotel (right) are seen much as they were left to the ghosts in the 1970s. Historical figures, from left to right in the first row above the buildings, are Remi Nadeau of Cerro Gordo Freighting Company; Pablo Flores, the Mexican miner credited with discovering the first ore; Lola Travis, a prostitute and the owner of Lola's Palace of Pleasure; mining mogul Mortimer Belshaw; and Victor Beaudry, Belshaw's mining mogul partner and general store owner. The top row portrays the general population of Cerro Gordo and its various professions with a prostitute, a musician, miners, a gunfighter, and a blacksmith. Pablo Flores and young Lola Travis are artists' renderings, as there are no known images of them. (Robert C. Likes Collection.)

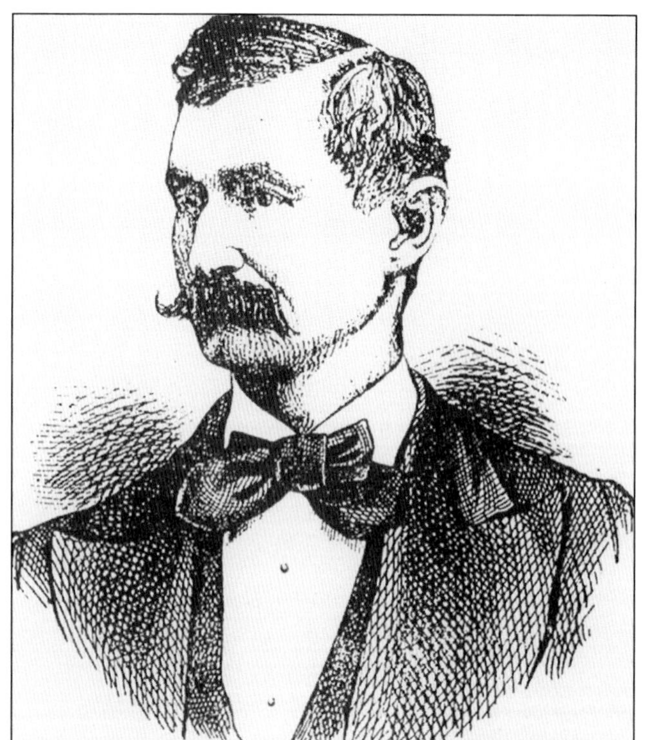

Victor Beaudry, a French Canadian, came to Cerro Gordo as a successful businessman from Camp Independence in Owens Valley. He opened his general store in 1866, providing a place for supplies on the mountain. As the early Mexican miners' debts for purchases came due, Beaudry wound up with their mining claims. He also built a smelter at the lower end of the mining camp, and eventually joined in partnership with Mortimer Belshaw. (Robert C. Likes Collection.)

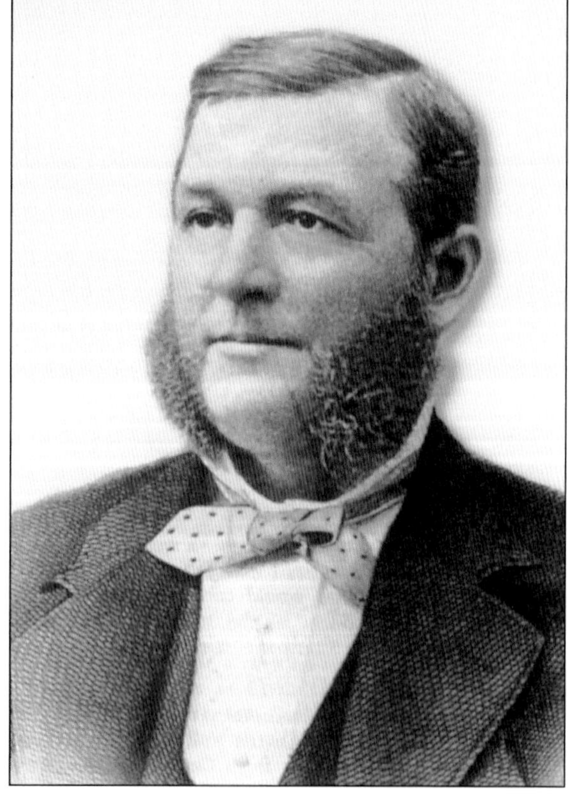

Mortimer Belshaw arrived in Cerro Gordo in April 1868, attracted by the galena ledges rich with 40 to 80 percent lead. By May 6, 1868, he acquired one-third interest in the Union Mine, partnering with Victor Beaudry. Belshaw's mining expertise, mechanical genius, and shrewd business sense gave him control of the silver-mining camp, earning him the title Silver Bullion King through the booming 1870s. (Cerro Gordo Collection.)

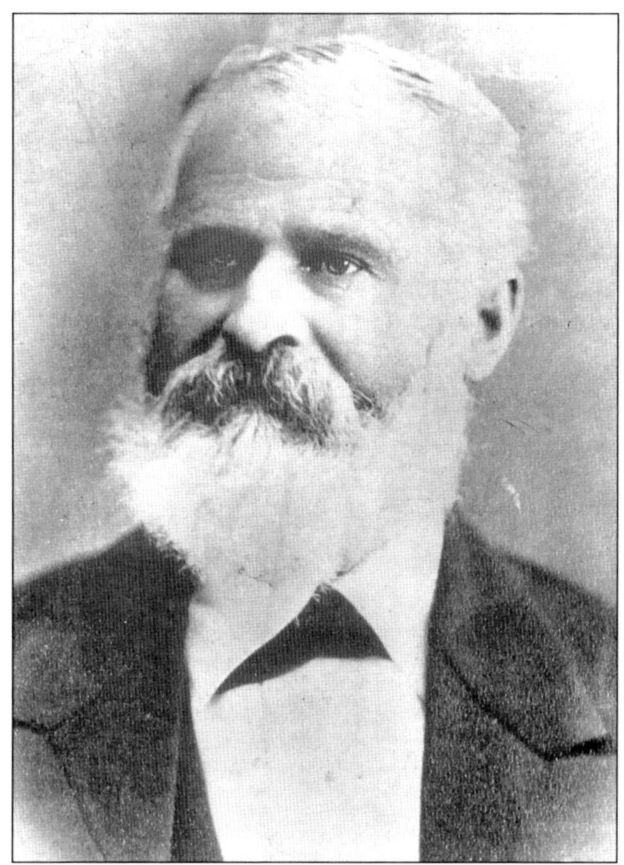

Another French-Canadian businessman, Remi Nadeau, controlled the freight wagons rolling up and down the Yellow Grade Road with loads of 19-inch, 85-pound silver lead ingots. From December 1868 to December 1871, Nadeau's Cerro Gordo Freighting Company traversed the 230 miles from Cerro Gordo to Los Angeles with silver and supplies. While there were other freighting companies, Nadeau's wagons dominated the trade. (Cerro Gordo Collection.)

Certificate of Partnership.

KNOW ALL MEN BY THESE PRESENTS that we, Mortimer William Belshaw, residing at the town of Cerro Gordo, County of Inyo, State of California, and Egbert Judson, residing in the City and County of San Francisco, State of California, and Remi Nadeau, residing at the City and County of Los Angeles, State of California, do hereby certify and declare that we have organized and formed ourselves into a co-partnership for the purpose of carrying on and conducting the business of General Forwarding and Freighting, under the firm name and style of "Cerro Gordo Freighting Company;" that the principal place of business of said co-partnership is situated in the County of Los Angeles, and State aforesaid; that the names of all the persons interested as partners in such business are above stated and signed hereto.

MORTIMER WILLIAM BELSHAW, [SEAL.]
EGBERT JUDSON, [SEAL.]
REMI NADEAU, [SEAL.]

STATE OF CALIFORNIA,
City and County of San Francisco. } ss.

On this seventeenth day of June, in the year eighteen hundred and seventy-four, before me, N. Proctor Smith, a Notary Public, in and for the said city and county, personally appeared Egbert Judson, known to me to be the same person whose name is subscribed to the foregoing instrument, and acknowledged to me that he executed the same.

[SEAL] N. PROCTOR SMITH,
Notary Public.

STATE OF CALIFORNIA,
County of Inyo. } ss.

On this ninth day of June, A. D, one thousand eight hundred and seventy-four, before me, Patrick Reddy, a Notary Public in and for the said County of Inyo, residing therein, duly, commissioned and sworn, personally appeared Mortimer William Belshaw, known to me to be the person described in, whose name is subscribed to, and who executed the within instrument, and who duly acknowledged to me that he executed the same.

In witness whereof, I have hereunto set my hand and affixed my official seal at my office, in the said Coun y of Inyo, the day and year first above written.

[SEAL.] PATRICK REDDY,
Notary Public,
Inyo county, California.

STATE OF CALIFORNIA,
County of Los Angeles. } ss.

On this twenty-second day of June, in the year one thousand eight hundred and seventy-four, before me, A. W. Potts, County Clerk and ex-offic.o Clerk of the County Court, in and for said coun'y, personally appeared Remi Nadeau, known to me to be the same person whose name is subscribed to the within instrument, and acknowledged to me that he executed the same.

In witness whereof, I have hereunto set my hand and affixed the seal of said Court, the day and year in this certificate first above writen.

[SEAL] A. W. POTTS,
County Clerk,
and ex-officio Clerk of said County Court.
je 23-4w

This June 27, 1874, newspaper clipping from the *Los Angeles Herald* is a legal notice of the new partnership between Nadeau, Belshaw, and Egbert Judson, the principal owners of the Cerro Gordo Mines, forming the Cerro Gordo Freighting Company. This allowed Nadeau to expand his freight operation between Cerro Gordo and Los Angeles. The document was drawn up by attorney Pat Reddy, who was well known throughout the Owens Valley for his legal acumen. (Explore Historic California Collection.)

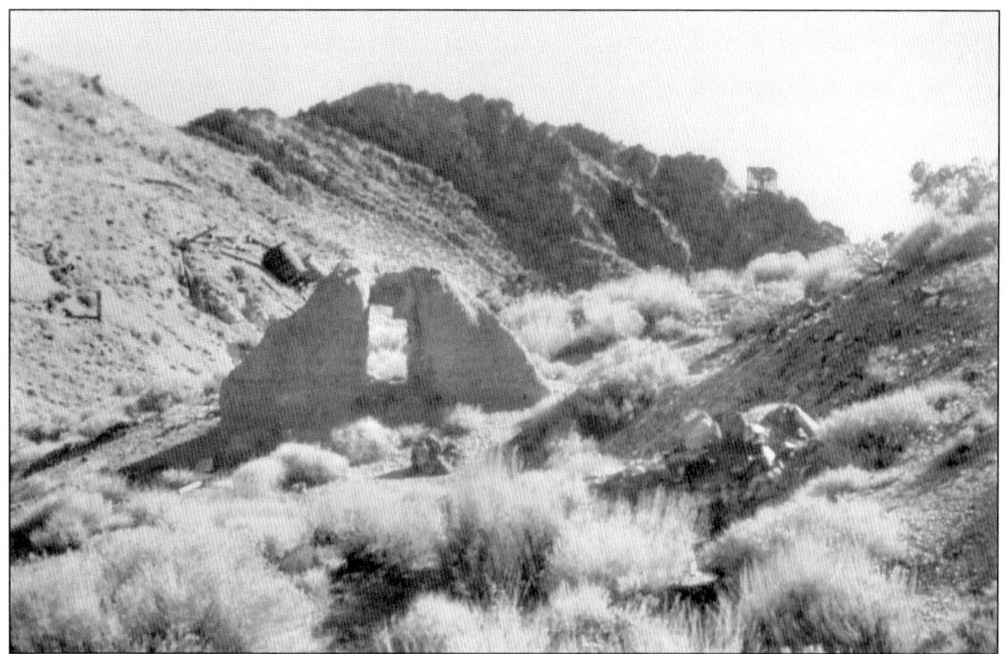

Evening shadows accentuate relics of the varied phases of Cerro Gordo's long and colorful history in this late-1960s photograph. Adobe furnace ruins in the foreground built by Mexican miners in the 1860s contrast against a tram tower on the ridgeline built in the early-1900s zinc era. (Robert C. Likes Collection.)

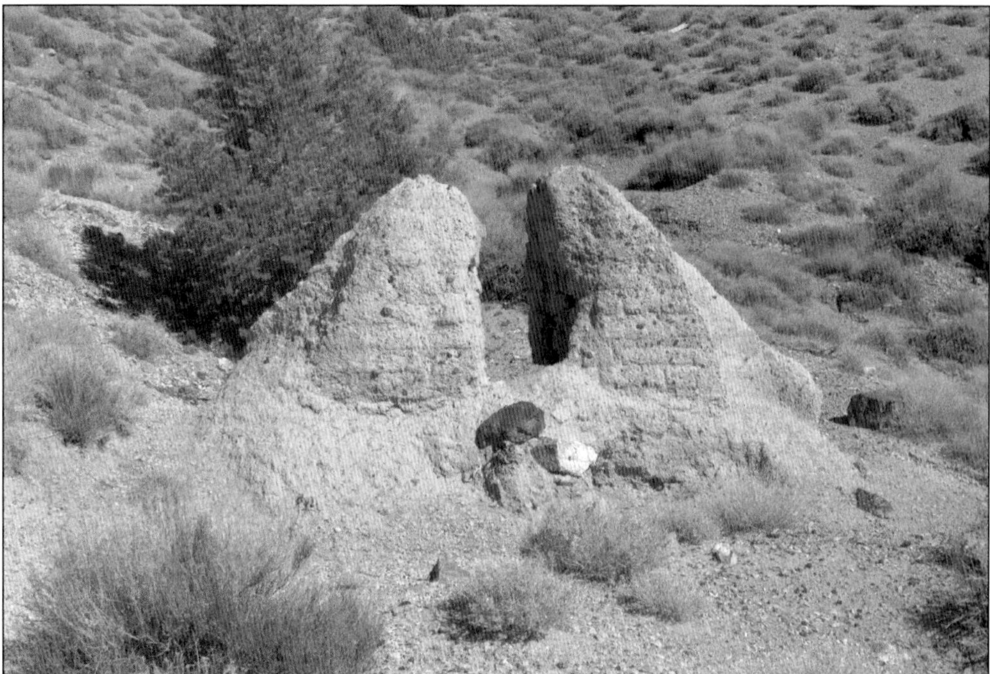

The Mexican miners used furnaces like this one, seen 50 years later, to partially refine (or concentrate) the lead and silver ores into metallic bars or buttons, which were easier to handle and transport out of the backcountry. (Explore Historic California Collection.)

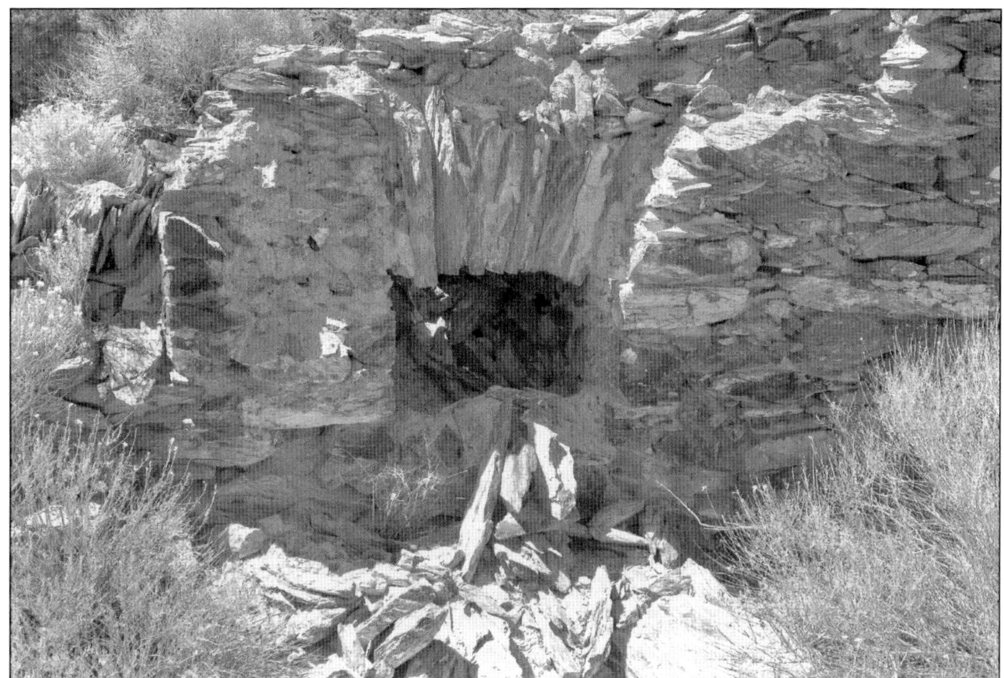

Shown here is another Mexican-style *vaso* furnace built in the early 1870s. Above is a close-up of the loading door area. Below is the furnace, with its vent chimney going uphill. The furnace was obsolete by the time it was completed and was never fired in. Similar furnaces produced slag used in early phases of the ore-reduction process. Modern blast furnaces built by Beaudry and Belshaw provided more efficient conversion from ore to silver-lead bullion than the old style *vasos* could. In the early 20th century, the dark-colored slag piles remaining from the furnaces were reworked to recover silver and lead. (Both, Explore Historic California Collection.)

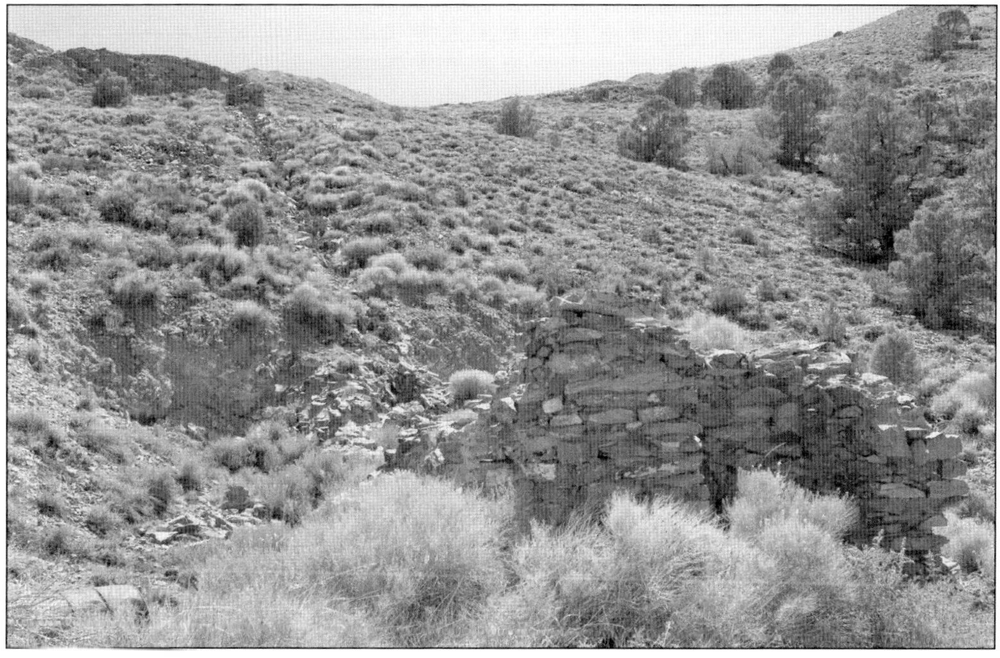

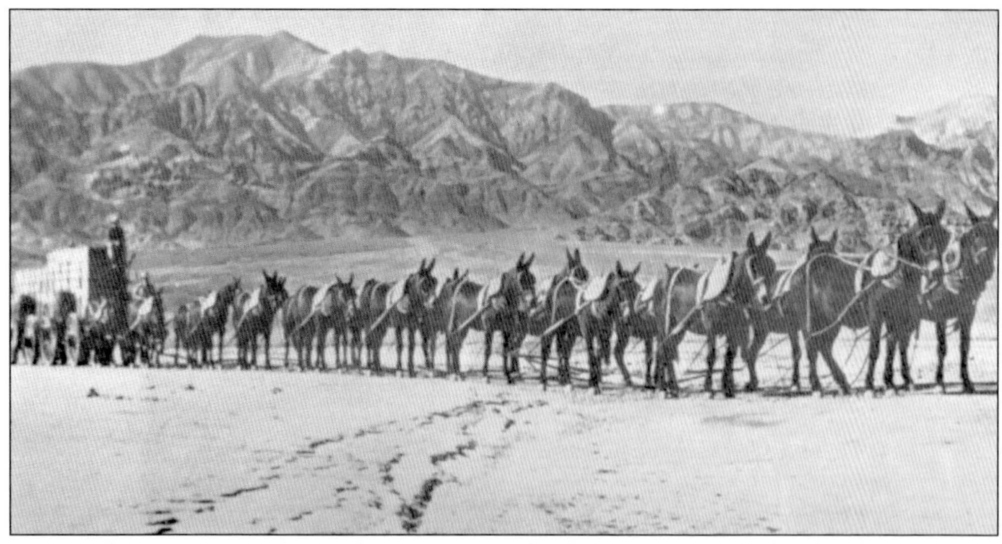

Remi Nadeau's Cerro Gordo Freighting Company landed the contract to freight silver and trade between Cerro Gordo and Los Angeles. His teams of 16 to 20 mules transported 18 tons of bullion across the desert. The 12-day trip included stops at 12 stations to refresh the teams, at intervals of 13 to 20 miles. From 1869 to 1874, two teams operated each lap, with one pair heading for Owens Valley and the other for Los Angeles. (Robert C. Likes Collection.)

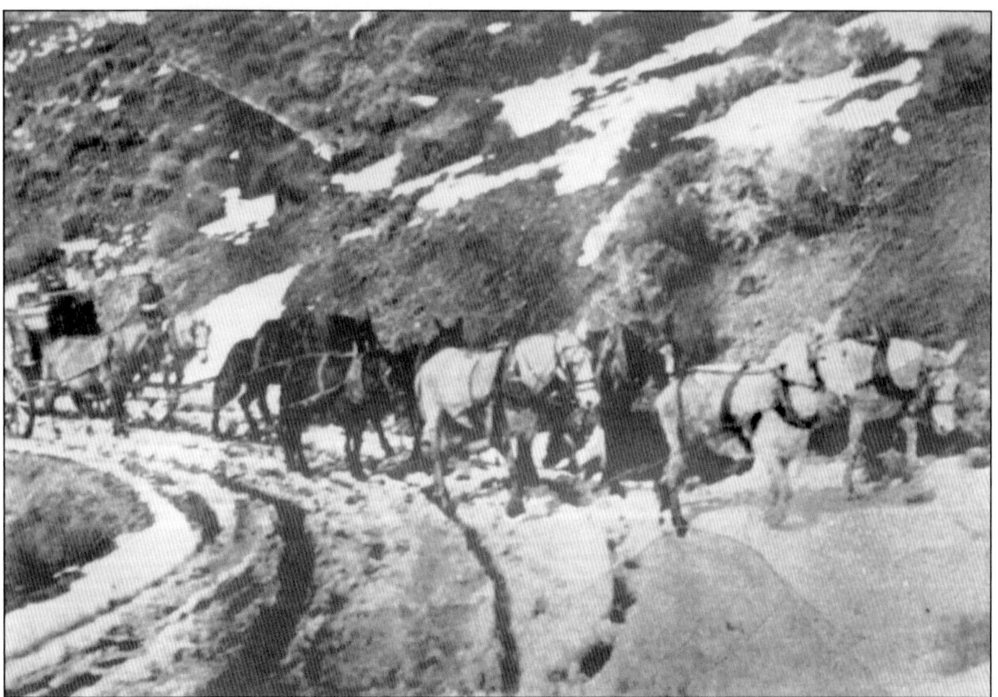

The two animals in front of the wagon are called "wheelers." Owen Dearborn, 17, perches atop one, checking the position of a freight wagon before signaling the team around a turn on the Yellow Grade Road. This is one of many arduous turns along the rugged eight-mile ascent to Cerro Gordo. The route was challenging in the winter, but Dearborn rose to the occasion and arrived safely with his load intact. (Robert C. Likes Collection.)

Tiburcio Vasquez was famous for his reign of terror throughout California, including on the Bullion Trail from Cerro Gordo to Los Angeles. When confirmation came that a stage was robbed in Coyote Wells just north of Mojave, Cerro Gordoans hid all their valuables in flour bins, baking powder cans, and mattresses. Children armed themselves with slingshots, pocket knives, and pipe pieces to rescue the bandit search party, but Vasquez never showed. (Robert C. Likes Collection.)

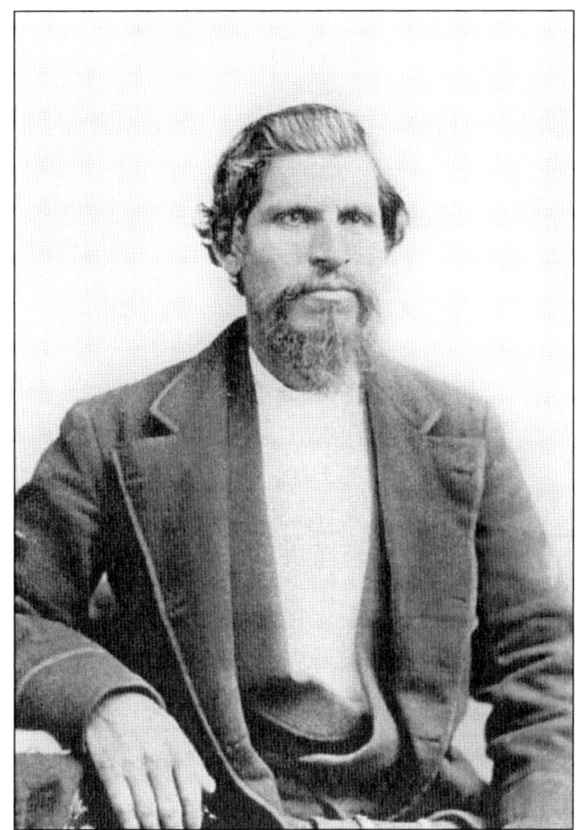

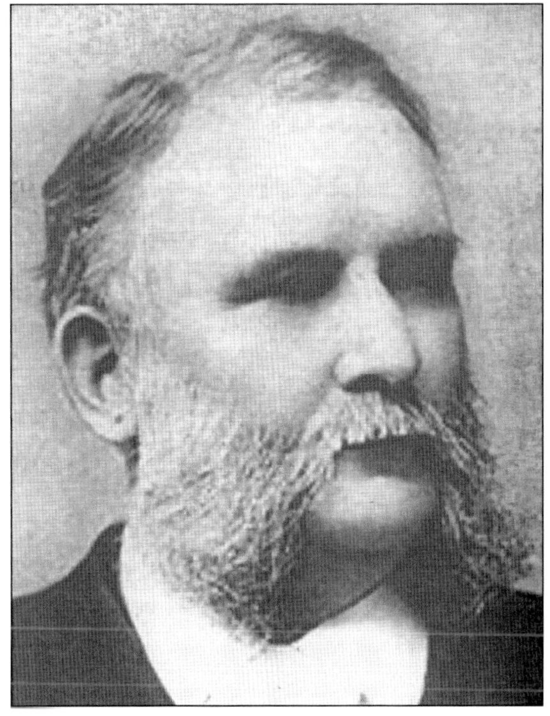

One-armed lawyer Pat Reddy defended Mortimer Belshaw in August 1872 when Inyo County supervisors were asked to buy his toll road and make it free. Reddy won the case, replying, "If it had not been for the owner of that trail practically there would have been no Cerro Gordo, or need of any road at all." In subsequent years, Belshaw continued to call on Reddy to defend his mining rights. (Robert C. Likes Collection.)

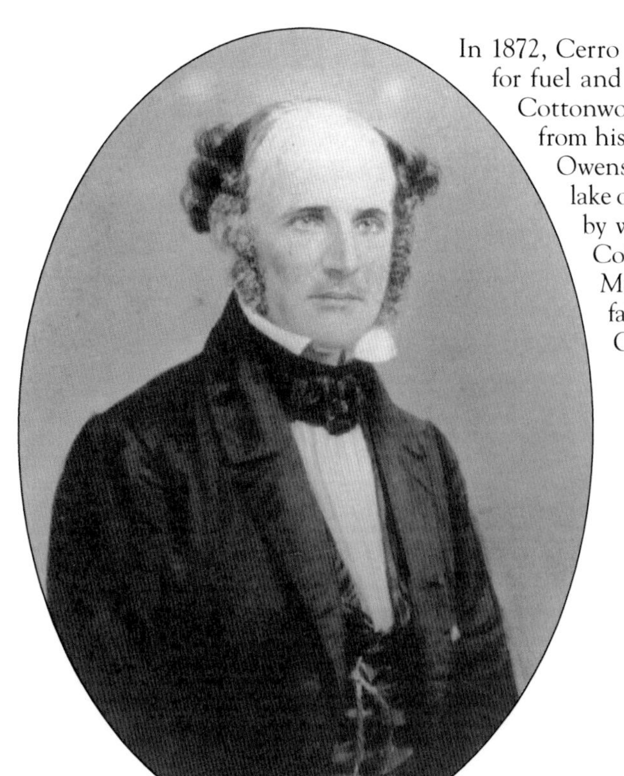

In 1872, Cerro Gordo smelters needed more wood for fuel and Col. Sherman Stevens found it in Cottonwood Canyon. A flume carried wood from his lumber mill to kilns on the shore of Owens Lake. Charcoal was taken across the lake on the *Bessie Brady* steamship and then by wagon to the mining town. By 1877, Colonel Stevens built his own ship, the *Mollie Stevens*, but within six months, faltering mines docked the boat. (Robert C. Likes Collection.)

Prolific gunfights and brawls at Maggie Moore's dancehall and the Lola Travis house earned Cerro Gordo the "man for breakfast" title. In March 1873, Judge John A. Hannah of Inyo County declared war against "these lawless ruffians who with murder in their hearts and the implements of death trapped upon their persons, congregate in public places ever ready to discharge their death dealing weapons upon the unoffending and unarmed citizen." (Robert C. Likes Collection.)

The only known photograph of Lola Travis shows her at 80 years old after she retired from her life as a renowned Cerro Gordo dancehall and brothel owner and was living respectably in Bakersfield. (Courtesy Robin Flinchum.)

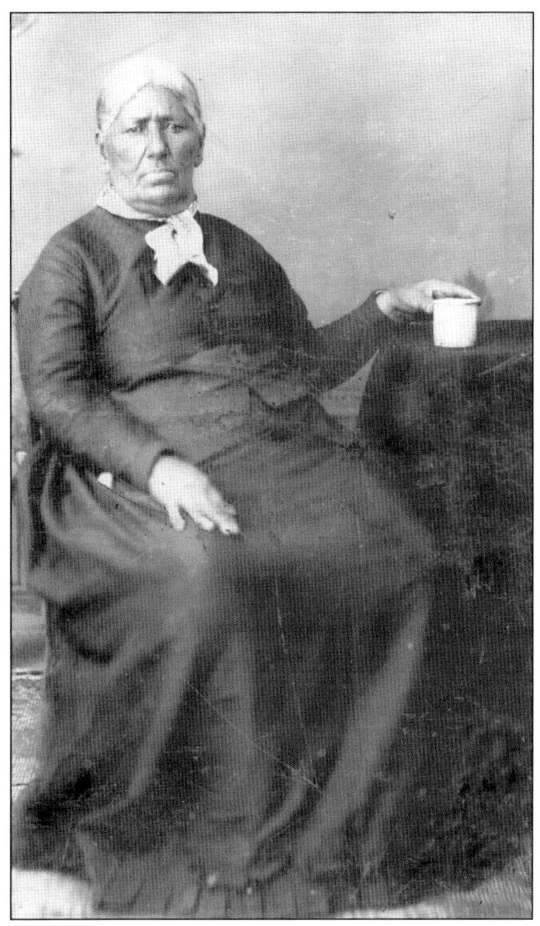

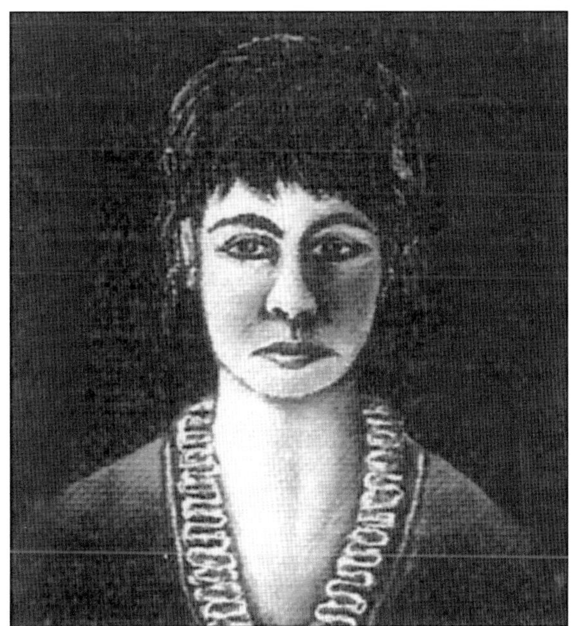

This Robert C. Likes drawing portrays what Travis may have looked like in her prime. Originally from Mexico, she came to the gold country at age four. She was married but became a widow with three children and found her forte in the saloons and dancehalls on both sides of the Sierras and near Death Valley. With little education but a great sense for business, she came to Cerro Gordo and opened up Lola's Palace of Pleasure sometime in 1867. She was noted in newspapers as being a great beauty, who wore gowns purchased on trips to San Francisco. She and the girls under her employment often appeared in local newspaper headlines, as gunfights and catfights broke out often in her establishment. (Robert C. Likes Collection.)

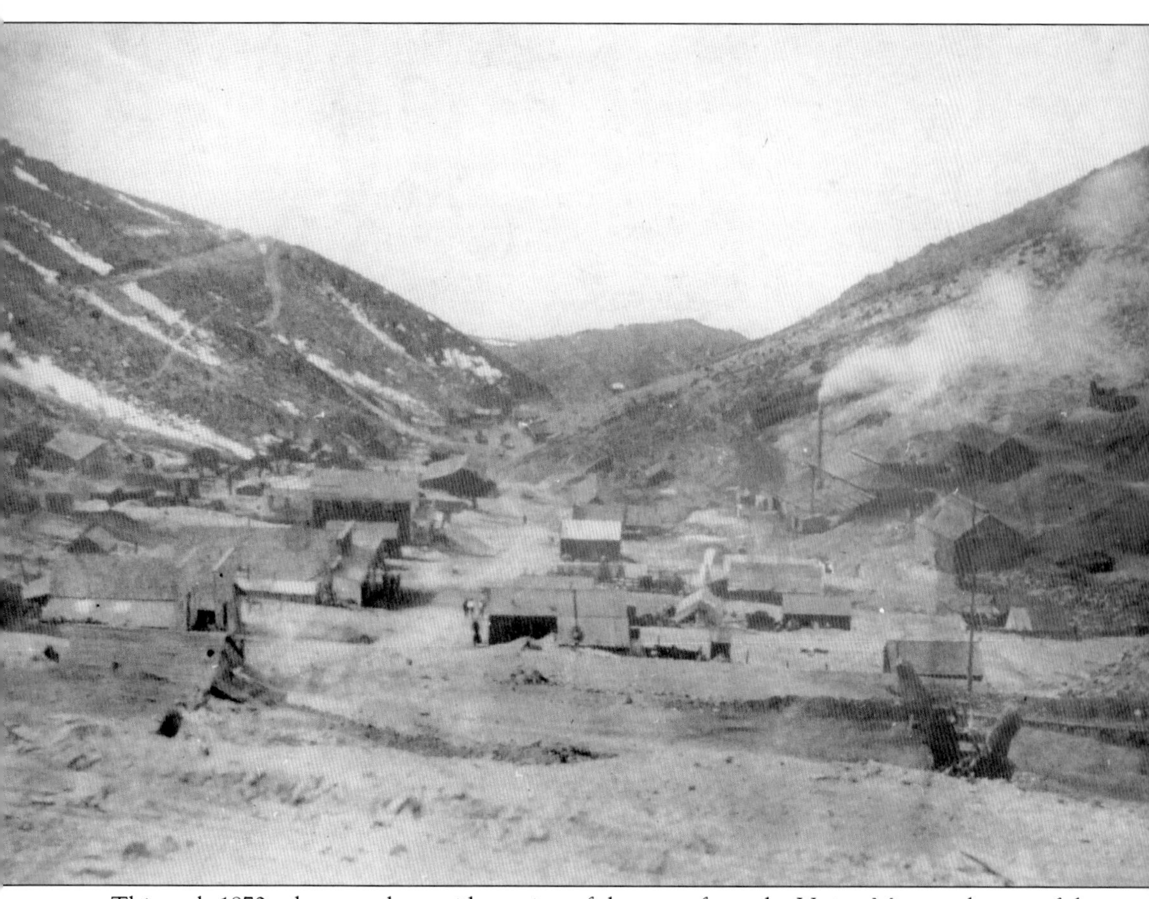

This early-1870s photograph provides a view of the town from the Union Mine at the top of the mountain. At right center, the chimney of Victor Beaudry's smelter shows a plume of smoke. Both Beaudry and the Belshaw smelters usually ran 24 hours a day and seven days a week. The gray skies created from the smoke earned Cerro Gordo the nickname "Old Smokey." The smelters burned charcoal in their blast furnaces, creating a lucrative sub-industry of woodcutters and charcoal burners. (Robert C. Likes Collection.)

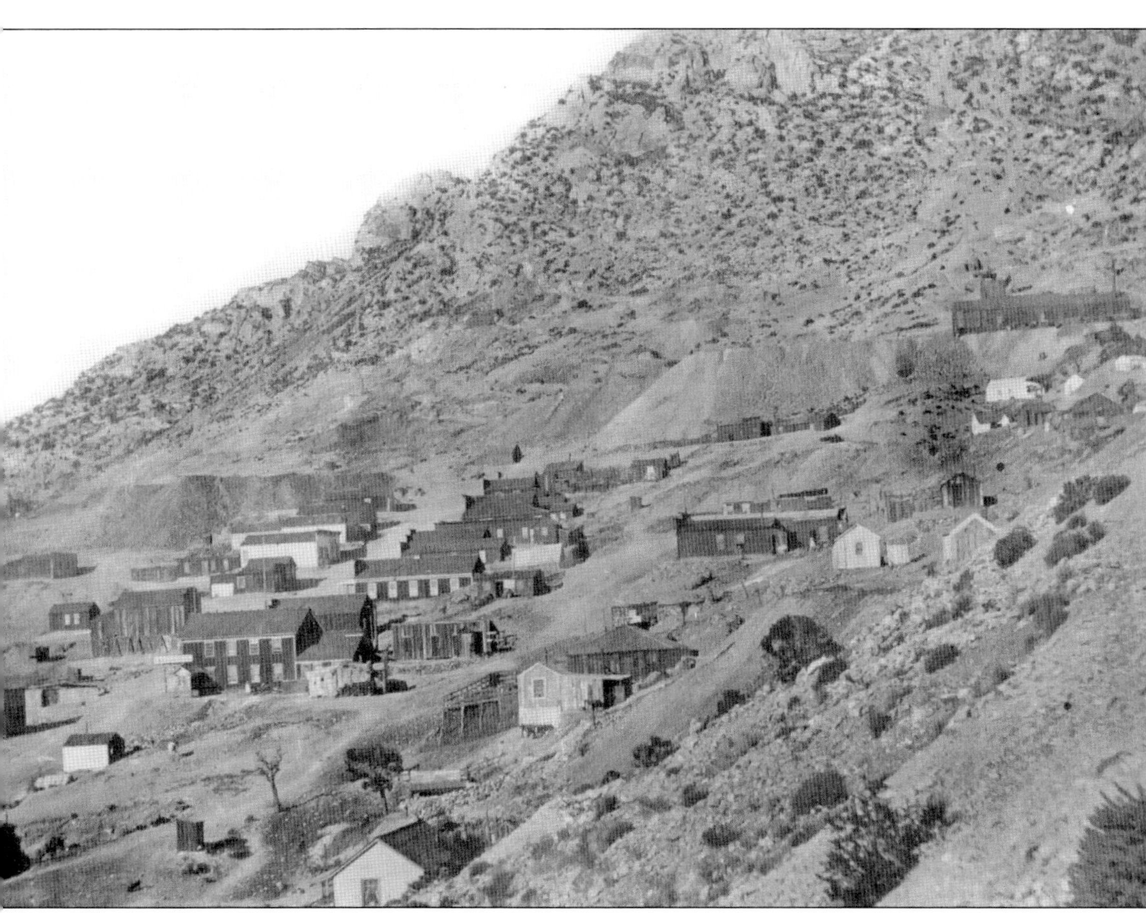

The town site of Cerro Gordo began to boom in the 1870s as silver was pulled out. Saloons, dancehalls, hotels, and various businesses were there for the needs of miners. Primarily a mining town, there were few women and children and never a school or a church. A circuit rider and teacher were available for preaching and teaching to those in need of such things. (L.D. Gordon Collection.)

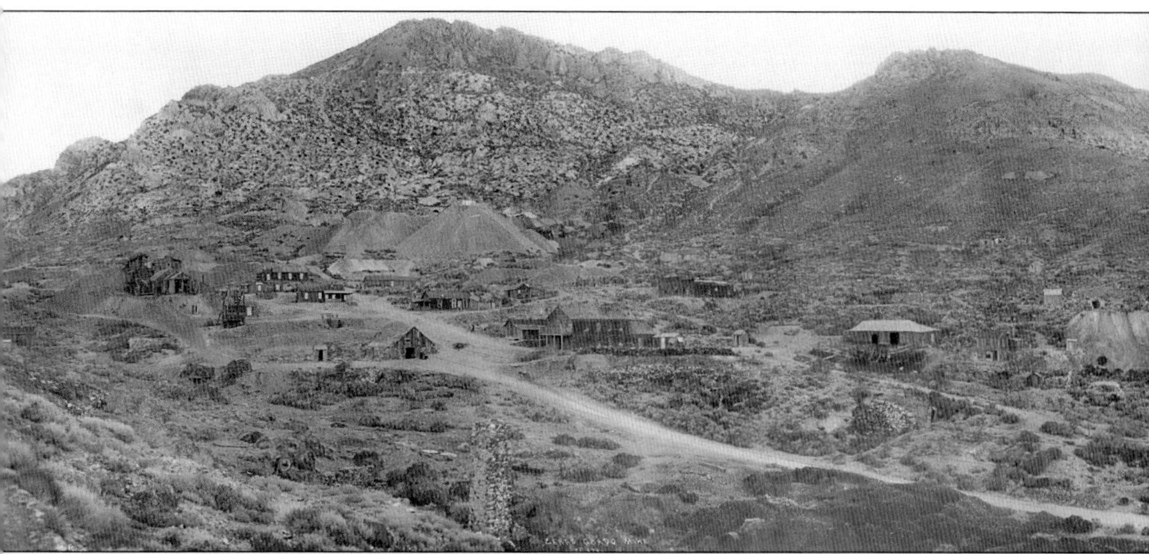

This composite panorama shows Cerro Gordo in the very early 1900s, after the Montgomery tram (far left) was built. Cerro Gordo's main street runs through the center of the photograph. Prior to L.D. Gordon's acquisition, Cerro Gordo was operated by the Western Ore Development

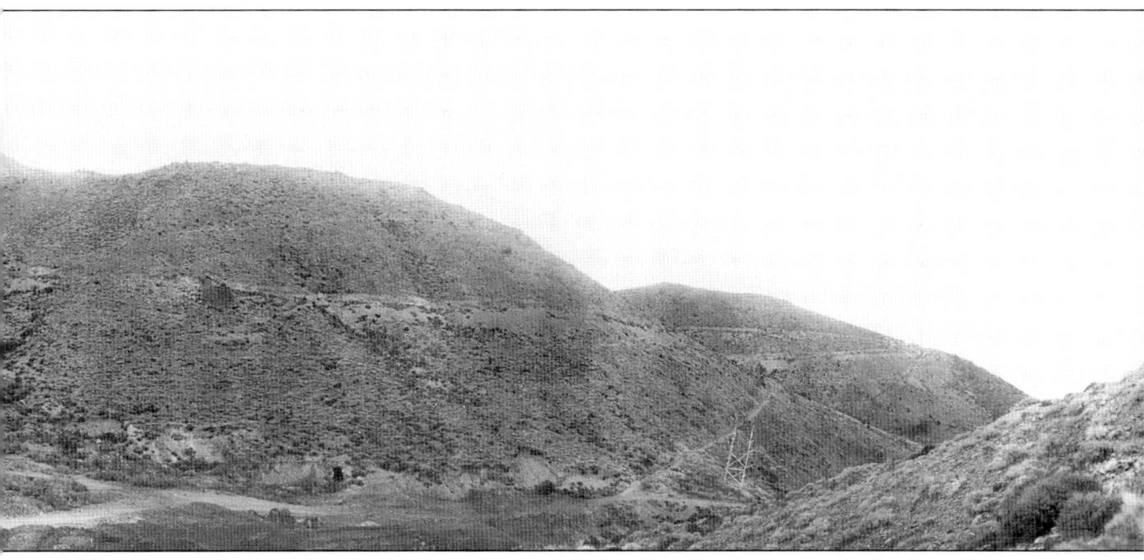

and Purchasing Co. and then by the Four Metals Mining Co. Gordon controlled it from 1911 to 1920. (L.D. Gordon Collection.)

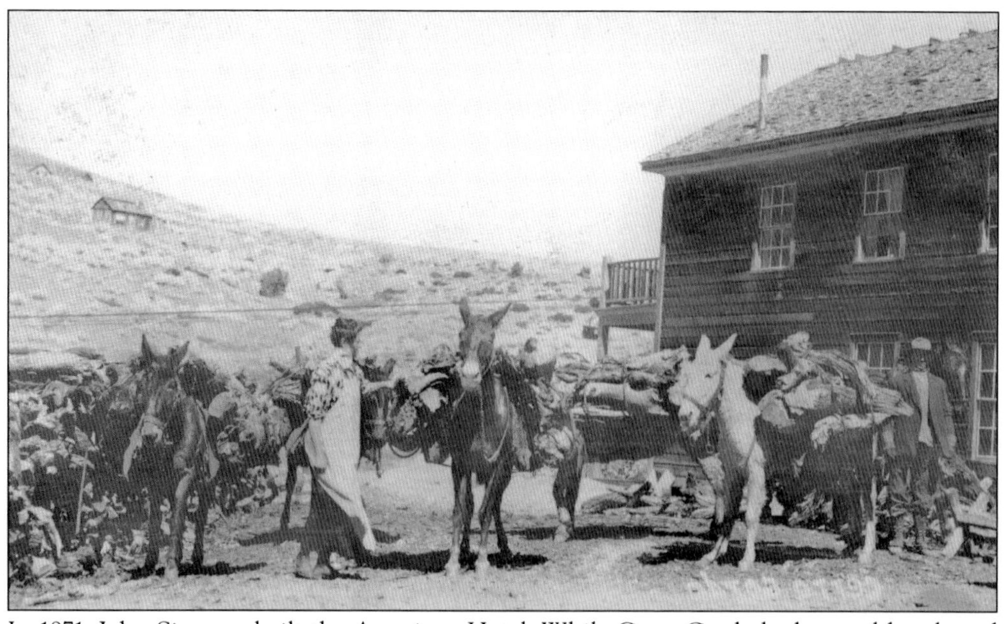

In 1871, John Simpson built the American Hotel. While Cerro Gordo had several hotels and numerous boardinghouses, the American is the only such structure remaining. Here, a hotel cook supervises the unloading of firewood from pack animals. This photograph probably dates from the early 1900s, as a tram cable can be seen. (L.D. Gordon Collection.)

AMERICAN HOTEL,

Cerro Gordo,

Inyo County, - . - - Cal.

MR. AND MRS. JOHN SIMPSON, HAVING established themselves in their new hotel, are prepared to accommodate the public, and respectfully solicit its patronage.

Cerro Gordo, June 15, 1871. je17y1

This advertisement from a June 1871 issue of the *Inyo Independent* announces the opening of the hotel. The hotel operated on and off, providing rooms and meals in the late 1800s and early 1900s. (Explore Historic California Collection.)

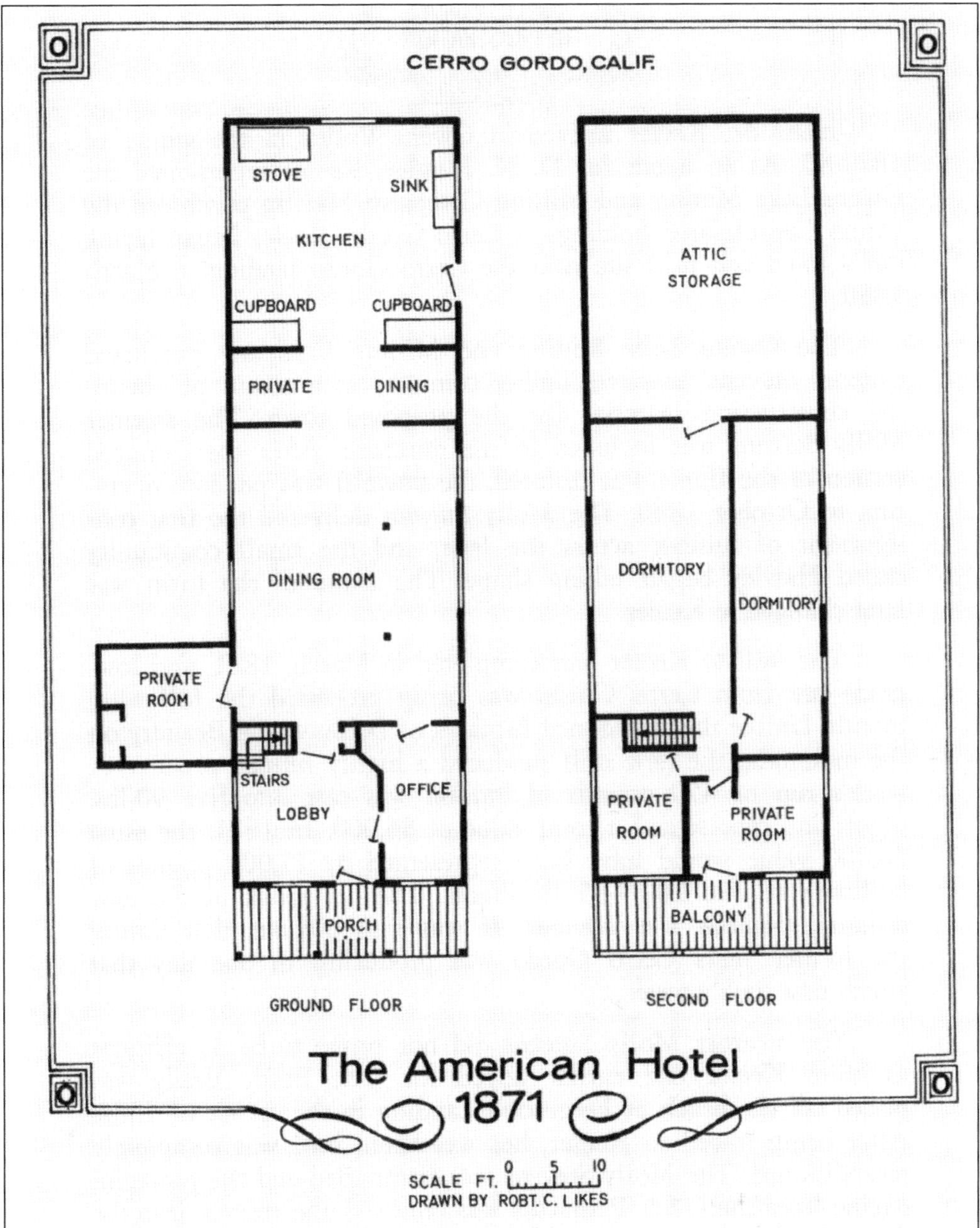

This diagram by Robert C. Likes shows the first and second floor of the American Hotel. There were three private rooms, one downstairs and two upstairs. A full dining room was downstairs with private dining between it and the kitchen. Dormitory-style rooms were upstairs between private rooms and attic storage. These dormitories more than likely had beds rented 12 hours at a time to tired and lonely miners who spent the rest of their time working or hanging around the saloons and dancehalls. The hotel was the scene of the wedding of Lulu Lewis and Al Wapplehorst in 1872. Lulu, the daughter of the proprietor, and her attendants dressed in one of the private rooms. The actual wedding was held in the dining room, which was covered in wildflowers native to the mountain. In later years, the balcony was used by Mortimer Belshaw and Victor Beaudry to speak to the masses in celebration of a legal victory over the mines. (Robert C. Likes Collection.)

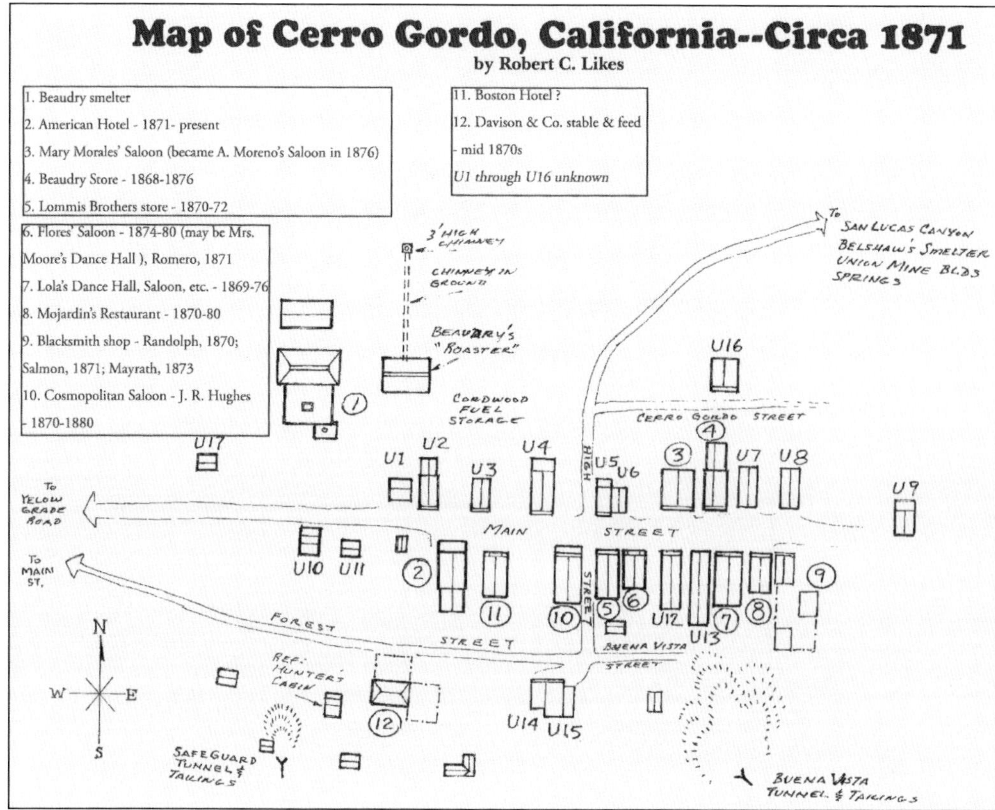

Author and historian Robert C. Likes put together this c. 1871 map, identifying both existing buildings and those gone to the ghosts. Upon receiving this rendition sometime in the first decade of the 21st century, the late Mike Patterson, owner of Cerro Gordo, declared politely, "He got it wrong." Many records are missing and there is a lot of guesswork involved; the truth probably lies somewhere between Likes's and Patterson's. (Robert C. Likes Collection.)

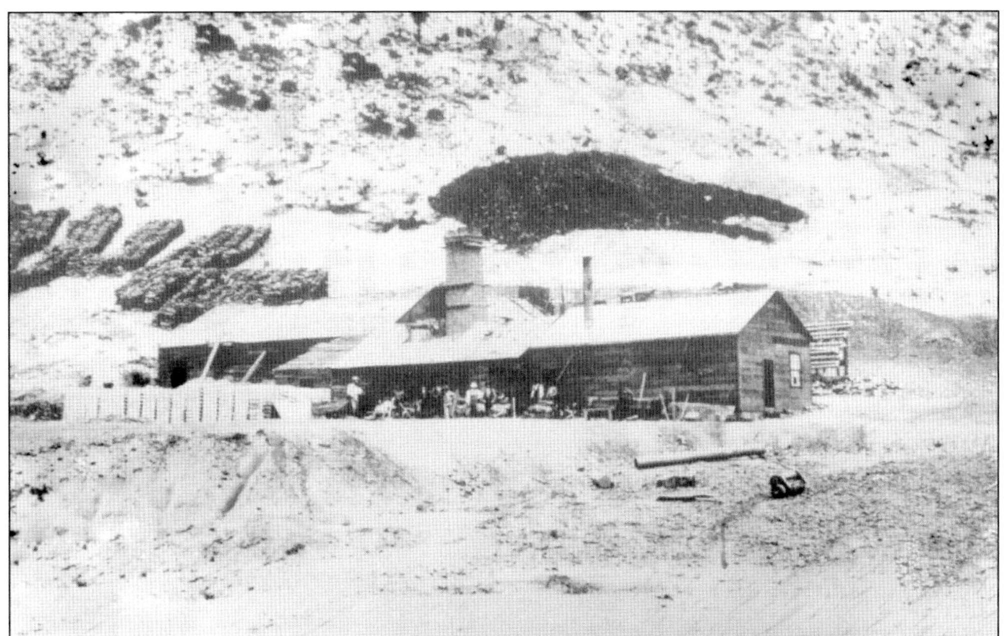

A stack of bullion bars can faintly be seen at the front left of this rare photograph of the Belshaw smelter. Cordwood fuel for the steam boiler is stacked on the mountainside at the back left of the building. Belshaw's blast furnaces were the highest technology of the day, producing 5.25 tons of bullion in 24 hours. Above the furnace chimney, the dark area that looks like smoke is actually an outcropping of rich galena that ran 15 to 70 feet wide and 750 feet deep. (Robert C. Likes Collection.)

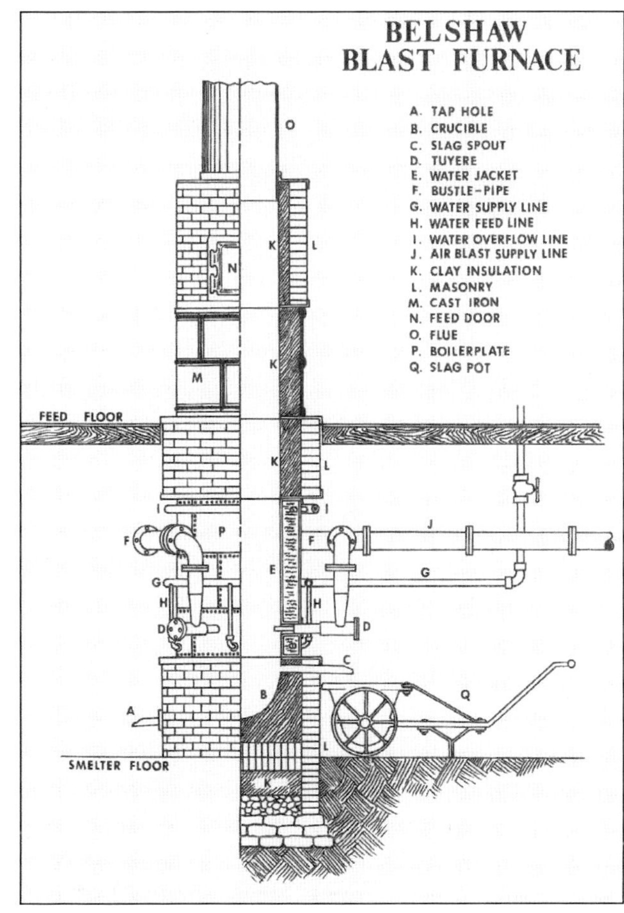

The inner workings of Belshaw's blast furnace are illustrated in this drawing by Robert C. Likes. Verbal descriptions from the state mineralogist reports and furnace construction methods common to the period aided Likes in his drawings. Today, only a few bricks, slag, and parts of a foundation mark the location of Belshaw's smelter on the saddle near the Union mine. (Robert C. Likes Collection.)

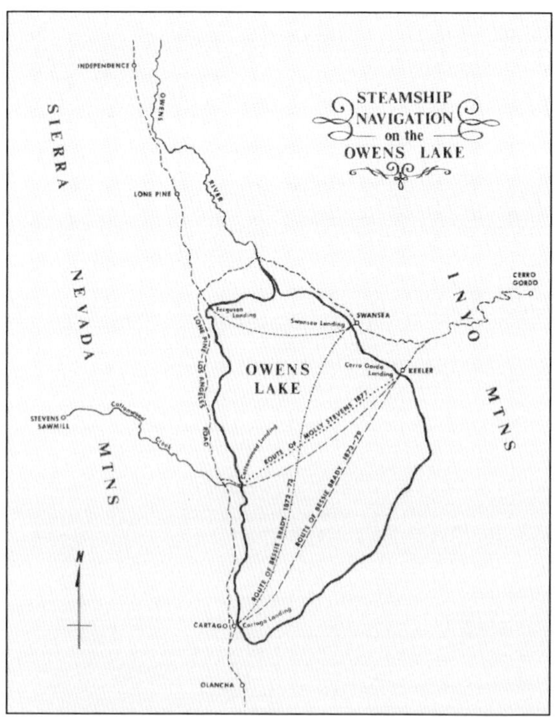

This Robert C. Likes map shows the routes of the two steamships, the *Bessie Brady* (upper right) and the *Mollie Stevens*, which were deployed to take bullion and wood across Owens Lake. The route saved three to five days of travel and was much smoother sailing than the sandy route around the lake. (Robert C. Likes Collection.)

This drawing of the steamship *Bessie Brady* by Robert C. Likes is based on a model built by Ralph J. Simonds and given to the Eastern California Museum in Independence. The *Bessie Brady* was launched on Owens Lake on June 27, 1872, with 700 bars of silver bullion, traveling from Swansea to the western side of the lake, where wagons awaited to transport the bullion across the desert to Los Angeles. The ship was christened as part of the Independence Day celebrations on July 4, 1872. (Robert C. Likes Collection.)

BESSIE BRADY 1872–79

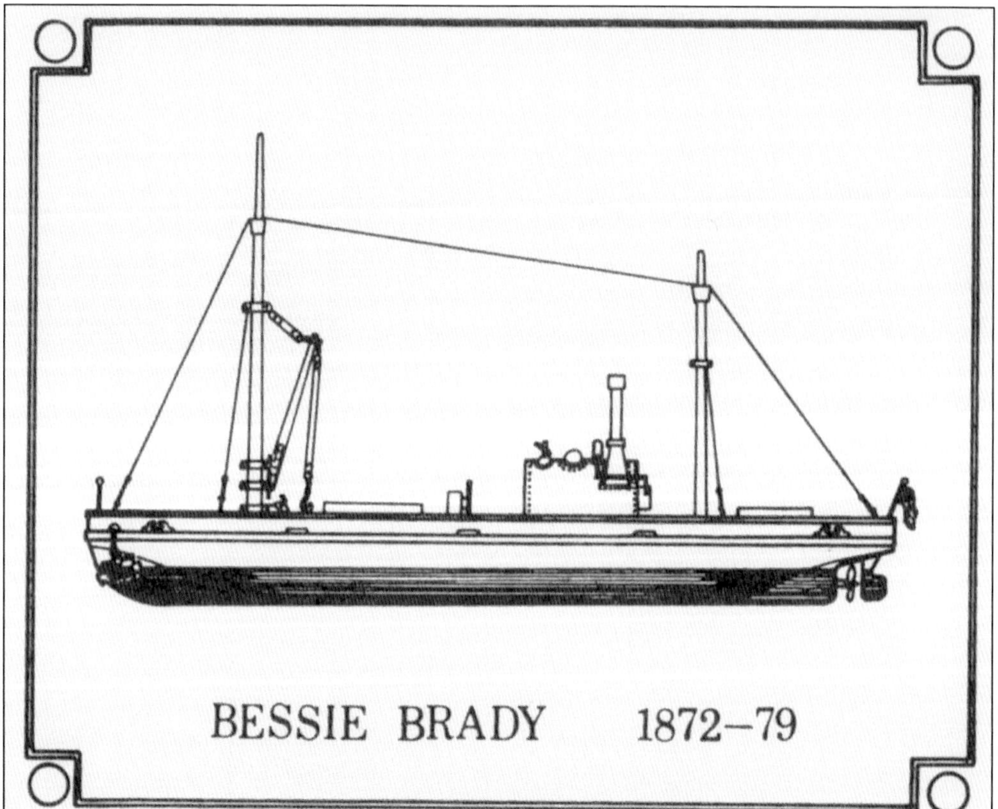

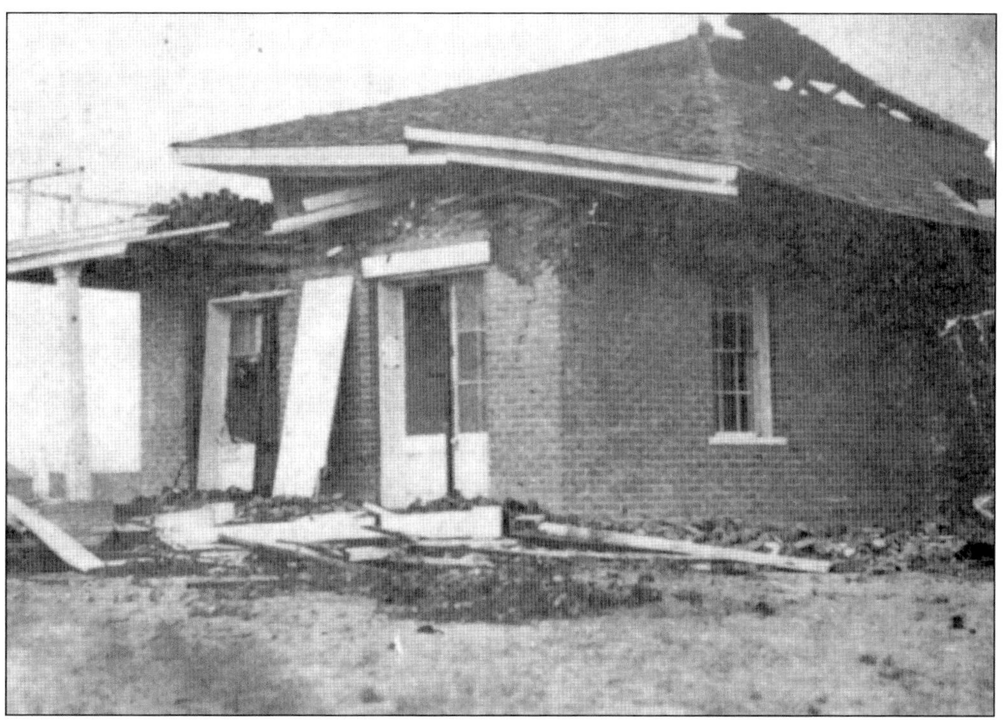

The earth shook violently on March 26, 1872, causing damage in much of Owens Valley and totally destroying the Inyo County Courthouse in Independence. Cerro Gordo, perched on the mountaintop, was more fortunate, and residents collected $800 for earthquake relief down below. The *Bessie Brady* steamship was under construction at this time, and the earthquake was just one of many factors delaying its completion. (Robert C. Likes Collection.)

HORRORS!!

Appalling Times!

EARTHQUAKES

Awful Loss of Life!

25 Persons Killed!

Earth Opens!

HOUSES PROSTRATED

LONE PINE!

ITS TERRIBLE CONDITION

MOST HEART-RENDING SCENES!

Miraculous Escapes!

Individual Heroism!

A Demoralized Printing Office.

Between 2 and 3 o'clock Tuesday morning last (March 26), the inhabi-

The front-page headline from the March 30, 1872, *Inyo Independent* tells of the disastrous quake. The newspaper's printing office was one of the structural casualties of the seismic event. (Courtesy Laws Railroad Museum.)

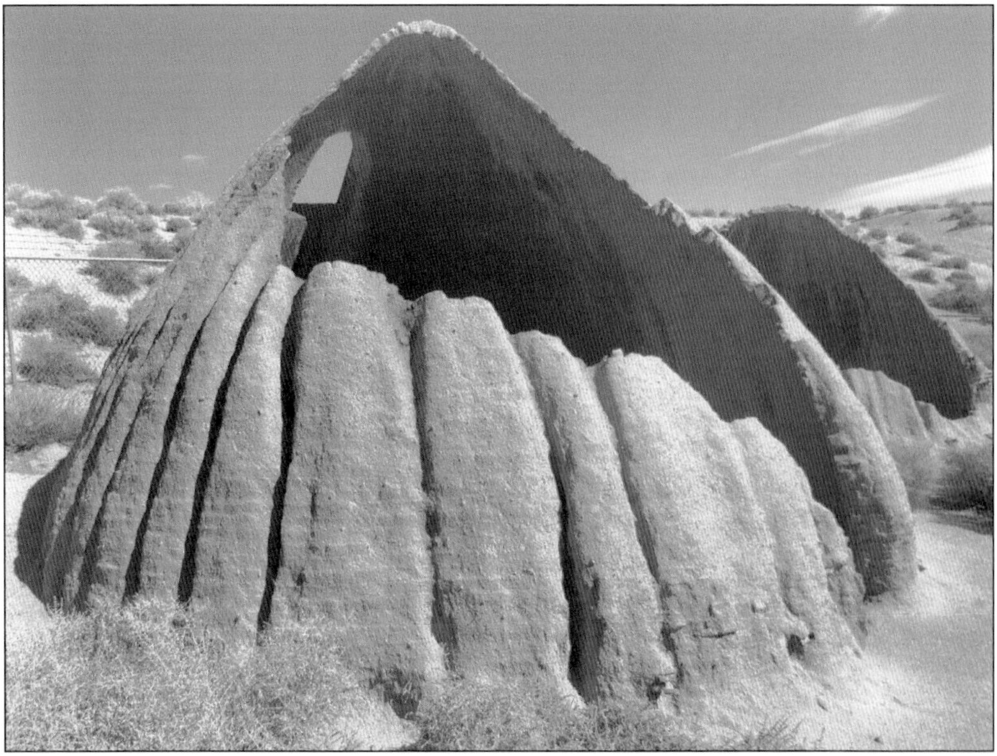

Under the direction of Col. Sherman Stevens, two charcoal kilns were built on the shore of Owens Lake just north of Cottonwood Creek in 1873. The kilns were constructed in beehive shapes of adobe bricks eight inches wide, two feet long, and two inches thick. Inside, it was 20 feet in diameter and 20 feet high. Wood cut from the forest above Cottonwood Canyon and transported down a water flume was shoved into the rear door of the kiln and converted to charcoal, then removed through the front door. The charcoal was shipped across Owens Lake on the *Bessie Brady* and later the *Mollie Stevens* and used to fuel the smelters of Cerro Gordo and Darwin. This photograph shows the kilns as they were in 2005. The kilns are accessible today by a dirt road east of Highway 395, south of Lone Pine. (Explore Historic California Collection.)

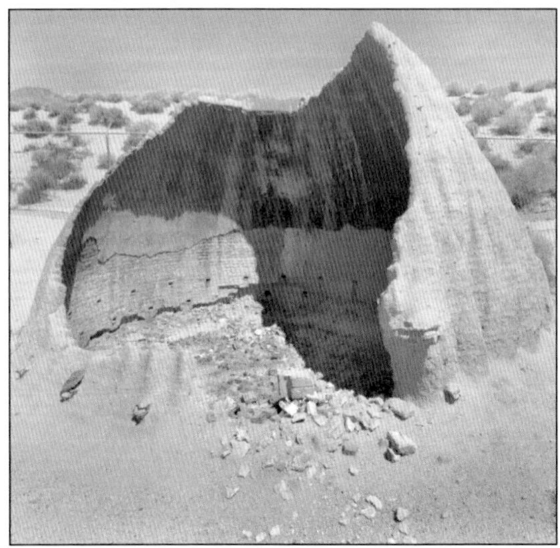

This 2006 image shows the adobe brickwork inside the beehive-shaped kilns. Vents at the bottom controlled the amount of air allowed in. The idea was to convert the wood to charcoal by partially burning it. Too much air would have allowed the wood to completely burn to ash. The charcoal provided both a source of heat and a chemical reaction for the furnaces. Wood was still used to fuel boilers to make steam, which in turn powered air compressors and other heavy equipment at the mines. (Explore Historic California Collection.)

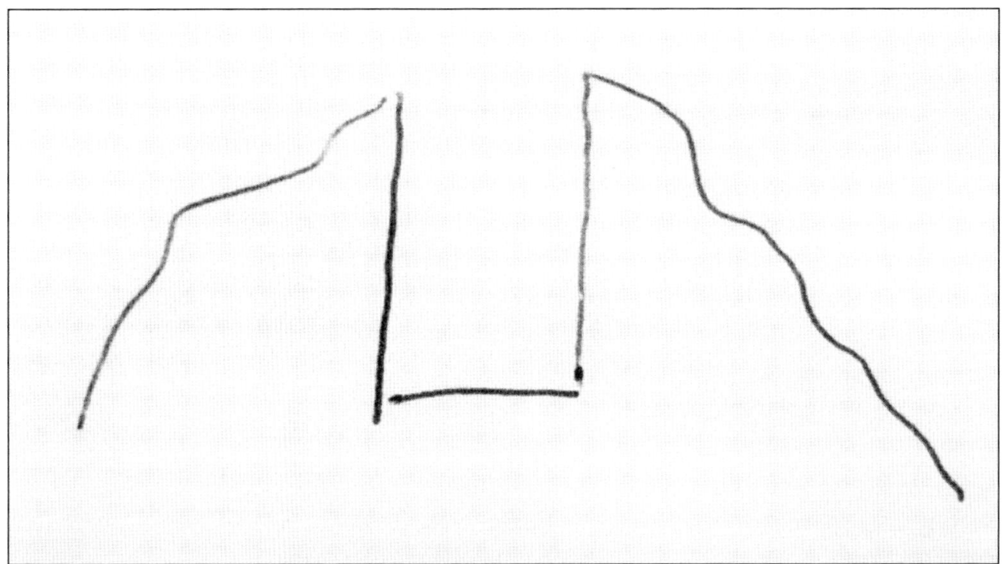

In 1849, cries of gold in the foothills of the western Sierras sent William Lewis Manly and the 49'ers across Death Valley to get to it. Along the way, one member of the party discovered what has become known as the "Lost Gunsight Mine." There is some confusion as to which actual gunsight the mine was named after. The late Mike Patterson, one of the most recent owners of Cerro Gordo, drew this crude picture of a mountain peak with a notch in it, which looks exactly like the gunsight of a rifle. (Explore Historic California Collection.)

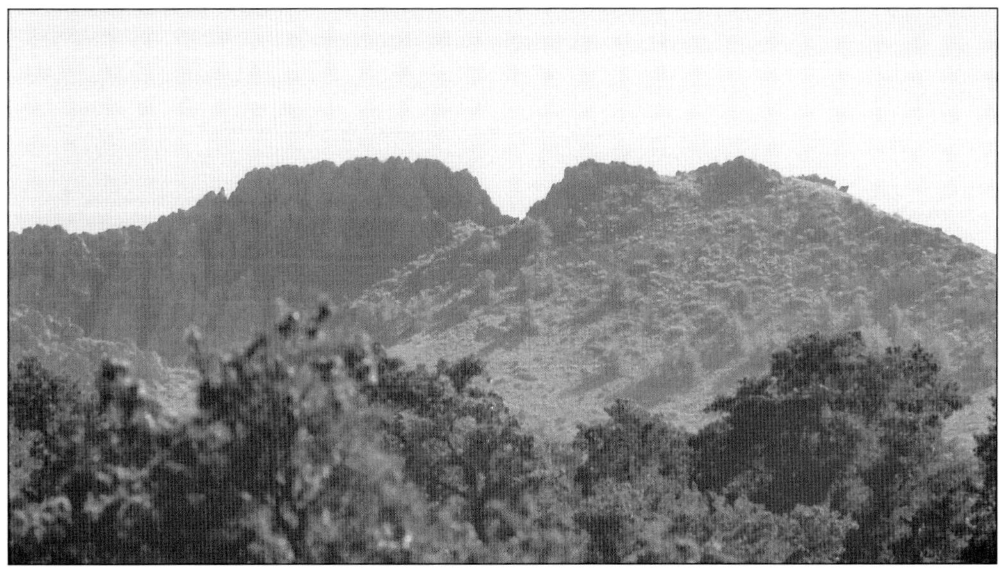

A notch in the Inyo Mountains that may be the "Lost Gunsight" of mining legend is seen here from the backside of Cerro Gordo. The image looks west from the Lee Flat/Saline Valley side of the Inyos. Perhaps Pablo Flores, the original discoverer of Cerro Gordo in 1865, gazed at the peak and realized he had found the fabled mine. Cerro Gordo's rich silver and lead fit certain aspects of the Lost Gunsight story, but other accounts place the location closer to the Death Valley area, southeast of Cerro Gordo. (Explore Historic California Collection.)

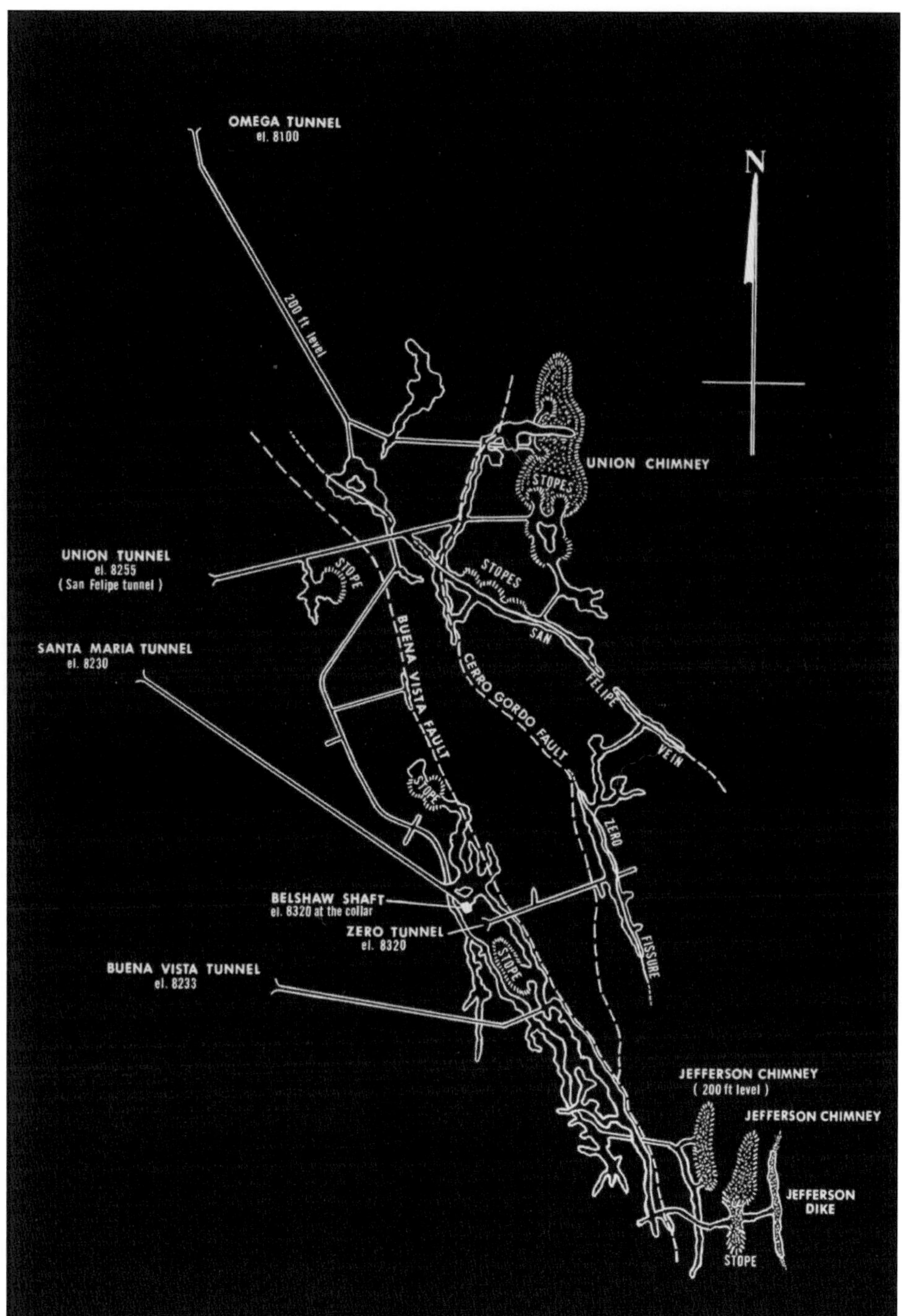

This map details the underground workings of the various mine tunnels dug by the Union Consolidated Company. The company was created on January 13, 1876, following long court battles. Mortimer Belshaw and Victor Beaudry held two-thirds interest, with G.M. Fisher of the San Felipe Company in control of the remaining third. With the struggles with the San Felipe Company at last resolved, full-scale production was in process, and rumors of exhausted supplies of ore were squelched. (Robert C. Likes Collection.)

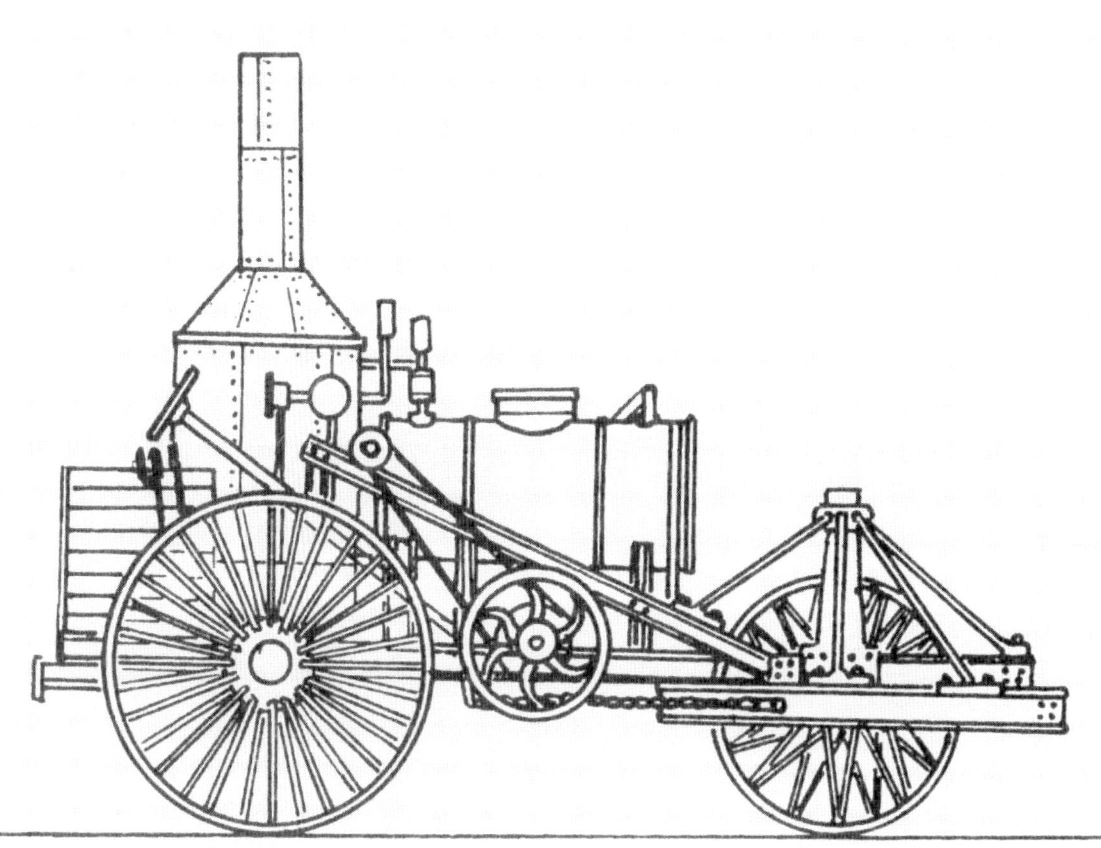

In 1906, the Great Western Ore and Reduction Company hired local teamsters to freight low-grade silver ore from dumps on the hill to their Keeler smelter. Modern technology in the form of a steam traction engine, drawn by Robert C. Likes, was introduced that spring, pulling four wagons of ore a day down the steep Yellow Grade. The engine ran only a short time, as heavily loaded wagons did not hold up on the rough road at increased speeds. (Robert C. Likes Collection.)

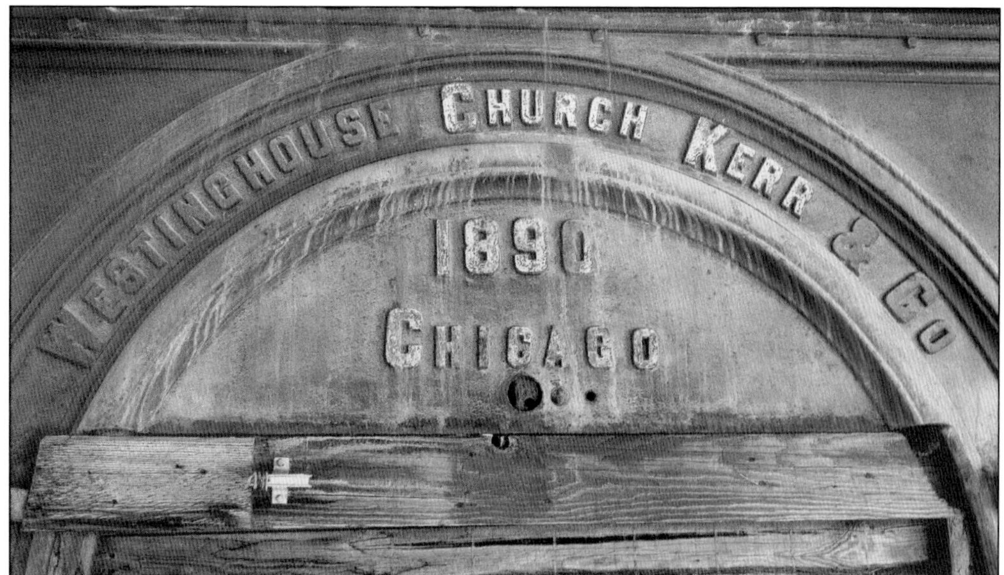

The sign from the 1890 steam plant is still intact, but the equipment is long gone. The original steam hoist operated under 70 horsepower with a 350-cubic-foot air compressor and a 130-horsepower boiler. When electricity came to the mountain, the old steam plant was maintained in case of power failure. (Explore Historic California Collection.)

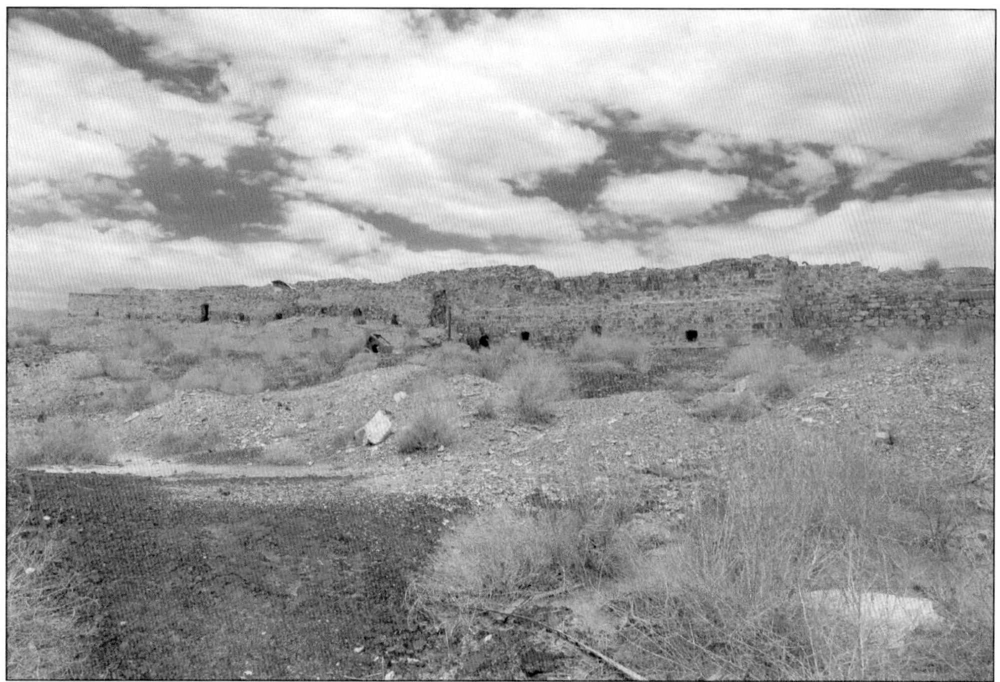
By the fall of 1907, the Four Metals Smelter Company erected a 200-ton smelter east of Keeler, the remnants of which still stand today. The smelter was operated by three shifts of 20 men each. Every day, 120 tons of silver ore, extracted from the previous owners' new discoveries below the 900-foot level of the Union Mine, were processed here. An aerial tramway to Cerro Gordo was built from the smelter to the mines. (Explore Historic California Collection.)

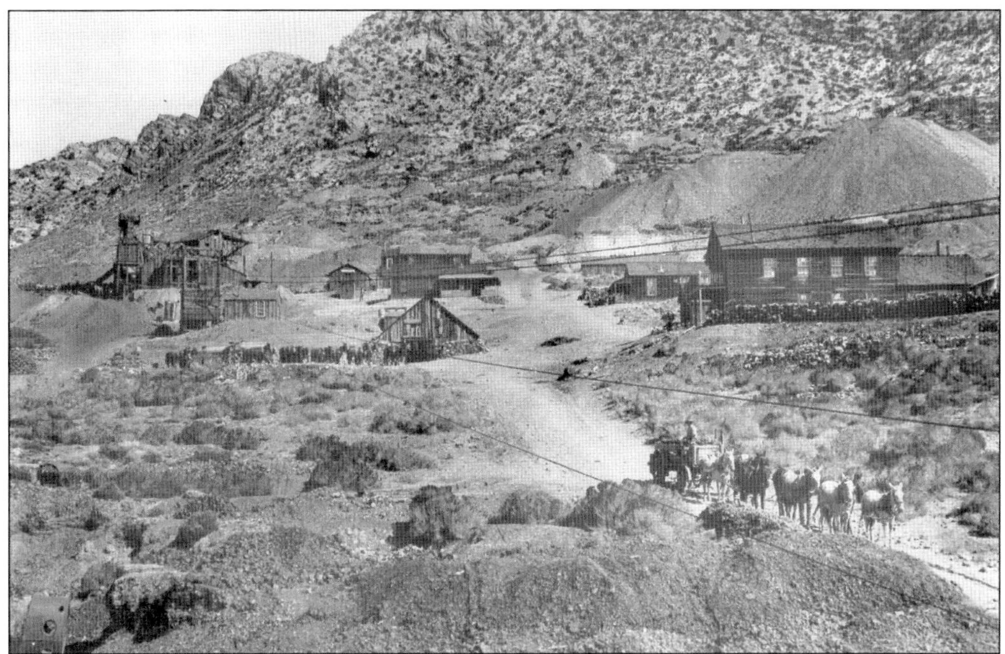

In this image, the station to the Montgomery Tramway is at upper left, and the cable, minus the ore bucket, is going from the station down the main street of Cerro Gordo, along with a mule team. The tram ran five miles as the crow flies, with its terminus just short of Keeler. (Robert C. Likes Collection.)

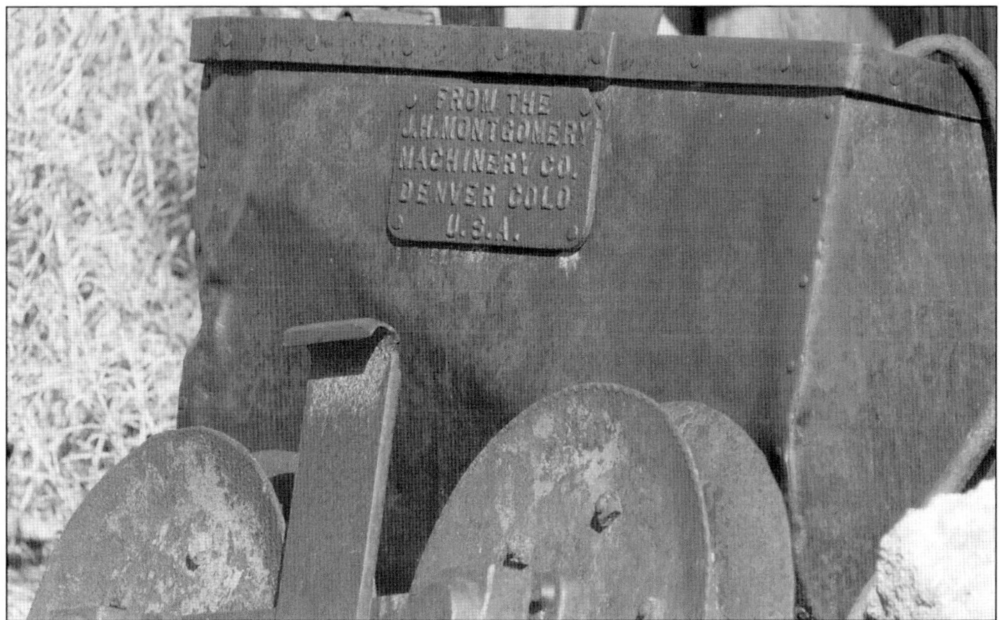

A Montgomery tram car remains intact for visitors to see in the ghost town of Cerro Gordo. Although designed for ore transport, many are the tales of drunken miners hopping on similar buckets following a night of whooping and hollering in Keeler. Stories abound of unlucky miners who forgot to lower their heads as the ore bucket came through the tram towers. (Explore Historic California Collection.)

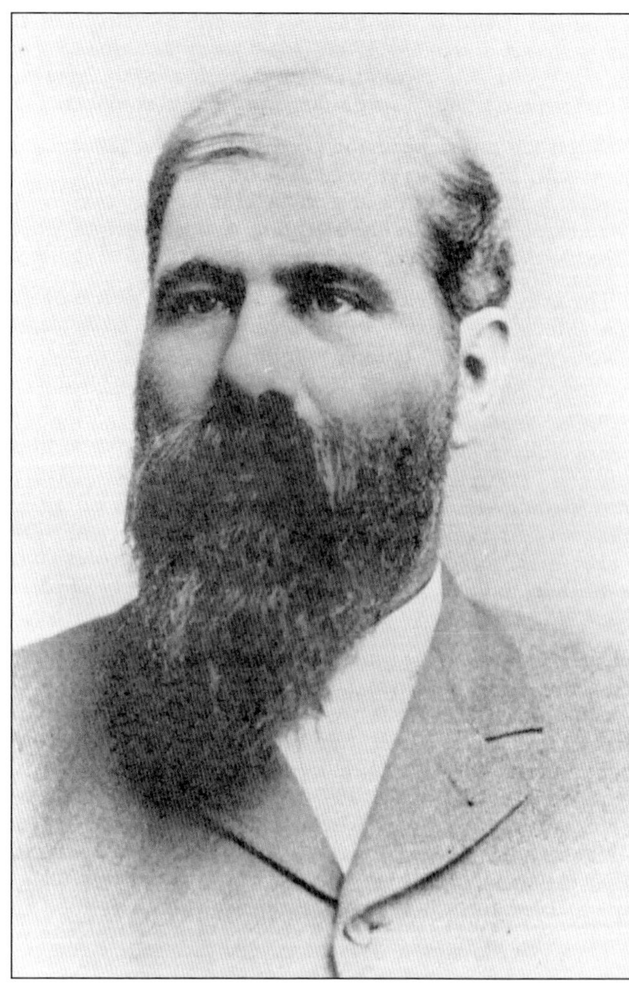

By the late 1880s, mining had all but ceased and Cerro Gordo was in danger of fading to the ghosts. Thomas Boland, chairman of the Inyo County supervisors and the owner of a general store in Keeler, began investing his money in further mining efforts. As owner of the Union Mine's lease, he succeeded in keeping the dream alive for 16 years, but failed in producing much more than small quantities of silver. (Robert C. Likes Collection.)

By 1896, the California state mineralogists announced the discontinuance of Cerro Gordo mining reports, and only 20 to 30 men on the mountain staying to eke out a meager existence trying to pull out what little ore they could. The smoke from Belshaw and Beaudry's smelters no longer billowed over the town, and the jingle bells of Nadeau's mules were no longer heard. Abandoned buildings struggled to hang on to the memory of what they had once been. (L.D. Gordon Collection.)

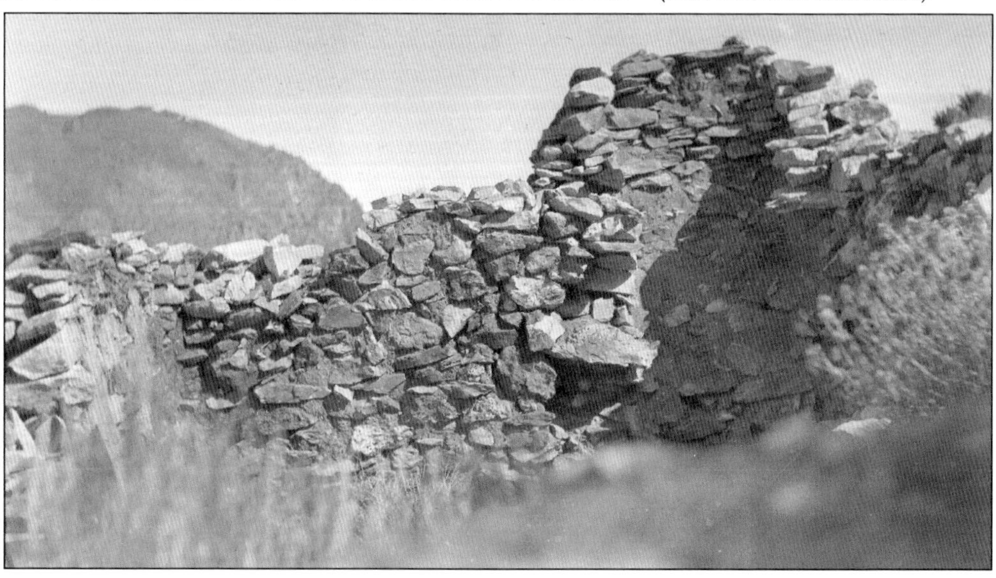

Two

The Gordon Family Album

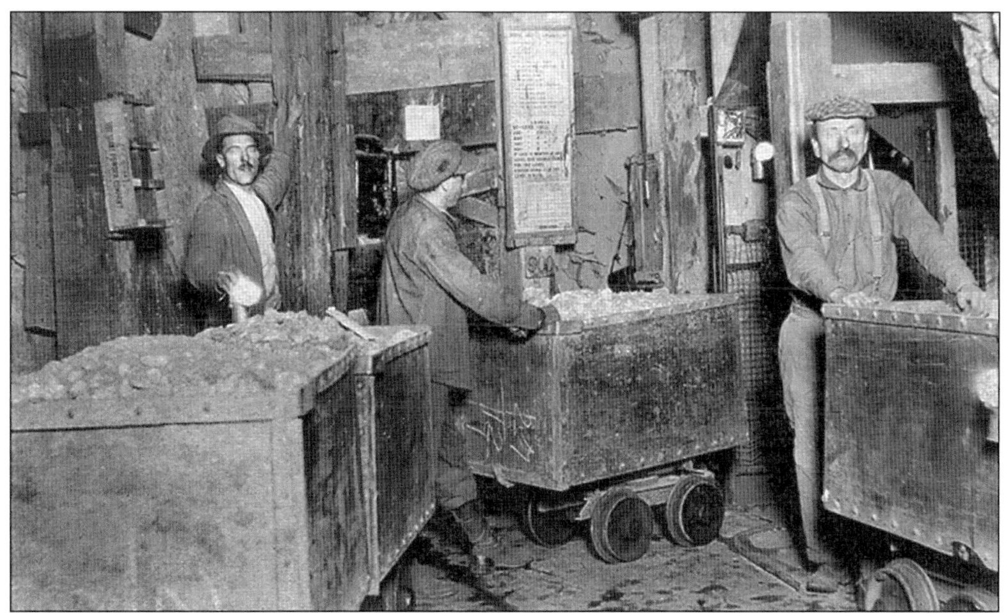

Louis D. Gordon (left) and two unidentified miners are underground in the Union Mine at the 900-foot level around 1915. Upon Gordon's arrival in 1911, the Union was little more than an abandoned pile of burned-out rubble. His mine surveys uncovered reasonable amounts of silver and galena. His close look at the zinc that had been tossed aside during the Belshaw and Beaudry years told him where Cerro Gordo's next fortune would come from. (L.D. Gordon Collection.)

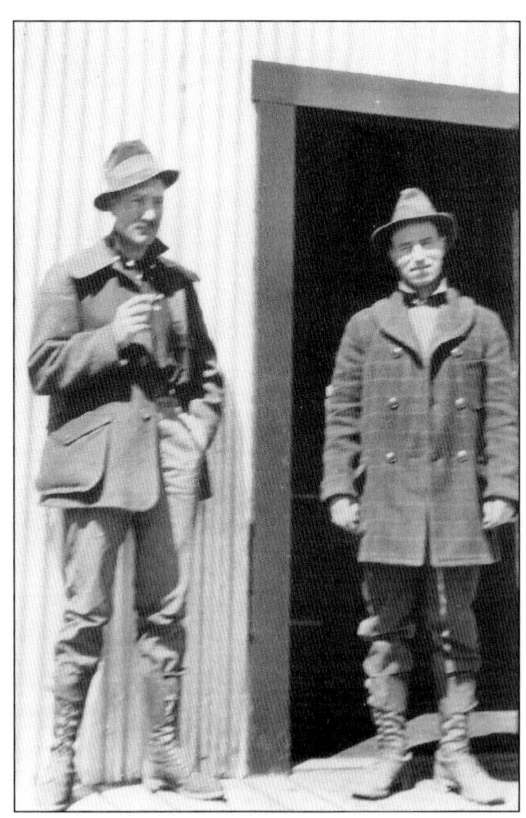

On the left, Louis D. Gordon (left) stands in front of one of Cerro Gordo's industrial buildings with an unidentified man. The photograph below shows the same man with a camera. Wherever Gordon went, a photographer accompanied him, recording his mining career. The majority of the images in this chapter are from this collection, which was passed down through the Gordon family and is now owned by Louis Gordon's grandson. (Both, L.D. Gordon Collection.)

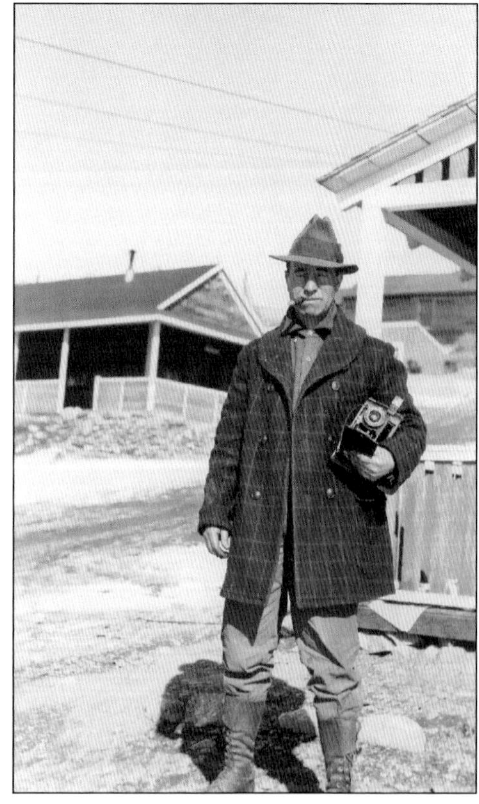

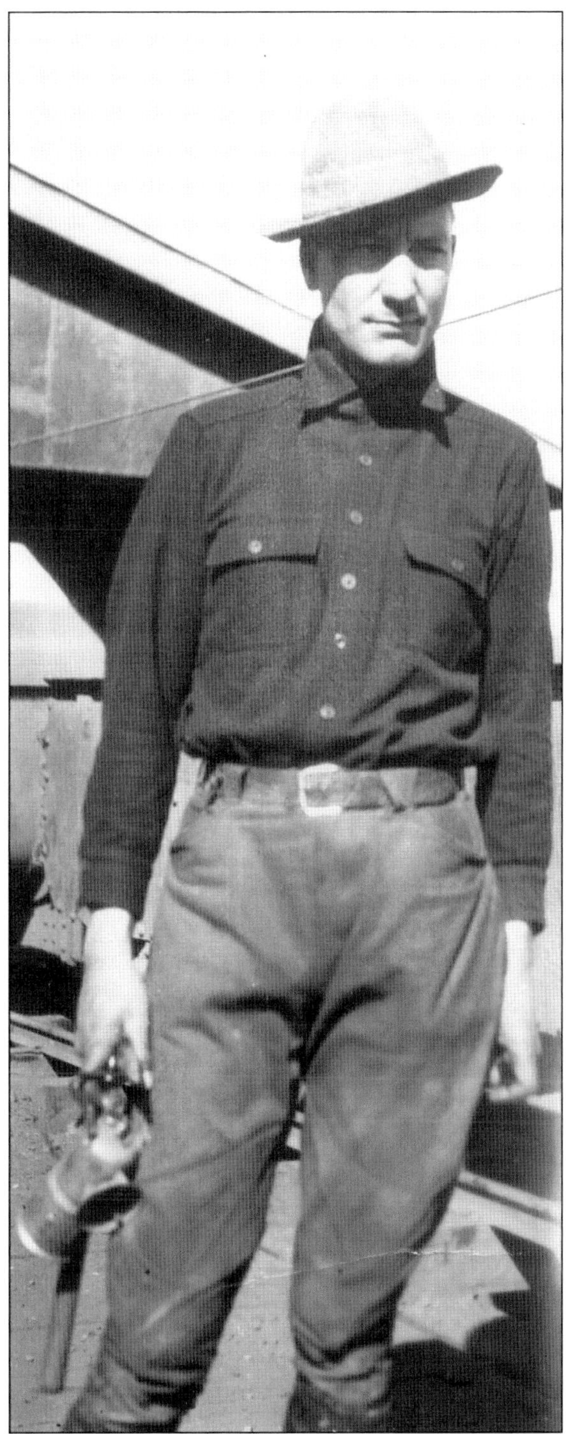

The Cerro Gordo Mines Company was incorporated on July 14, 1911, with Louis D. Gordon as both vice president and general manager. Gordon ran a well-organized operation and was not afraid to spend money to make money or to work beside his men. Gordon is seen here with a miner's lamp in his hand, perhaps getting ready to descend into the mines himself. (L.D. Gordon Collection.)

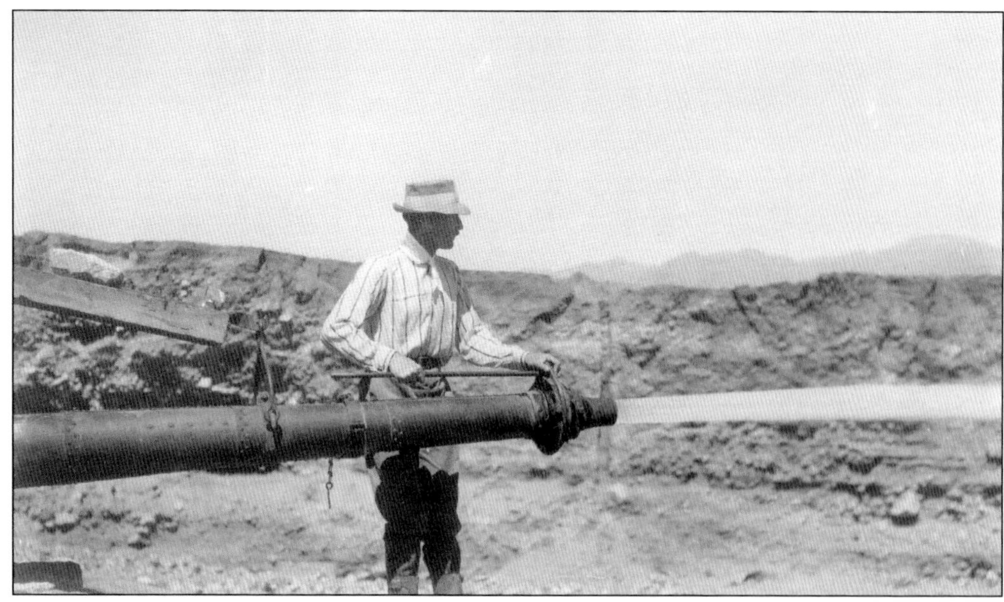

Louis D. Gordon (above) and his wife, Cornelia, take turns posing in front of a hydraulic monitor at Round Mountain, Nevada. Prior to his arrival in Cerro Gordo, Gordon and two other men discovered high-grade gold ore 65 miles north of Tonopah, Nevada. The first camp that sprouted at the base of the mountain was named after Gordon. By March 1906, the Round Mountain Mining Company was incorporated, with Gordon as president and general manager. Nearly 1,000 acres of mining claims ranging from gold to silver, from lode deposits to placers, would earn Gordon the title "Father of Round Mountain." When it was feasible, Cornelia and their family would follow him from mining camp to mining camp. The Gordons also had residences in Los Angeles and Salt Lake City. (Both, L.D. Gordon Collection.)

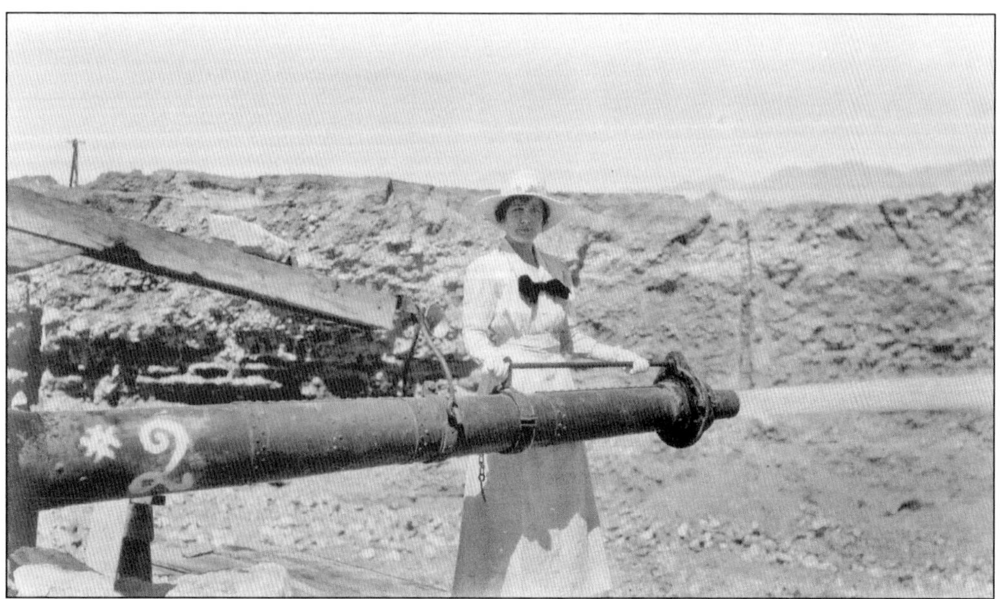

This picture may show one of the Gordons' two sons (right) with an unidentified man in front of what is known today as the Mortimer Belshaw House. It's quite possible that this is the "sad little cabin" that greeted Cornelia and her infant son upon arrival. She lived here temporarily until more comfortable housing could be built by her husband's employees. (L.D. Gordon Collection.)

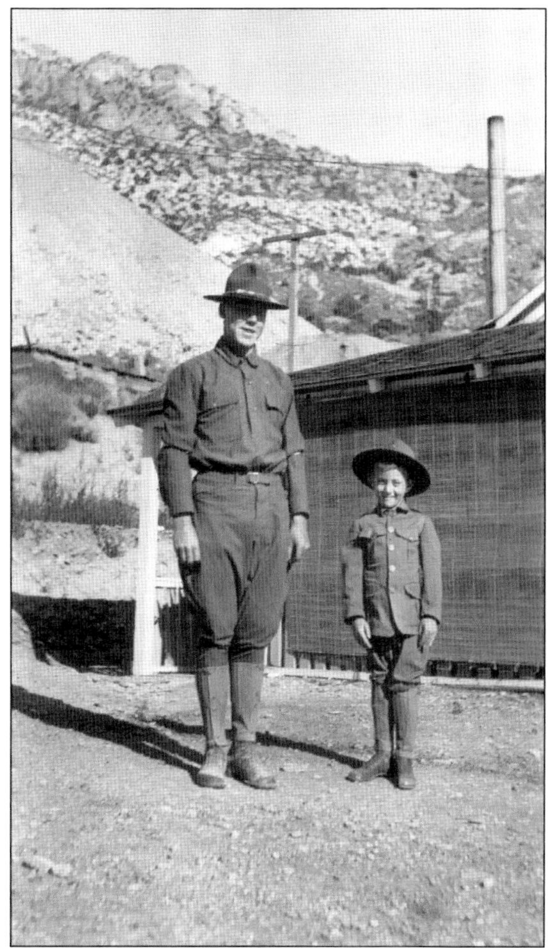

In 1911, when Cornelia Gordon first arrived at the Cerro Gordo Mines, she stepped out of a wagon and turned to the view of Keeler and Owens Lake down below, which she later described as the "dry soda lake turned most heavenly blue . . . blue as sapphire," with the Sierras towering in the distance. (L.D. Gordon Collection.)

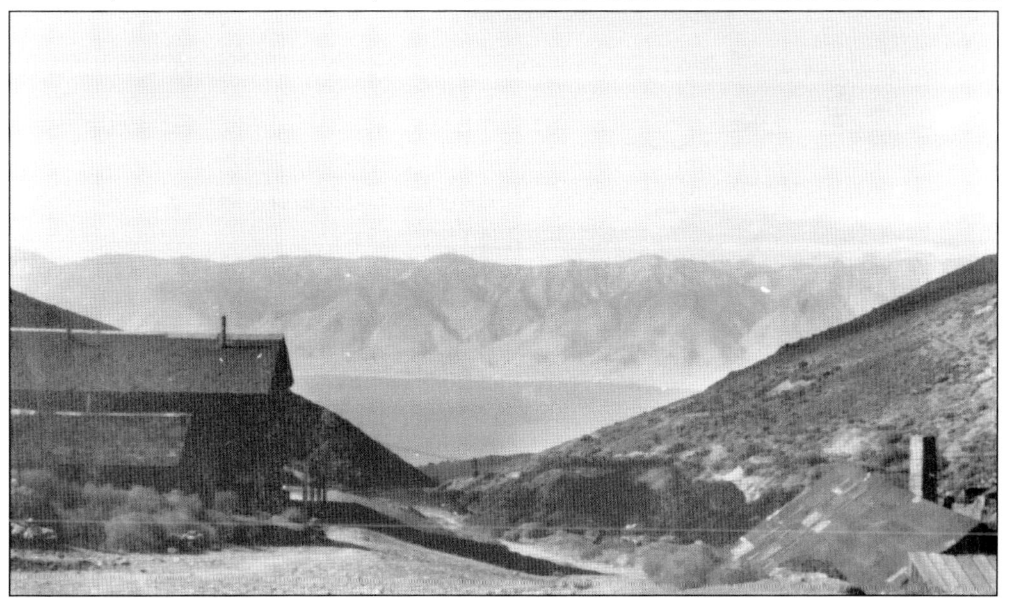

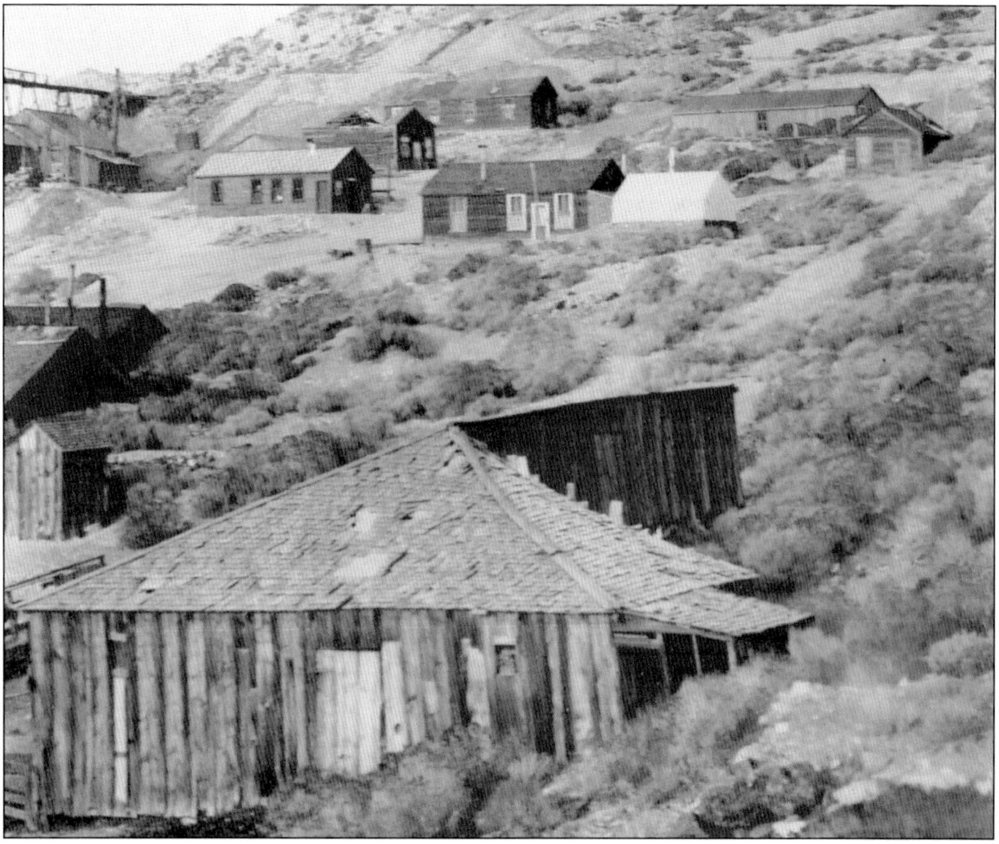

When the Gordon family arrived in Cerro Gordo, the view above looking up the canyon to the right of the main road would have greeted them. In the upper left distance, the remnants of the Montgomery tram are seen. A tent cabin sits behind the Belshaw House in the center of the image. The empty space between it and the little cabin across the road to the right, known as the Chinaman's shack, is the site where the Gordons' two-story modern home was later built. Below, men dig a trench as construction begins. (Both, L.D. Gordon Collection.)

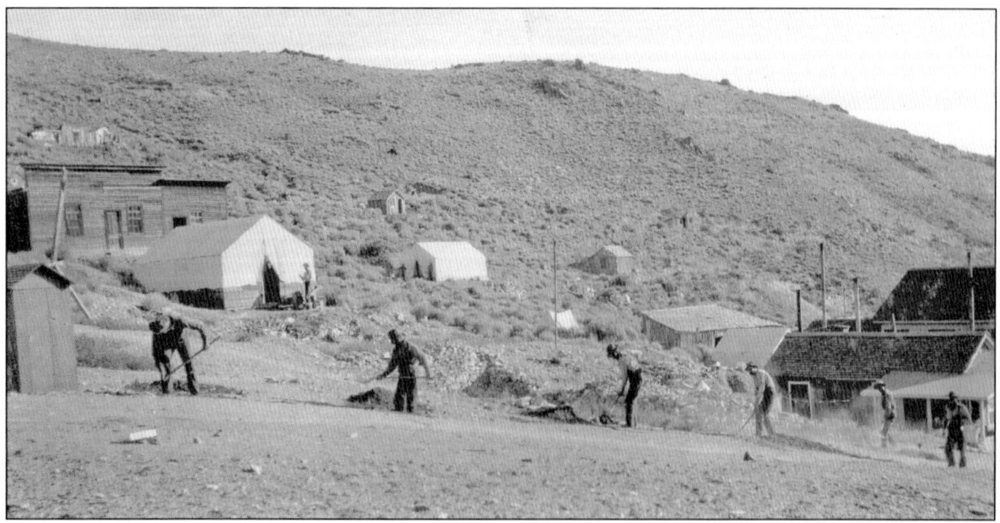

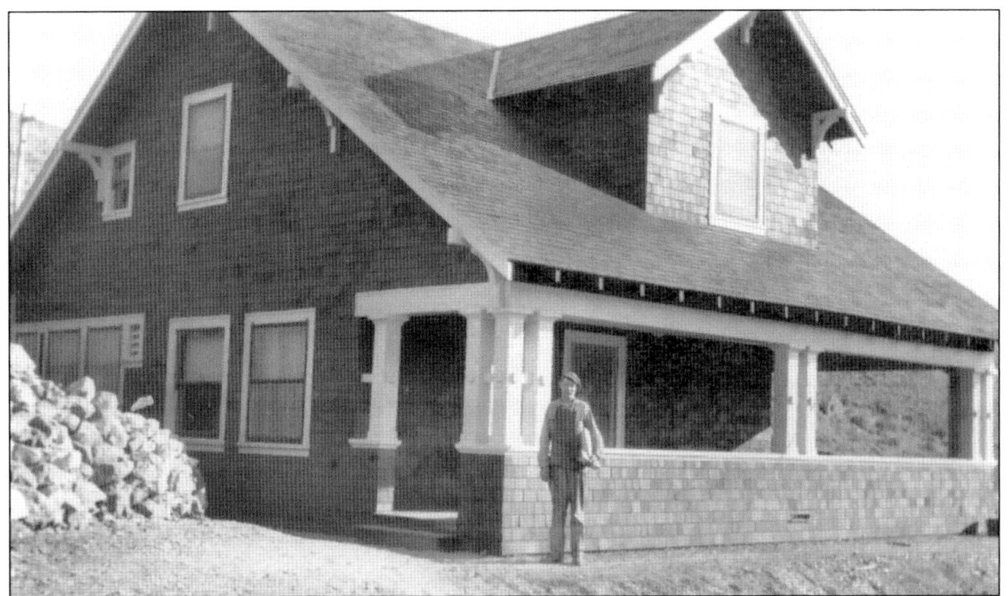

A workman poses in front of the nearly completed Louis D. Gordon house. Although Cornelia's diaries contain no information about the house, it would have been quite an upgrade from the shack she lived in until this was completed. It was more than likely outfitted with modern conveniences of the day like electricity, which was brought to Cerro Gordo from across Owens Valley during Gordon's reign. Over the years, the structure was used as a residence and office. It later became the home of Jody Stewart and Mike Patterson during their ownership of Cerro Gordo. (L.D. Gordon Collection.)

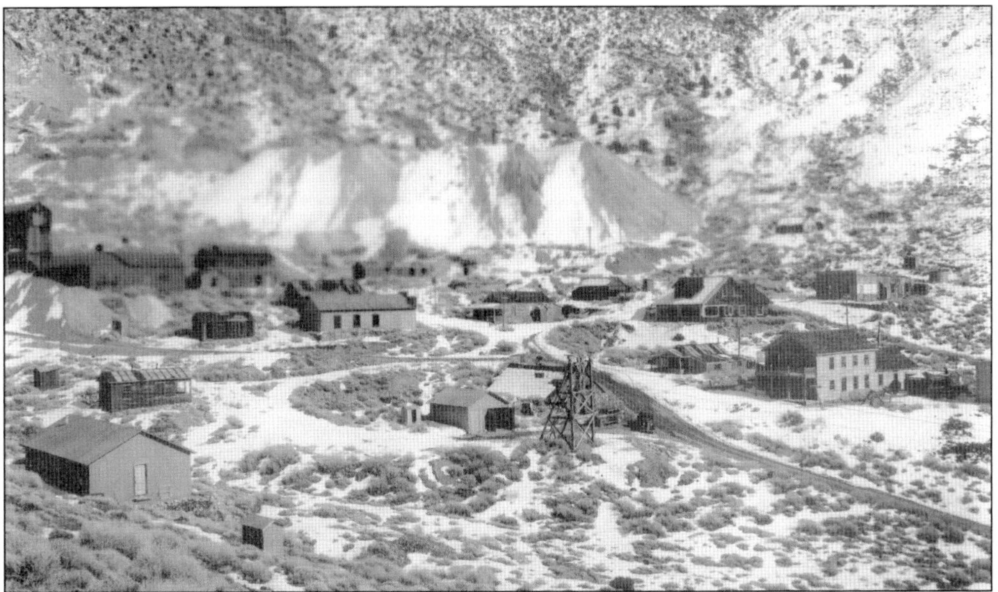

This photograph was taken after a snow, with the Gordon House completed in the middle. The American Hotel is shown a block below, still in use for meals. The hoist house and mines are hidden by the huge amount of tailings pulled out. Utility lines confirm this was taken after electricity was introduced in 1916. Tram towers are standing, but there do not appear to be any buckets in transit on the system. (L.D. Gordon Collection.)

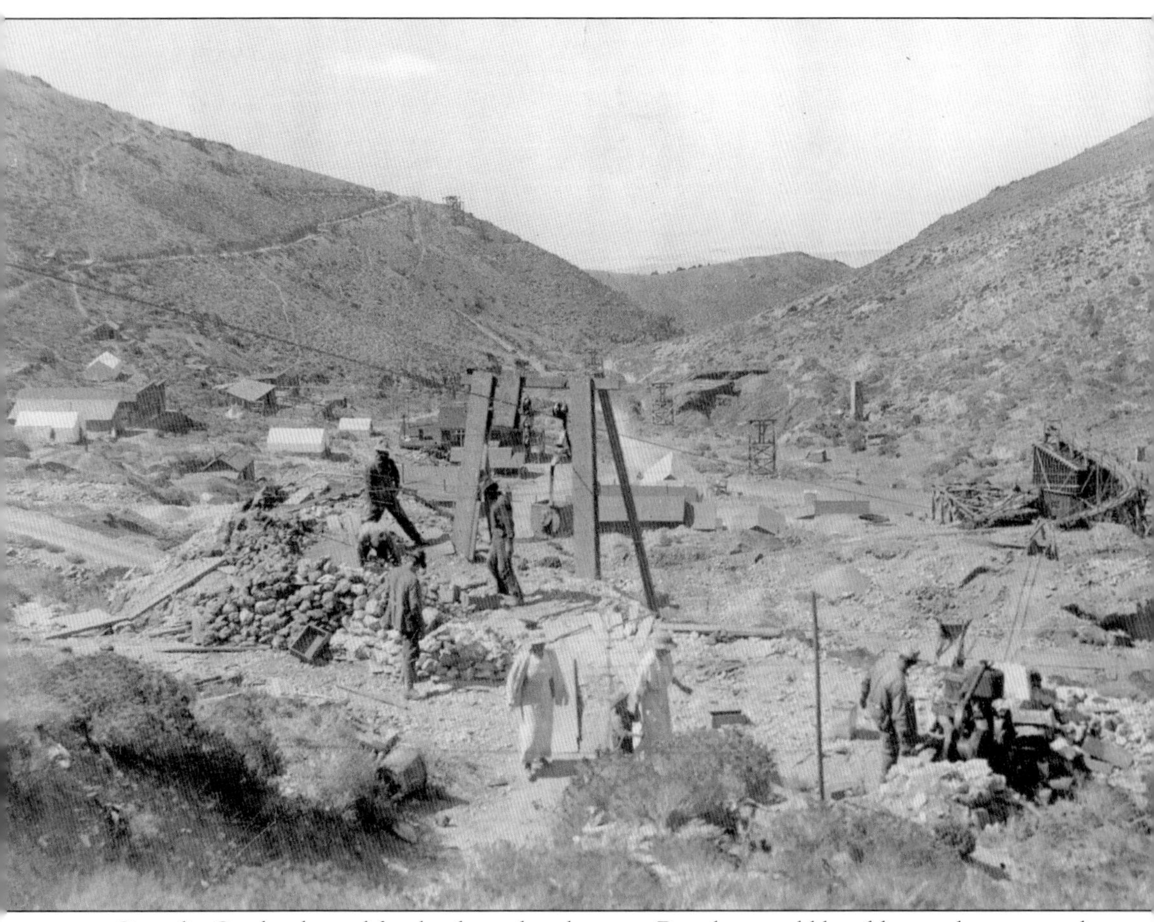

Cornelia Gordon longed for the days when her son, Douglas, would be old enough to go on the trails. In this picture, she holds his hand as they explore the area north of town above the tram station. The woman with her is more than likely the nursemaid. At far right, men work on a temporary tramway above the main tram terminal, as the Gordons head into the brush in search of wildflowers. (L.D. Gordon Collection.)

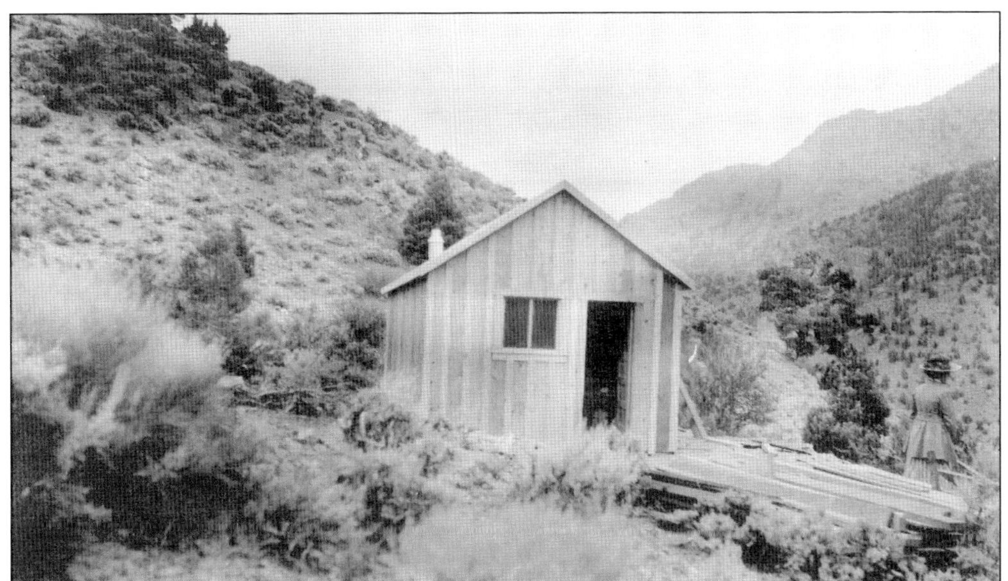

This cabin under construction is in Newtown on the Lee Flat side of Cerro Gordo. The woman to the right, with her back to the woodpile, may be Cornelia Gordon. On one of her rides, near a shed similar to this, her horse, Prince, shied at the sight of a large rattlesnake. Fear of snakes and heights on the narrow trails never stopped her from breaking the monotony of her days on the mountain. (L.D. Gordon Collection.)

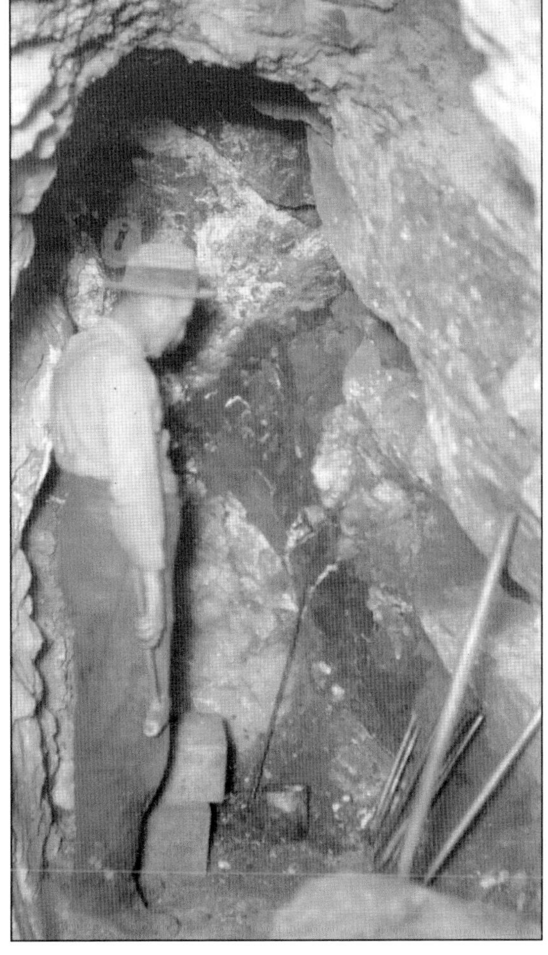

Cornelia spent many lonely days as one of the few women in the faded mining town of Cerro Gordo, while her husband, Louis, was busy around the mines with his workmen. Here he is inside one of the mines. Every day at 5:00 p.m., he would go down in the mine, leaving his wife and his baby son to eat dinner by themselves. (L.D. Gordon Collection.)

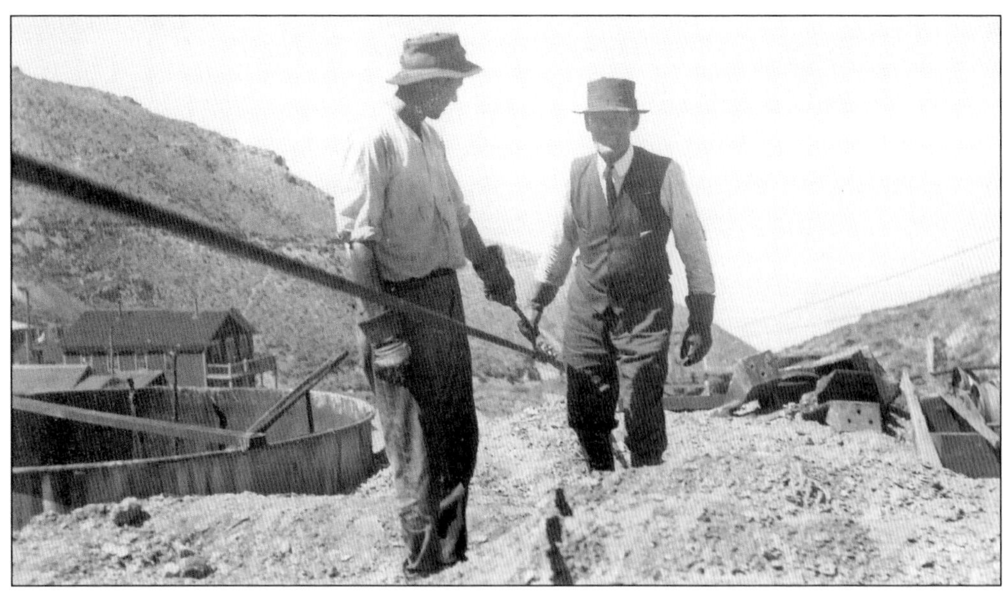

Louis D. Gordon was not afraid to get his hands dirty. Above, he is seen with a workman at the tram line with the American Hotel in the background. Below, Gordon poses at a makeshift tent housing compressor equipment. Under his persistent and patient direction, Cerro Gordo became the largest producer of lead and the second largest producer of zinc in California. Gordon introduced electricity to the mines and replaced the original Montgomery tramway with a new and improved Leschen model. A Joshua Hendy 100-horsepower electric hoist, an Ingersoll-Rand Imperial Type 10 compressor, and a 150-horsepower constant speed motor were installed during his supervision. Under Gordon, Cerro Gordo was a quiet company town compared to the Wild West atmosphere prevailing in the Beaudry and Belshaw silver era. (Both, L.D. Gordon Collection.)

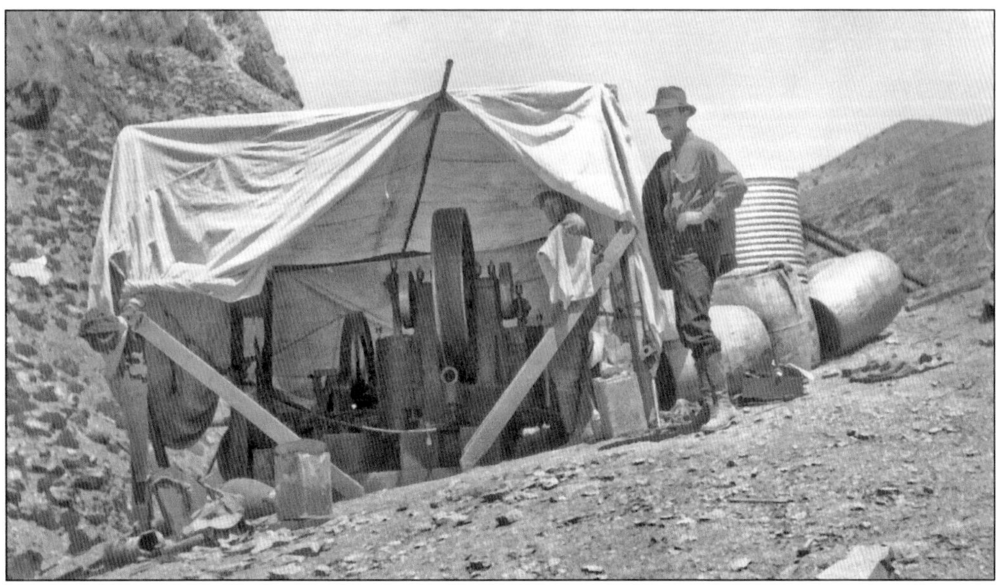

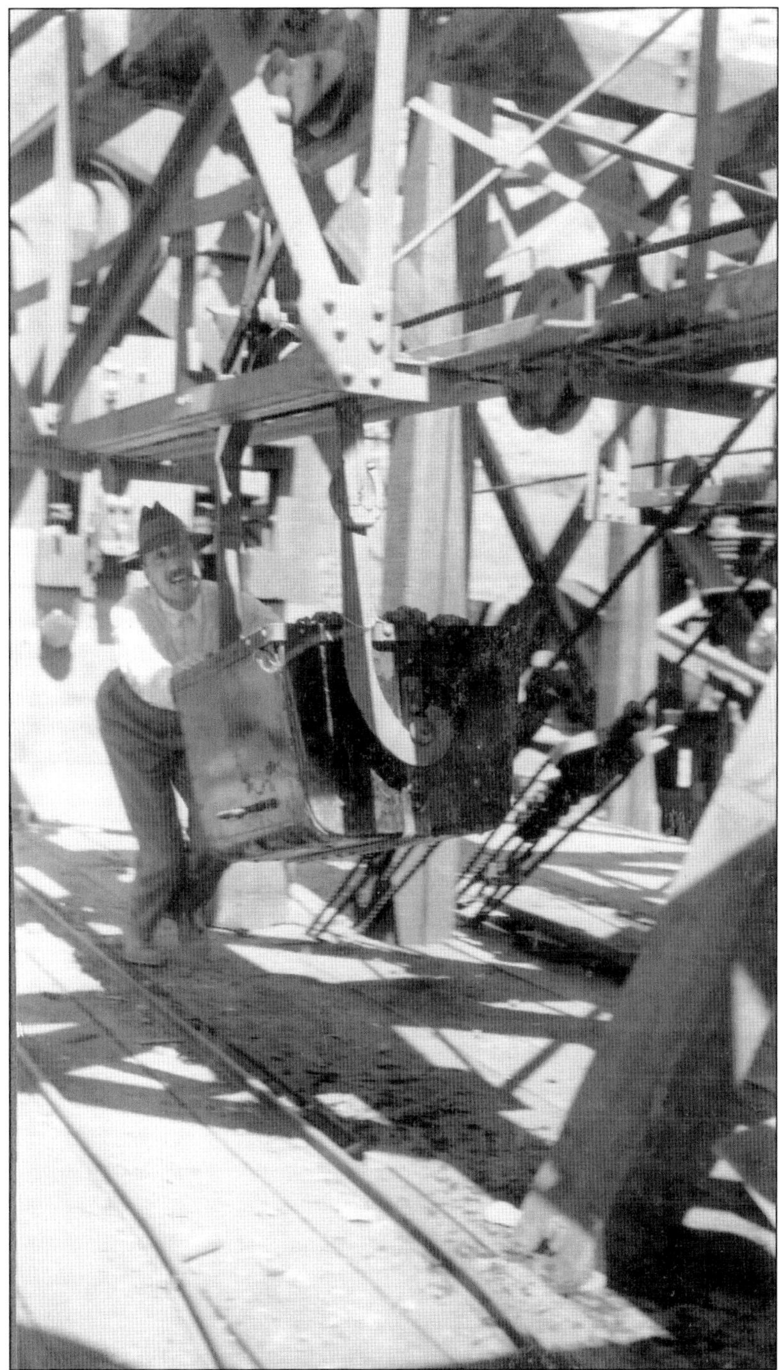

Louis D. Gordon pushes one of the Leschen tramway ore buckets. The tram brought ore down to the shores of Owens Lake at Keeler and much-needed supplies back up the mountain. Cornelia would put her grocery list on the cart, including requests for baby's milk, which spoiled in the heat on the ride back. Once, a magazine advertisement for baby formula caught her eye and she sent a note down on the ore cart for it. From time to time, a few brave miners chose to ride the six miles on the ore buckets. (L.D. Gordon Collection.)

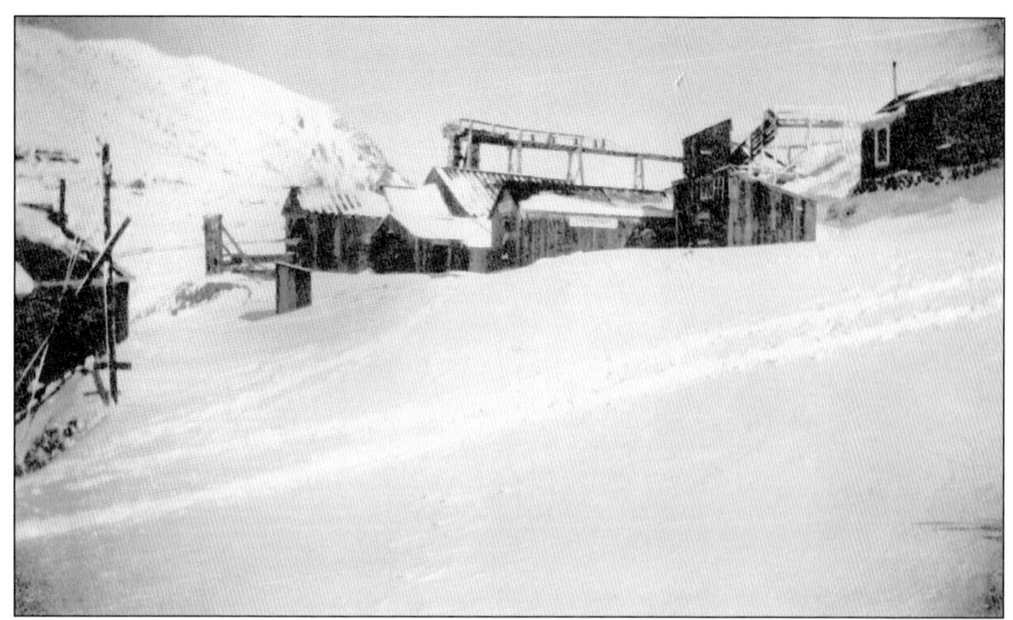

These two photographs show Cerro Gordo's tram stations during different winters with heavy snowfall. The image above shows the old Montgomery tram terminal and support buildings. The image below, with a handwritten description, shows the later Leschen tram. The writing reads, "This is not Alaska. Cerro Gordo Mines Co. ore bins & tram terminal, Keeler, Calif. It's not summer, all winter, this winter." The tram terminals are located approximately 8,300 feet above sea level. The Gordon family spent at least one Christmas at the mines; a pine tree was cut and brought to the family by the miners and decorated with both bought and homemade decorations. In her diaries, Cornelia reminisced about the beautiful weather, sunny and clear, with snow all around. (Both, L.D. Gordon Collection.)

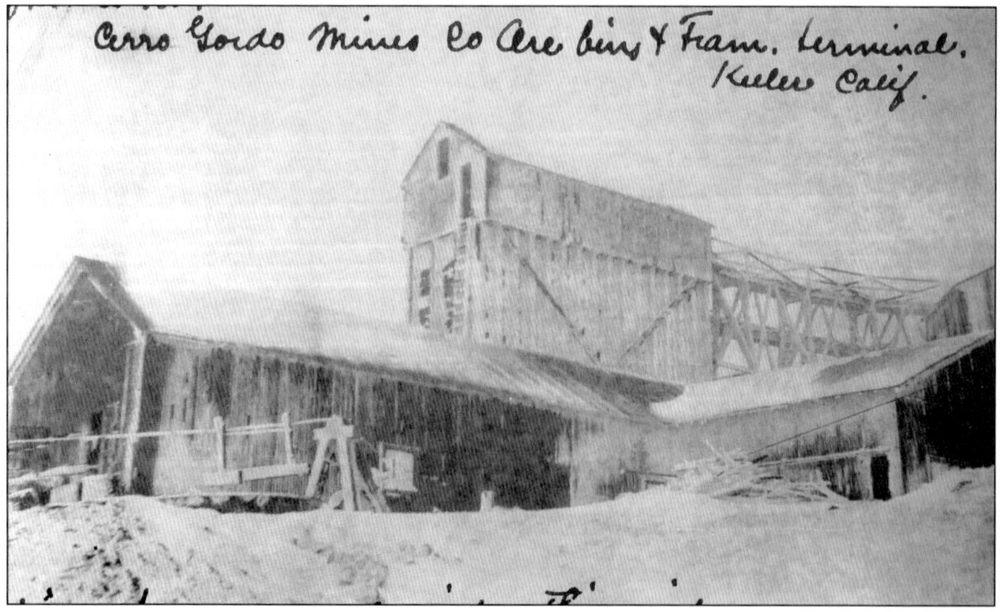

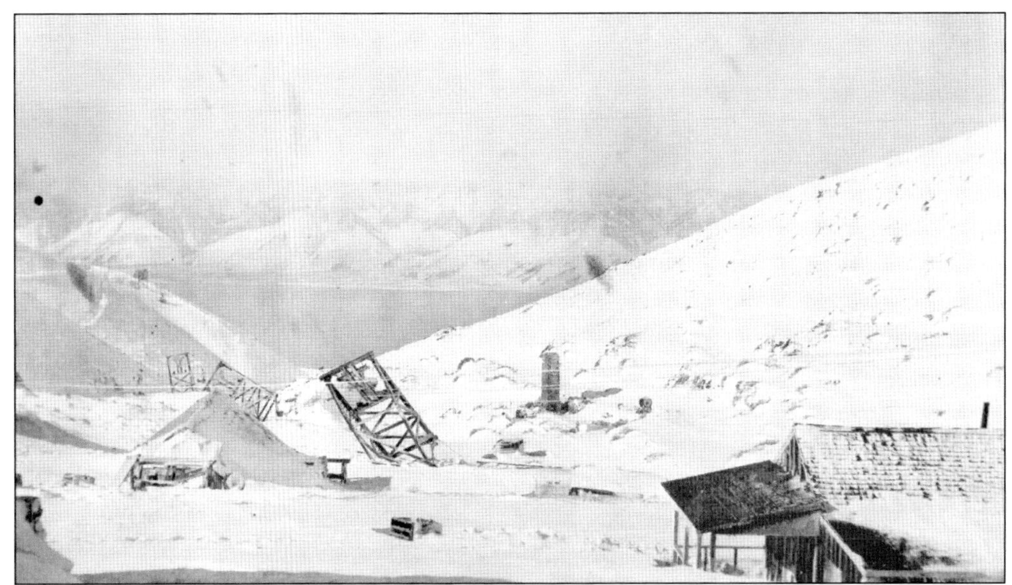

Snow began falling early in the afternoon on Christmas Day in 1916. High winds ripped through canyons and ridges, downing power lines. Some of the tram towers were covered in snow and the town was out of coal for heat. Telegrams were sent to Keeler letting them know the power was off and telephone lines were on the ground in several places. Since the mine was out of coal, backup steam power could not be used. It would not have mattered, because the wind blew too fiercely and the snow was too heavy to repair the downed tram towers. Nine steel power towers were blown over and it took six days to get everything in working order once again. Soon after the storm, reports went out that a rich vein had widened out in the mines, with six inches of ore at the 150-foot level assaying at $228 per ton and 20 inches at $3,000 per ton. The tram was running in full swing, filling 20 railroad cars per day down in Keeler. The image below shows snow-covered Cerro Gordo looking over Owen Lake obscured with heavy cloud cover. (Both, L.D. Gordon Collection.)

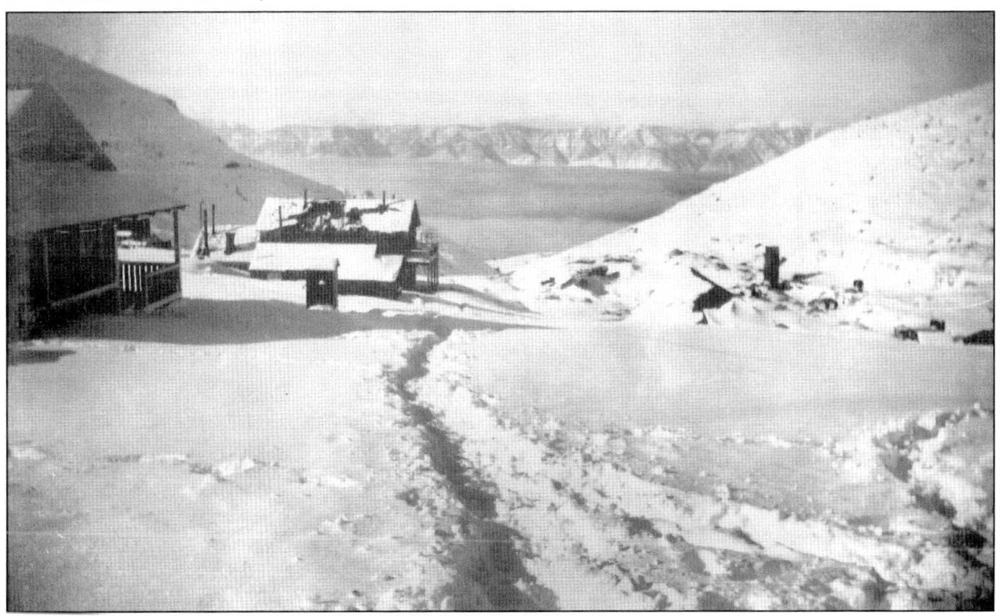

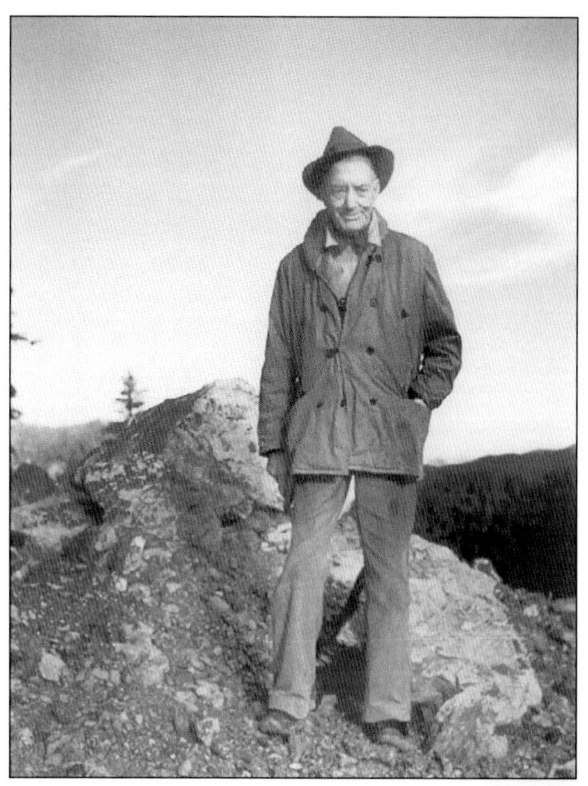

On May 3, 1964, after Louis D. Gordon's death, newspapers paid tribute to him and his many contributions to the mining industry. Gordon was born in Austin, Nevada, on June 23, 1885, and died at the age of 79 in Reno. In addition to interests in Round Mountain and the Cerro Gordo Mines, he was the executive secretary of the Nevada Mining Association, an organizer of the California Metal and Mineral Producer Association, and a member of the executive committee of the Nevada Mine Operators Association, the American Institute of Mining and Metallurgical Engineers, and the American Economic Society. Under his management, Cerro Gordo became the largest producer of lead and second largest producer of zinc in California, producing $6 million worth of ore. During World War II, Gordon worked for the federal Reconstruction Finance Corporation. (Both, L.D. Gordon Collection.)

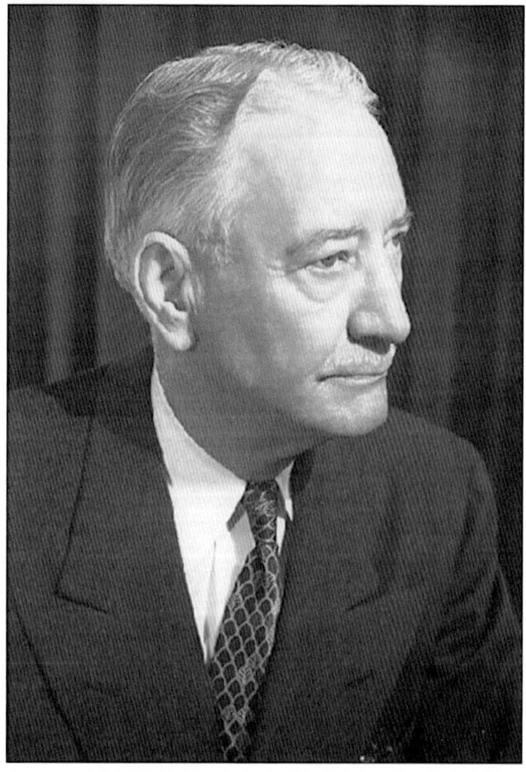

Three

Tram It Up

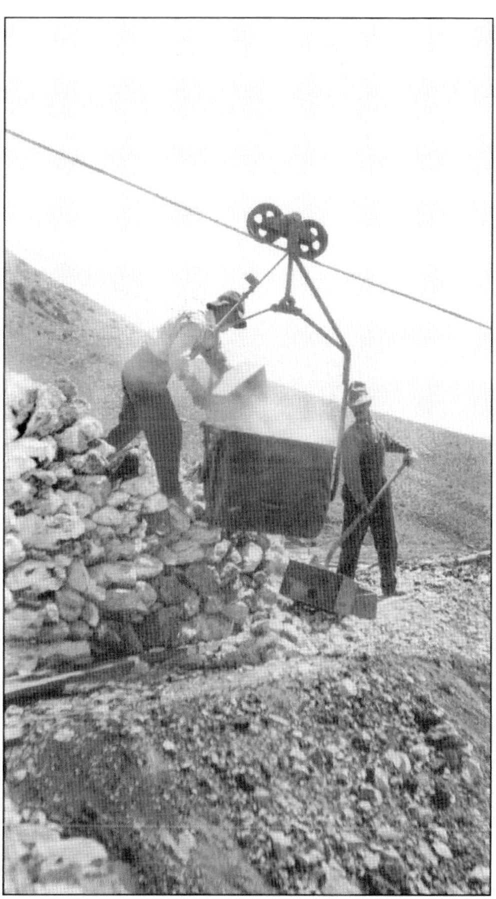

Miners shovel rocks into a tram bucket suspended on a wire rope in a temporary tram operation during the zinc period. Sometime in 1907, before Louis D. Gordon's arrival, the Four Metals Company acquired holdings in Cerro Gordo. The J.H. Montgomery Machinery Company of Colorado was contracted to build what it touted as the finest aerial tram in the United States, which, according to a 1908 Los Angeles newspaper story, cost $70,000 to build. The Montgomery tram never worked properly and was replaced with a Leschen tram in 1915–1916. (L.D. Gordon Collection.)

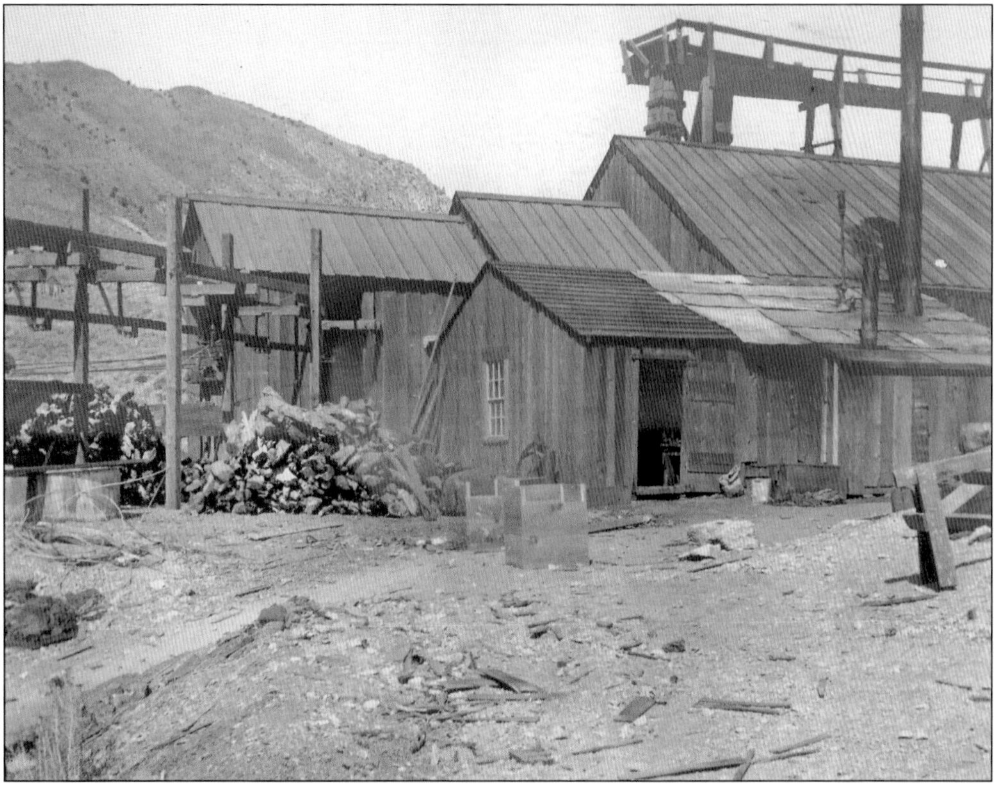

The Montgomery tram was five miles long, from below the main mine to the terminus just short of the town of Keeler, where the smelter was built. A total of 100 men were hired to build the tram, which had a capacity of 50 tons a day. The Four Metals Company smelter opened in December 1908 but the tramway did not begin operation until the spring of 1909. The photograph below shows the tram terminal and its associated buildings. The machinery was steam powered. (Both, L.D. Gordon Collection.)

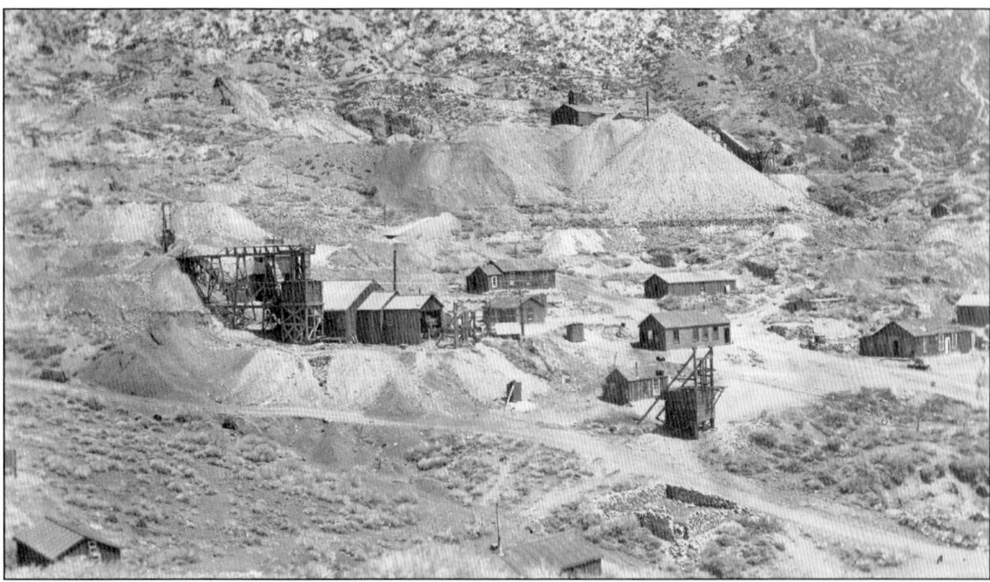

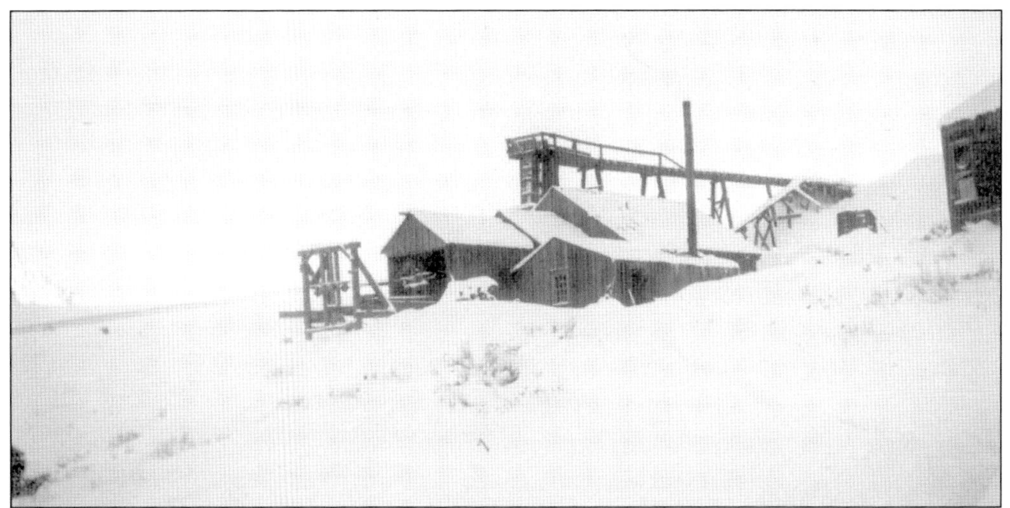

Sometime after 1911, a snowstorm half-buried the tram terminal offices, which had been shut down since the spring of 1910. The Four Metals Company reached the 1,200-foot level of the mines, found the body of ore was not as great as expected, and began having financial problems. Previously, in September 1909, as much as 1,000 tons of high-grade silver ore had been transported from the Union mine dumps. (L.D. Gordon Collection.)

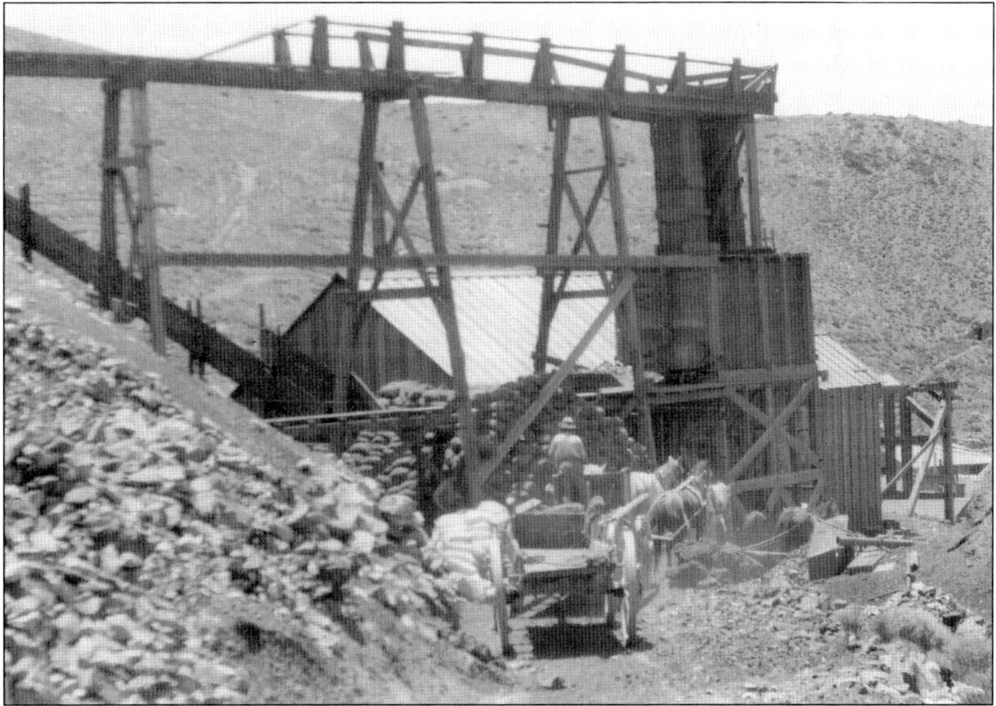

A horse-drawn wagon passes the ore hopper and the Montgomery tramway terminal. A good team of horses or mules with a wagon full of silver ore took four hours to travel the eight miles up or down the Yellow Grade Road. A steam traction engine temporarily replaced the wagons, cutting the trip to two hours, but it proved unstable on the precipitous route. The tram took three miles off the trip, traveled faster, and was more cost-effective. However, the first Montgomery tram was plagued with engineering problems and was eventually replaced. (L.D. Gordon Collection.)

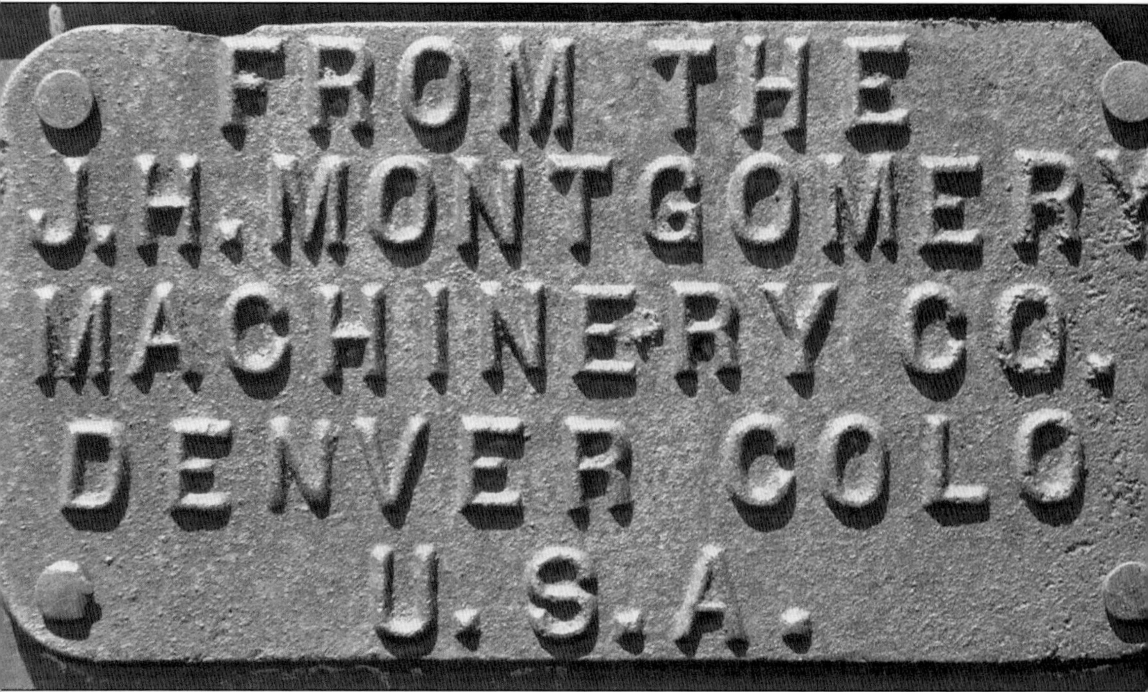

This is a close-up of the manufacturer identification plate from one of the J.H. Montgomery Co. tram buckets. Many of the Montgomery buckets were still used after the tram system was re-engineered by the Leschen and Sons Wire Rope Co. to increase speed, capacity, and reliability. (Explore Historic California Collection.)

AUTOMATIC WIRE ROPE TRAMWAYS

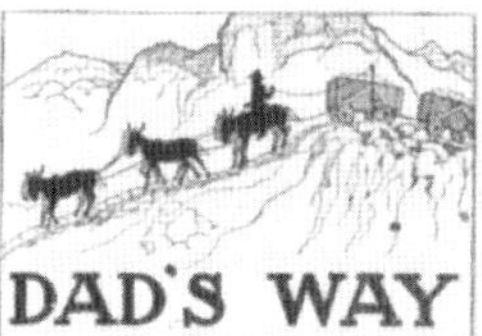

Dad employed the cheapest and best way to move ore there was in his day

DAD WAS ALWAYS UP TO DATE

The cheapest and best way to move ore NOW is with MONTGOMERY'S IMPROVED AUTOMATIC TRAMWAYS. R. Jones of the Revenue mine, near Pitkin, Colo., was doing it Dad's way with two teams at $24.00 per day, hauling quartz for their 10-stamp mill. He installed a Montgomery tramway for $1,100.00, now one man two hours cost $1.00; does the same work; saves the mine $23.00 per day. If YOU are doing it Dad's Way better write or see Monty at once.

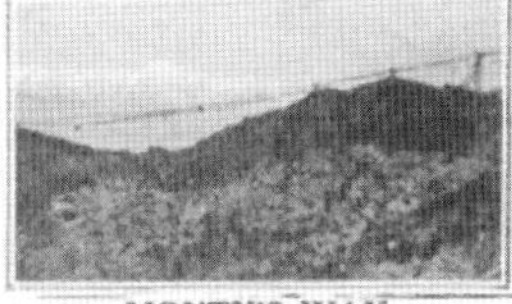

MONTY'S WAY

THE J. H. MONTGOMERY MACHINERY CO., 1445 Thirteenth St., Denver, Colo., P. O. Box 498

The Leschen tram replaced the Montgomery tram around 1915–1916. This advertisement for the J.H. Montgomery Machinery Co. tram ran in the December 29, 1910, issue of *Mining Science*. In the 19th-century mining boom, equipment and bullion was hauled to and from Cerro Gordo "Dad's Way." The 20th century brought "Monty's Way" of mechanized transport. However, the Montgomery tram was not very efficient or reliable and was eventually replaced with equipment from A. Leschen & Sons. (Explore Historic California Collection.)

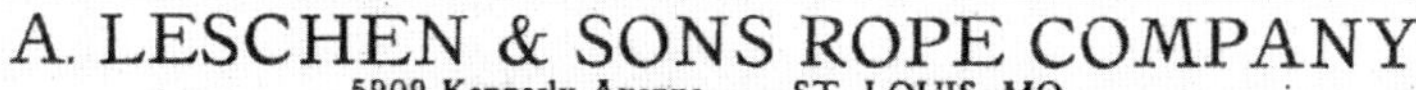

A. LESCHEN & SONS ROPE COMPANY

5909 Kennerly Avenue ST. LOUIS, MO.

Branches

NEW YORK CHICAGO DENVER SAN FRANCISCO

Manufacturers of

Aerial Wire Rope Tramways For All Purposes

(See Pages 488 and 489 for Data on Leschen Wire Rope)

Products and Services

Designers and manufacturers of Aerial Tramways in the following systems:

The Leschen Heavy Duty Friction Grip System. For heavy capacities, long distances and general use.

The Leschen Special Automatic System. Where labor is scarce or expensive.

The Leschen Two-Bucket System. For short lines—heavy or light capacities.

The Leschen Single Carrier System. For small capacities.

Special Designs to Suit Particular Conditions. Our Aerial Tramways are built for hard service. They are especially noted for their low upkeep cost.

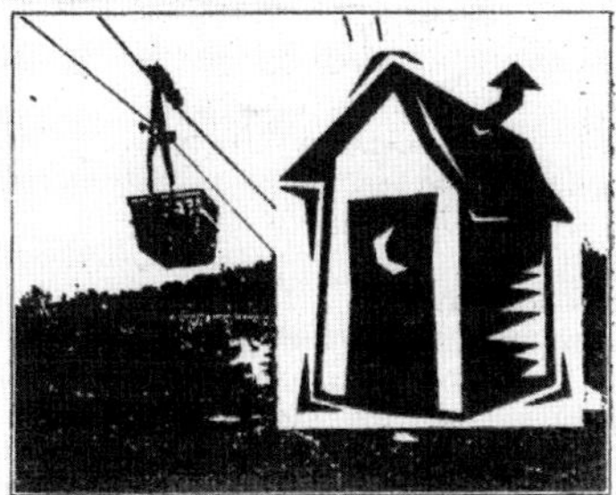

This installation carries 150 tons of crushed rock per hour from quarry to mixing plant on a large concrete job in New York State. On this particular project we furnished three aerial tramways for handling the stone, sand and cement. The contractor has told us that these tramways give him less trouble than any piece of equipment on the job.

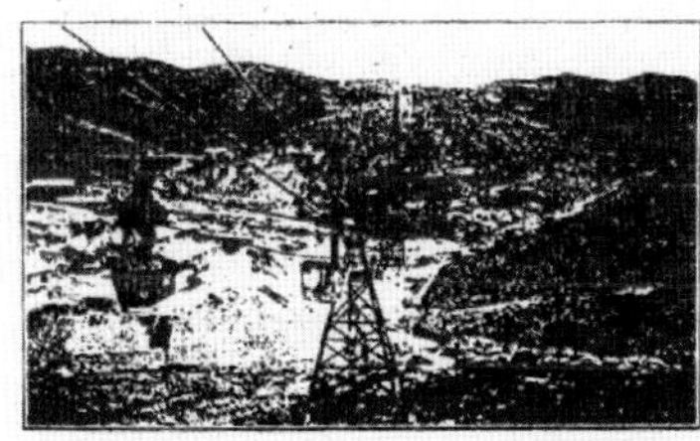

This line in Mexico is four miles long and has a capacity of 100 tons per hour of silver ore. Note the extremely rough country, where the cost of any other means of transportation would have been prohibitive.

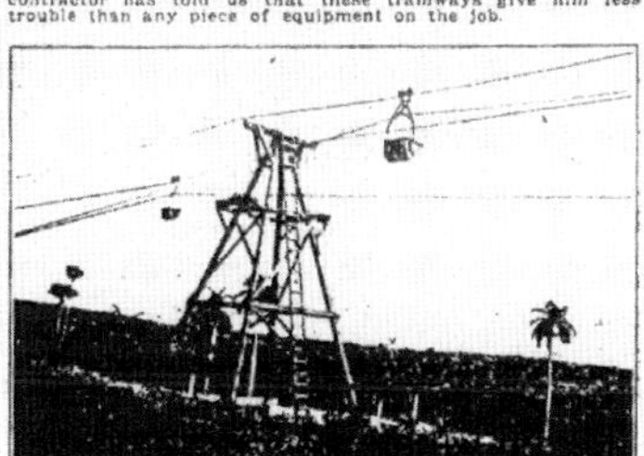

View along line of a six-mile tramway in Cuba for transporting copper ore. This installation reduced transportation cost from over $2.00 per ton to 35c per ton. Cost of installation returned in a year's saving.

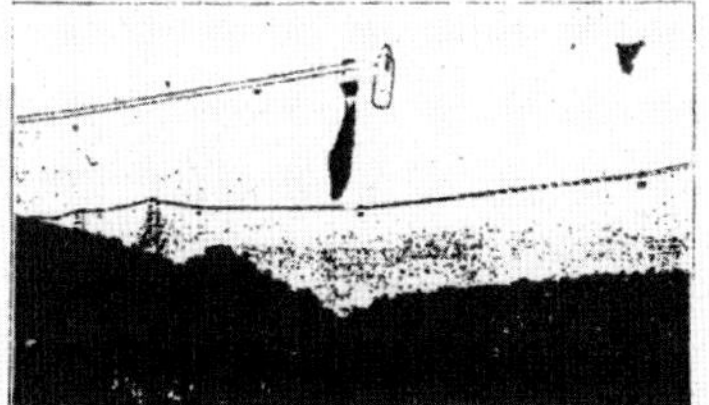

This Leschen Heavy Duty Friction Grip Tramway carries 100 tons of ashes per hour from a power plant of the West Penn Power Company and deposits them in a distant ravine. The line is automatic, except at the loading terminal, and the carriers pass around three angle stations.

If you are contemplating the purchase of an aerial tramway, or if you are having transportation troubles, our Engineering Department will gladly advise whether a tramway will solve your problem, and if so, they will suggest the system best suited to your conditions, and will furnish you an approximate estimate of cost.

See page 500 for your convenience in sending in your requirements.

We have designed and manufactured Aerial Wire Rope Tramways for twenty-five years, therefore our various tramway systems are the product of practical experience.

SECTION X KEYSTONE-CATALOG

This ad for the A. Leschen & Sons Rope Company out of St. Louis, Missouri, was found by Jody Stewart and Mike Patterson during their research on the tramway when Cerro Gordo was under their ownership as a ghost town in more recent times. The advertisement touts the Leschen heavy-duty friction grip system, its special automatic system, two-bucket system, and single carrier system, all designed for hard services and low upkeep. The Leschen tram survived until it was dismantled in the late 1950s and moved to Candelaria, Nevada. (Cerro Gordo Collection.)

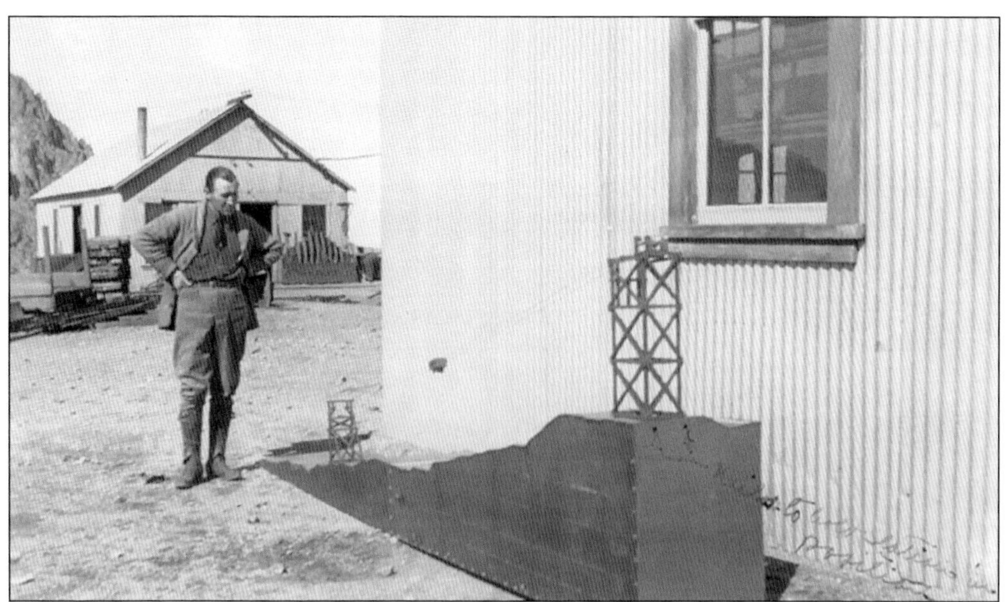

The A. Leschen & Sons Rope Company was hired to replace the Montgomery tram. Above, a design engineer displays his model—29,560 feet in length and capable of moving 16 to 20 tons a day. The force of gravity pulled loaded ore buckets down the mountain and empty buckets up. A brake housed at Cerro Gordo controlled the speed with three bands, using an electric motor to move things along. The Leschen sign below was found in 1995 while volunteers excavated the vault of an old outhouse at Cerro Gordo. (Above, L.D. Gordon Collection; below, Explore Historic California Collection.)

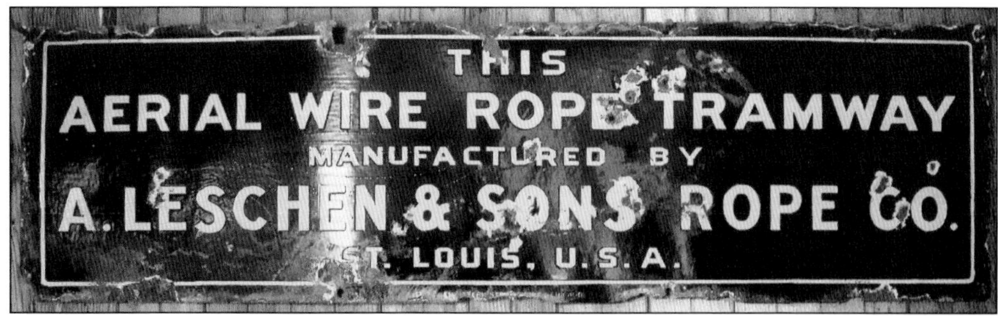

A temporary line was put in to transport slag from the smelter to the ore bins at the Leschen. A one-ton standard ore car was used to run on tracks in and around the mines and was fitted with two wheels on each side so that it would roll on stationary cables suspended in the air on modified tram towers. The front of the car was attached by cable, and motor driven up to the ore bins. Gravity brought the car back down to the slag dump once the winch was disengaged; a makeshift brake was used to control the car's descent. (L.D. Gordon Collection.)

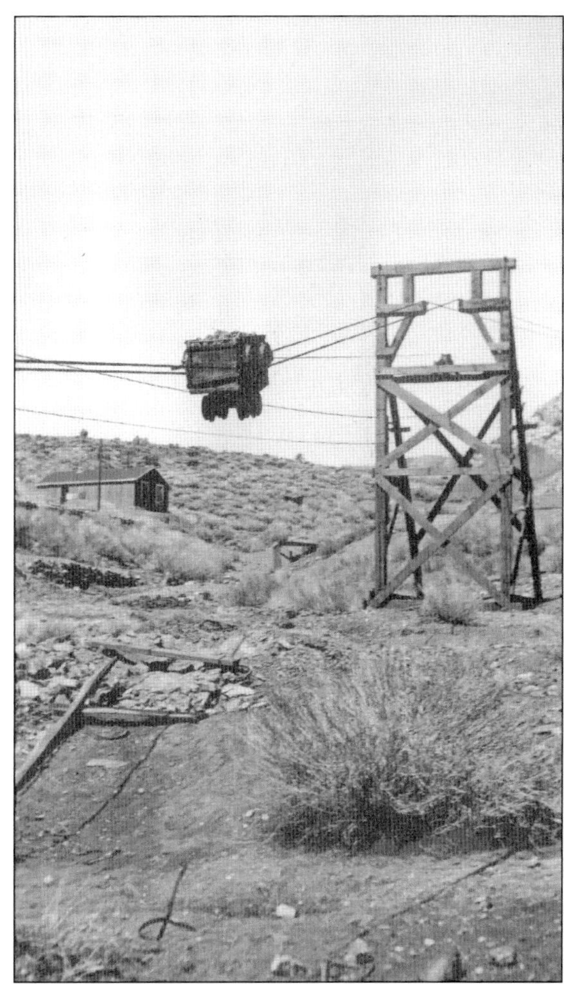

This is a close-up of the hybrid tramcar with Leschen terminal and Cerro Gordo's old mule barn in the background. According to historian Robert C. Likes, this system was an accident waiting to happen. He was proven correct on July 22, 1916, when Hannah Ryan was taking her burro for a ride. As she passed under the tram, the cable broke and hit her, knocking her off the burro headfirst and entangling both her feet in the burro's saddle stirrups. Among her injuries was a dislocated and swollen shoulder and severe skin abrasions. A lawsuit went on for four or five years, but the outcome has been lost to history. (L.D. Gordon Collection.)

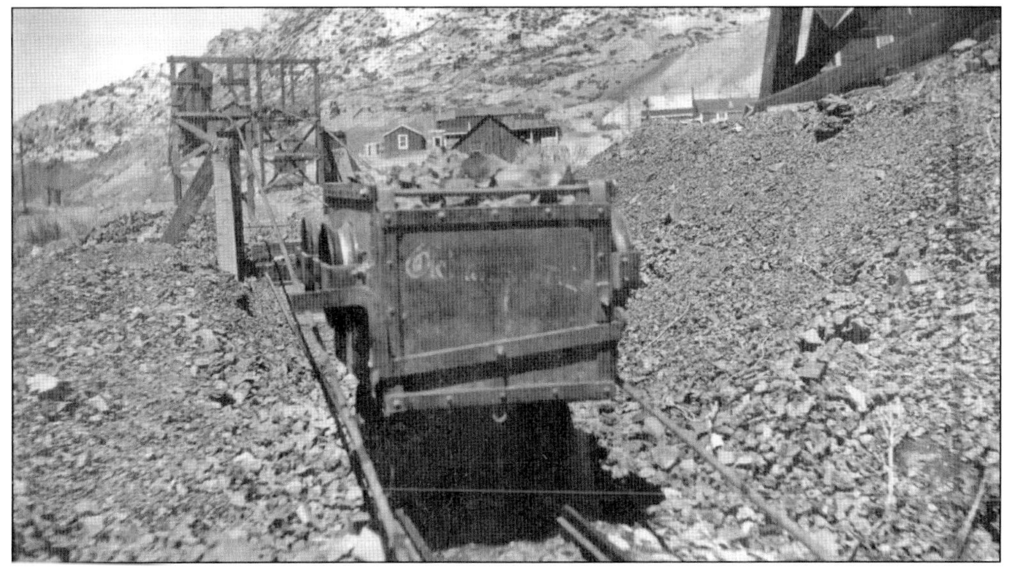

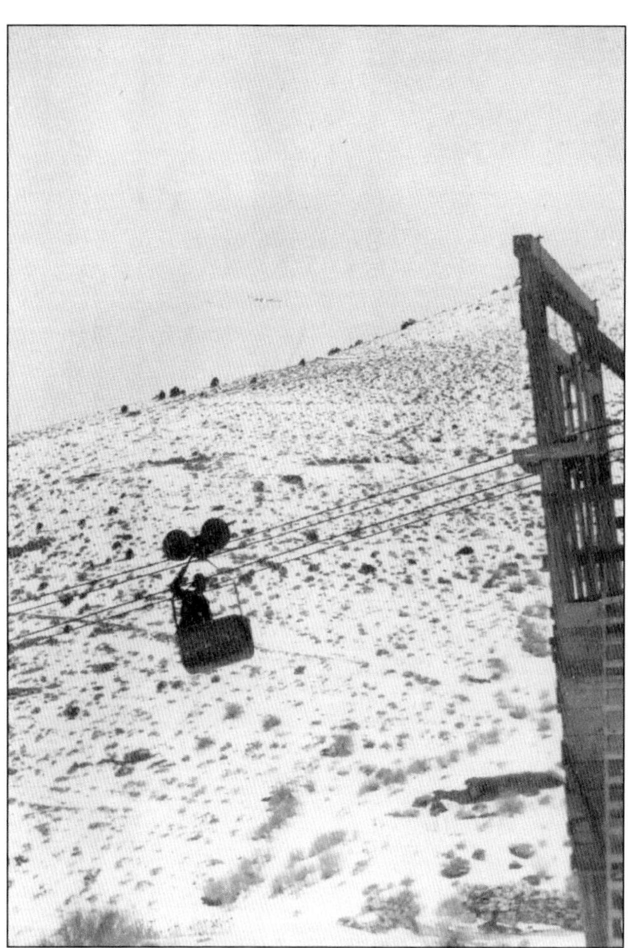

The man riding the ore bucket could possibly be the doctor who was called to Cerro Gordo to attend to Hannah Ryan after her accident. The doctor has been described as a properly attired gentleman, carrying a black leather bag equipped with medicine and a quart of local brew painkiller. Following his ride on the bucket, he said, "It was a fast trip, but never ask me to do it again." (L.D. Gordon Collection.)

A special rig was built using a chain and ratcheted device to carry heavy pieces of equipment from the railhead. Other devices such as this wood carrier were also used. This wood carrier is seen on a temporary tram system used during the construction of the Leschen tram. (L.D. Gordon Collection.)

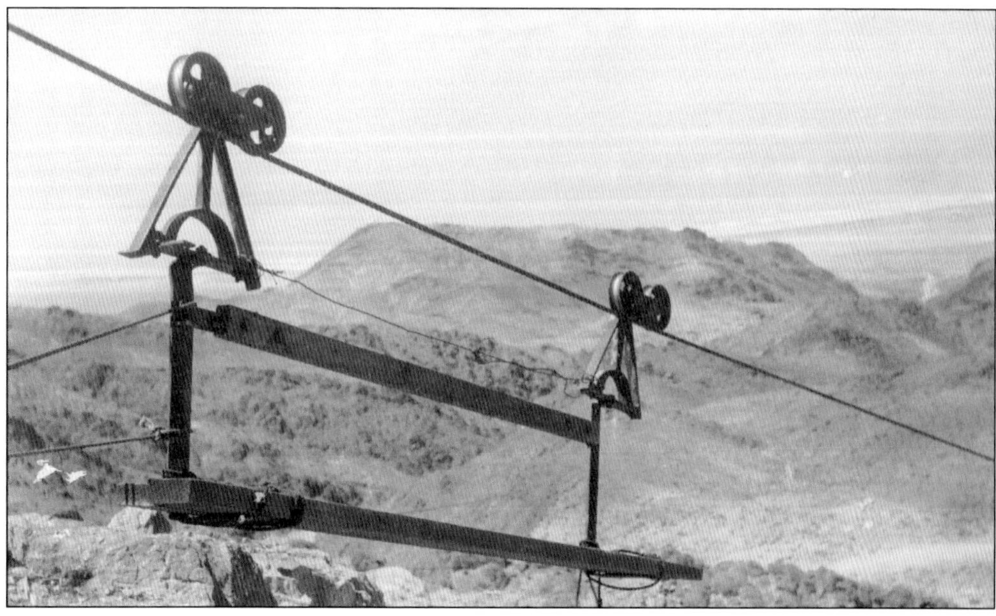

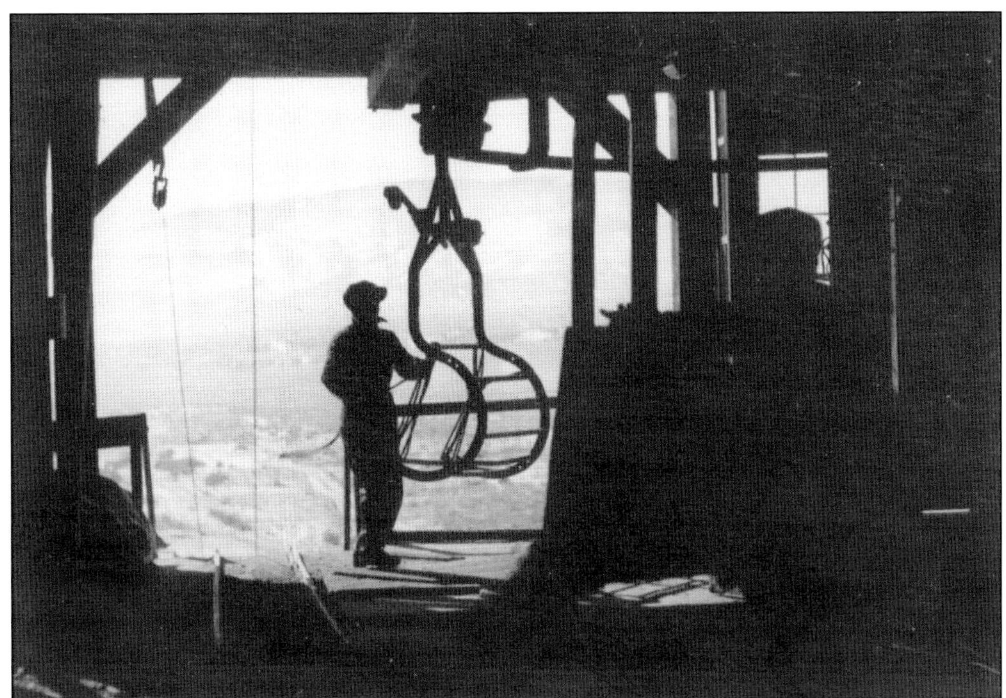

Specialized carriers were designed to be switched on or off the cable at either end of the line. Above, a workman is silhouetted at the edge of the tram terminal as he maneuvers an empty barrel carrier. One design carried barrels of grease, oil or other liquids, and could also carry wrapped and bundled supplies. Below, a barrel carrier glides along the wire rope tramway at Cerro Gordo. (Both, L.D. Gordon Collection.)

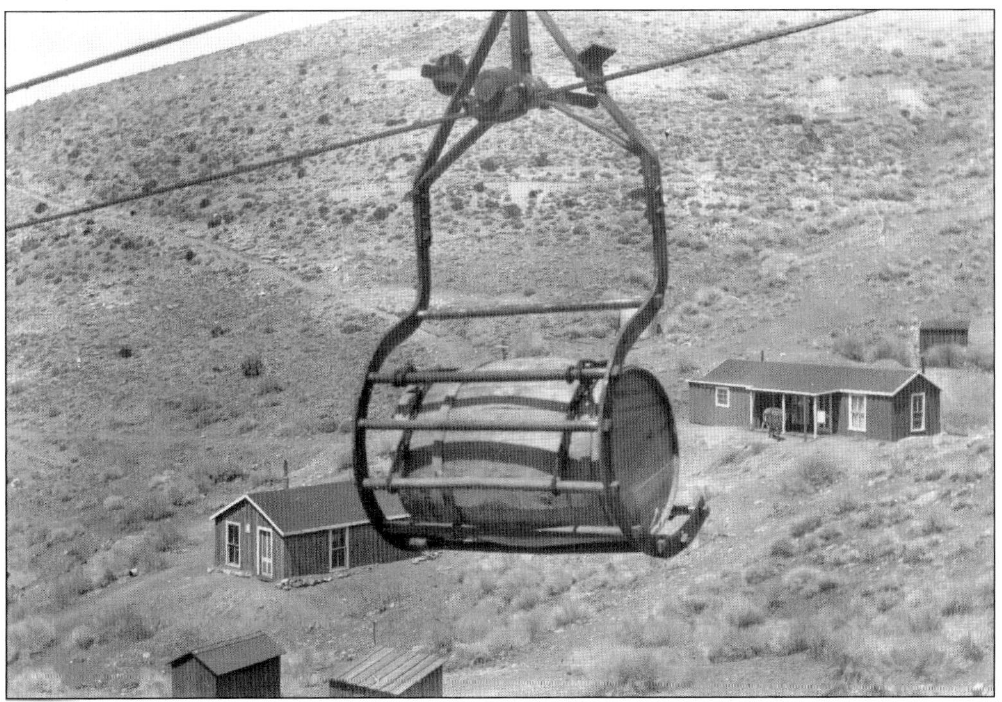

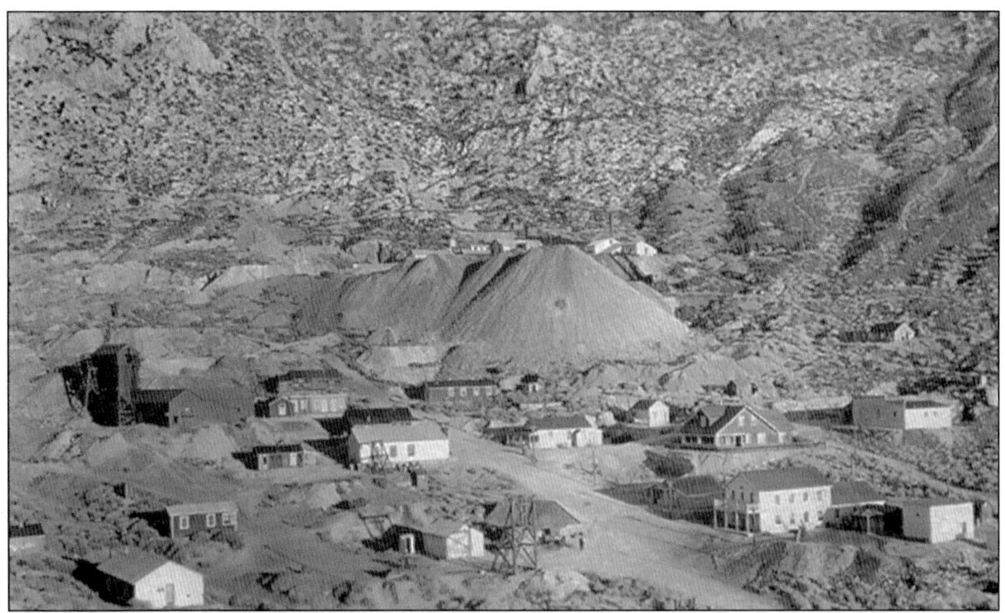

This view of Cerro Gordo is from after 1916. The Leschen tram terminal is the dark structure at far left. The American Hotel, one of Cerro Gordo's original buildings, from 1871, is in the lower right corner along with its newfangled icehouse (the first commercial ice plant in Inyo County). (L.D. Gordon Collection.)

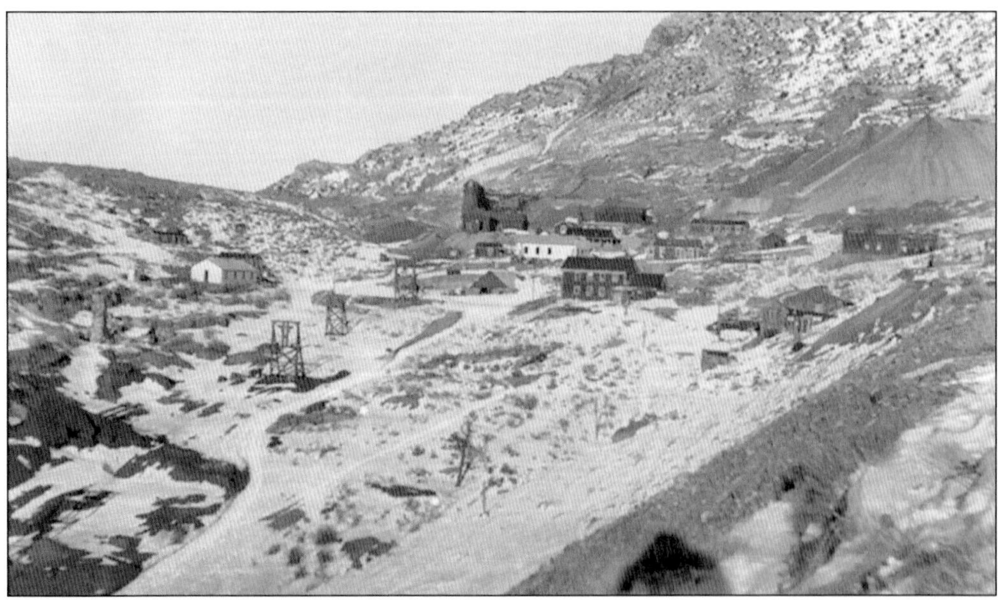

Tram towers extend westward from the Leschen terminal building (center) past the remnants of Victor Beaudry's smelter (left). The light-colored building to the left of the tram towers is the bunkhouse, which still stands today. The A-frame building between the tram towers and the American Hotel is a mule barn. (L.D. Gordon Collection.)

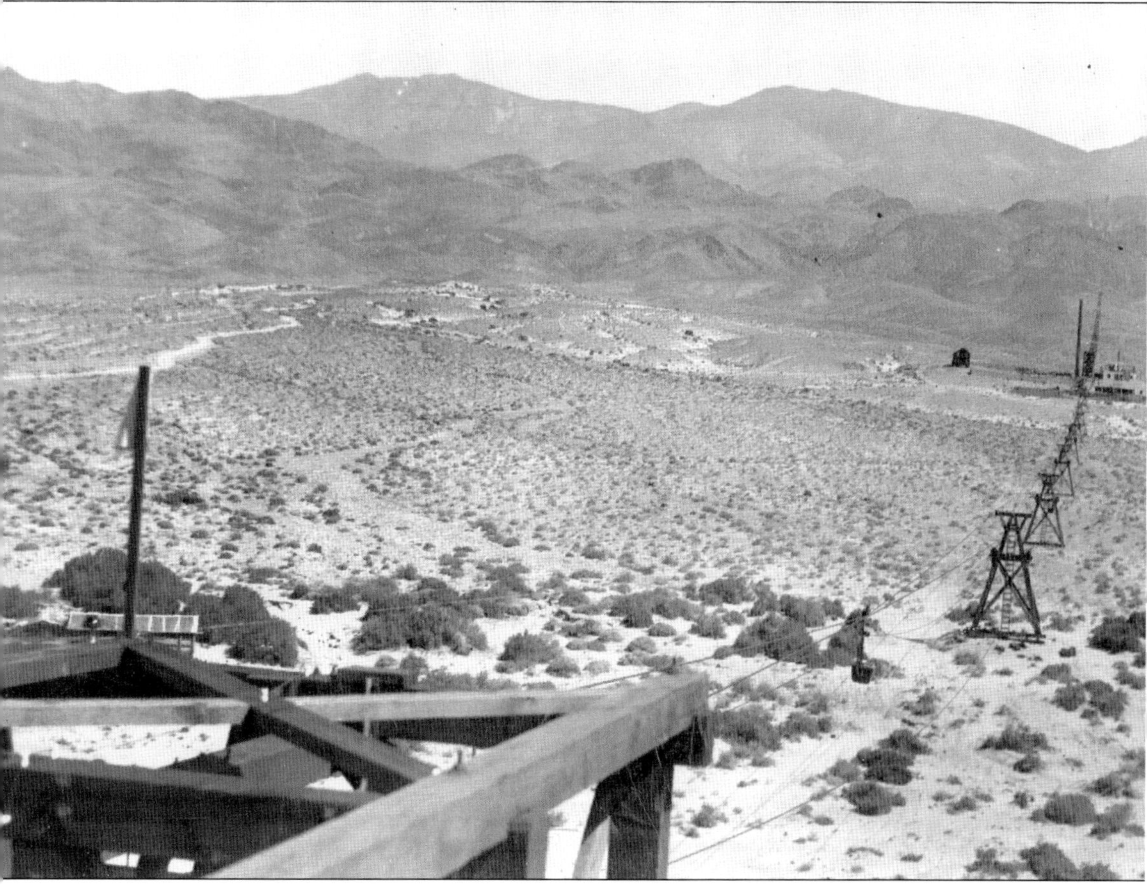

Wooden tram towers and steel cables appear to march in a single-file line downhill towards the old Four Metals smelter and beyond to Keeler. The total length of the tram was 5.5 miles, the last two miles a straight line over gently sloping terrain at the foothills of the Inyo Mountains. The proximity of the Southern Pacific narrow-gauge railroad in Keeler helped deliver construction supplies close to where they were needed. The Leschen tram was built at an estimated cost of $225,000 and the new tram was in service by 1916. (L.D. Gordon Collection.)

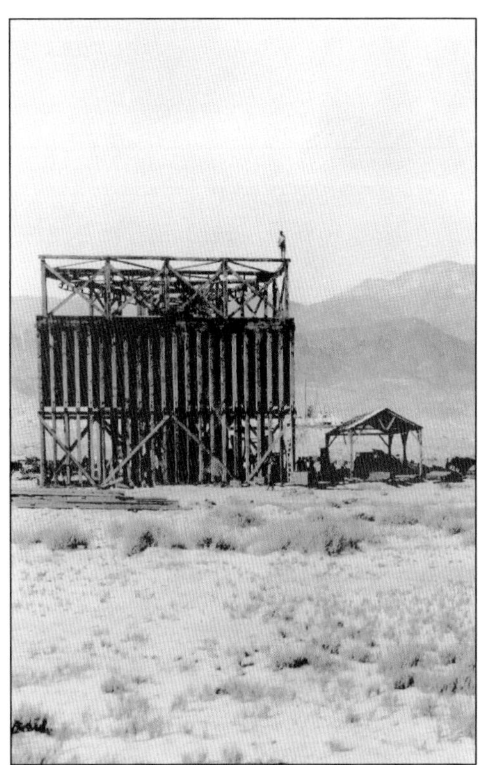

A man stands precariously on the right edge of the Keeler tram terminal while it is still under construction. This view looks west and the line of towers can be seen at the edge of the terminal leading to the old Four Metals smelter and uphill 5.5 miles into the Inyo Mountains and Cerro Gordo. (L.D. Gordon Collection.)

Three railcars full of ore await shipment on the Southern Pacific narrow gauge rail line out of Keeler. The tram was powered by electricity and gravity. The zinc ore was shipped to Kansas for processing. (L.D. Gordon Collection.)

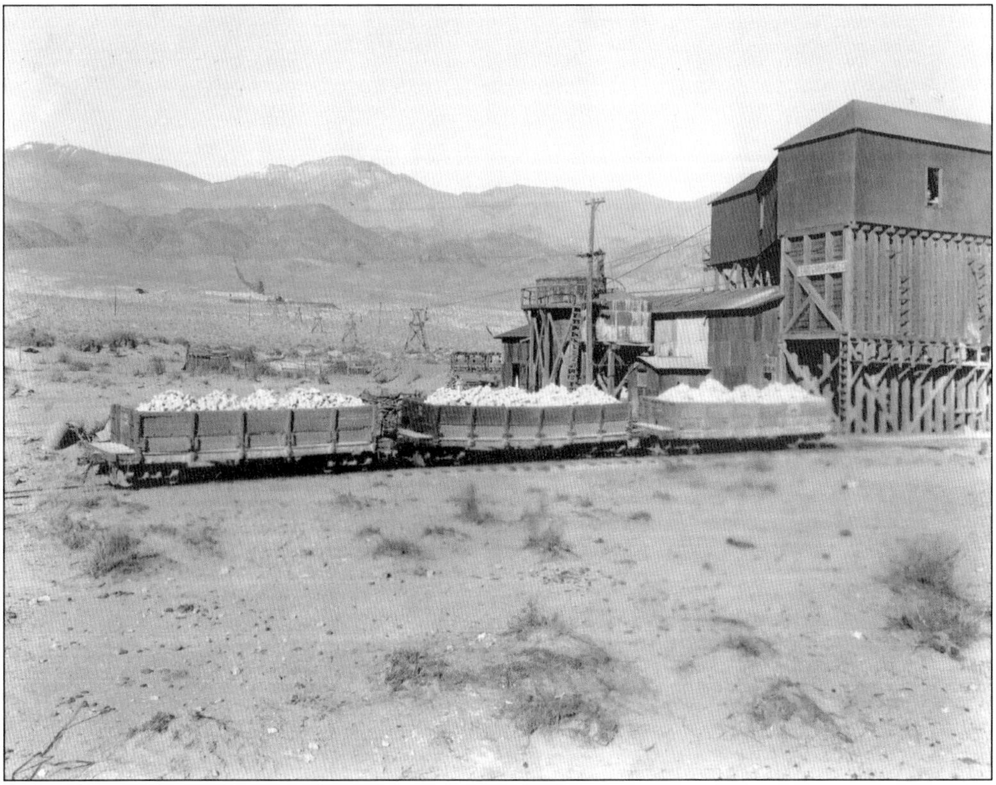

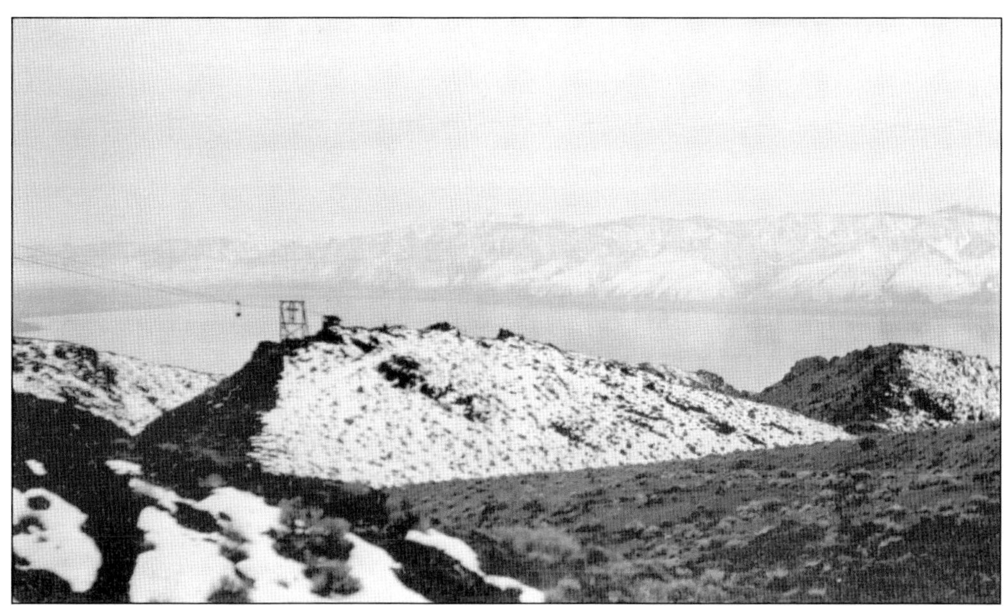

The route of the tram traversed the snow-powdered Inyo Mountains, with a view of Owens Lake down below. In the distance, the Sierra Nevada Mountains—also snow covered—can be seen. The lake was starting to fade long before Los Angeles diverted water from contributing streams, but it was still a far cry from the dry lake it has become. The image below is a rare photograph of the Owens Lake shoreline with the Inyo Mountains and Keeler reflecting in the water. Cornelia Gordon described her first view of the lake: "[the] water was as blue as a sapphire. I shall never forget my first look at it after we reached the top of the hill." (Both, L.D. Gordon Collection.)

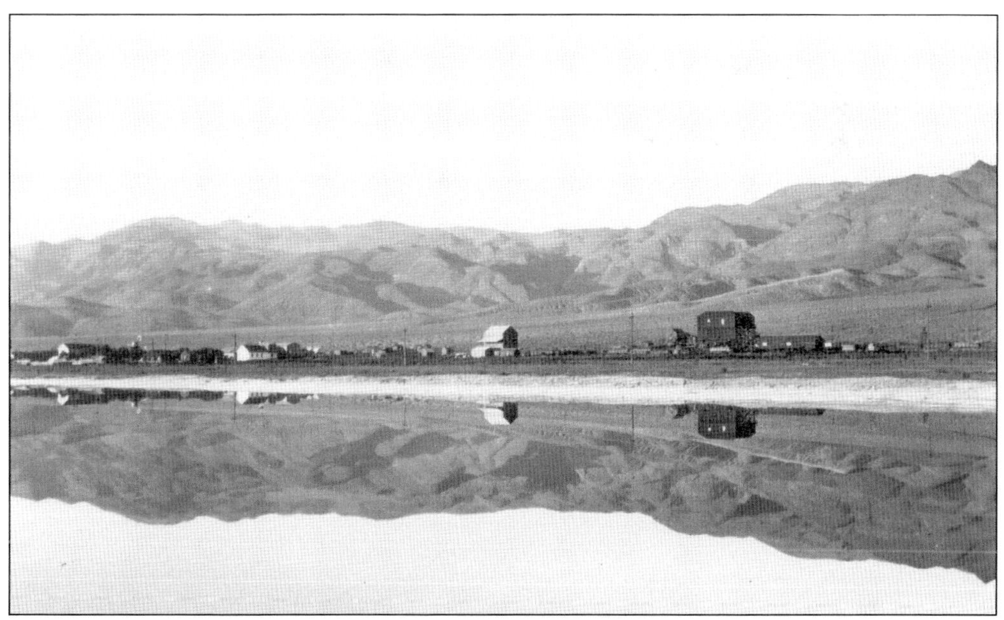

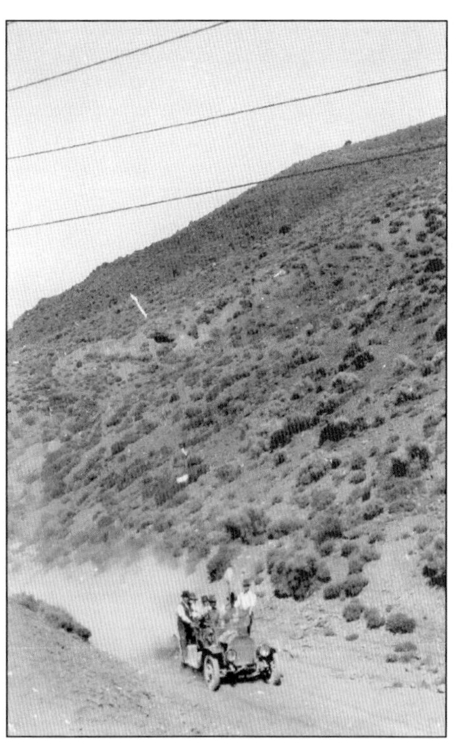

Six men and assorted hand tools ride an automobile under tram cables to Cerro Gordo. The steep and rocky roads were better suited to horses and wagons, as cars suffered frequent mechanical problems or flat tires and repair parts were not easy to find. (L.D. Gordon Collection.)

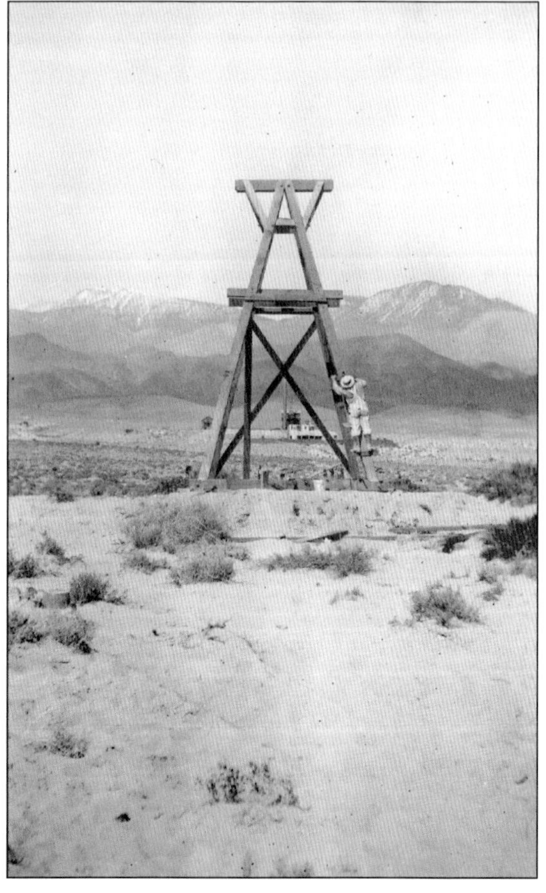

Cerro Gordo's tram system ran from ridge to ridge, spanning canyons. Sturdy wooden towers were constructed to support the cables and related equipment. The few trees that grow in the vicinity of Cerro Gordo are unsuitable for such construction, so lumber had to be hauled in from other areas. Fortunately, the Southern Pacific's narrow gauge rail line terminated at Keeler from points north. The Southern Pacific, known as the Espee, also connected Owens Valley with Southern California once its standard gauge line was completed in October 1910. Other than the soft ground, tower construction in the flat country near Keeler was relatively straightforward. However, transporting the heavy timbers into the Inyo Mountains was another story, as the main road was still the steep Yellow Grade Road built in the late 1800s. Internal combustion vehicles of that era were not up to the task and mule teams were relied upon for the heavy work. (L.D. Gordon Collection.)

A man poses on a wooden tram tower at Cerro Gordo. The towers were made of heavy wooden beams fastened together with steel bolts. Since few trees grow near Cerro Gordo, all the wood had to be hauled in from long distances, including the arduous eight-mile ride up the Yellow Grade Road, or on specially designed tram carriers. (L.D. Gordon Collection.)

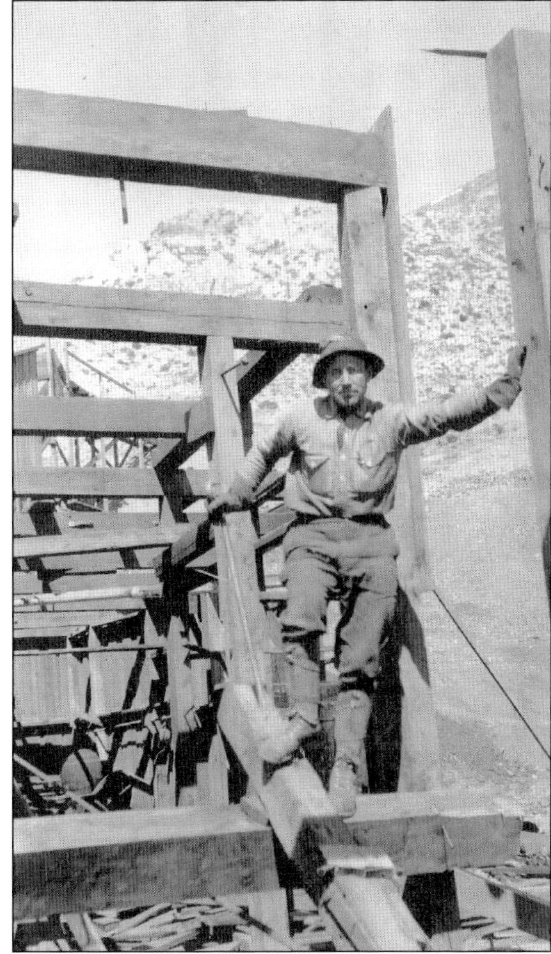

Temporary trams were used in the construction of the main tram system. This photograph shows the apparent collapse of one of the temporary stations. The main tram system used two cables strung between the towers, one for "track" and the other for motion. The temporary trams used a single track cable and the loads were pulled along by rope or smaller wire cable. (L.D. Gordon Collection.)

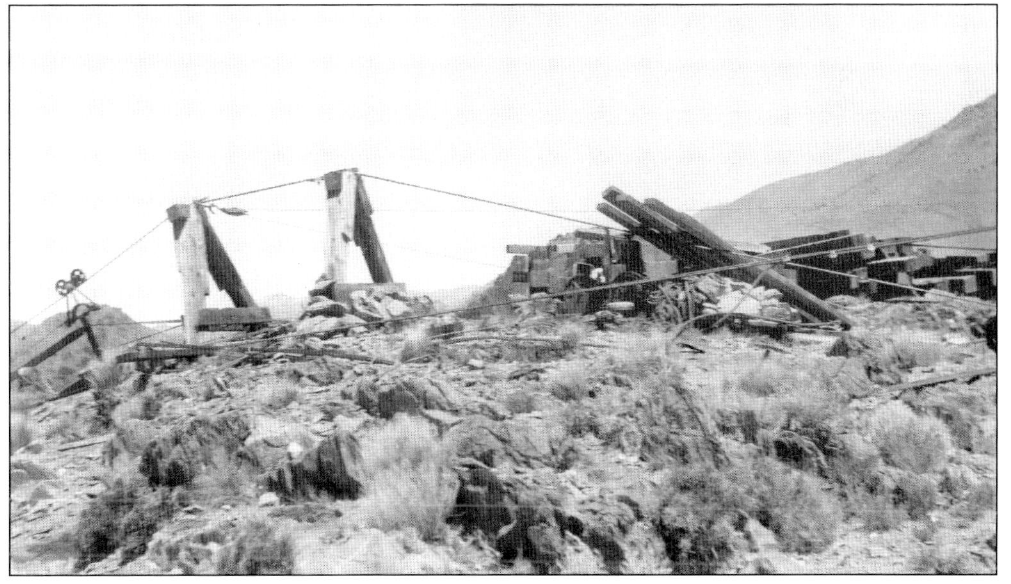

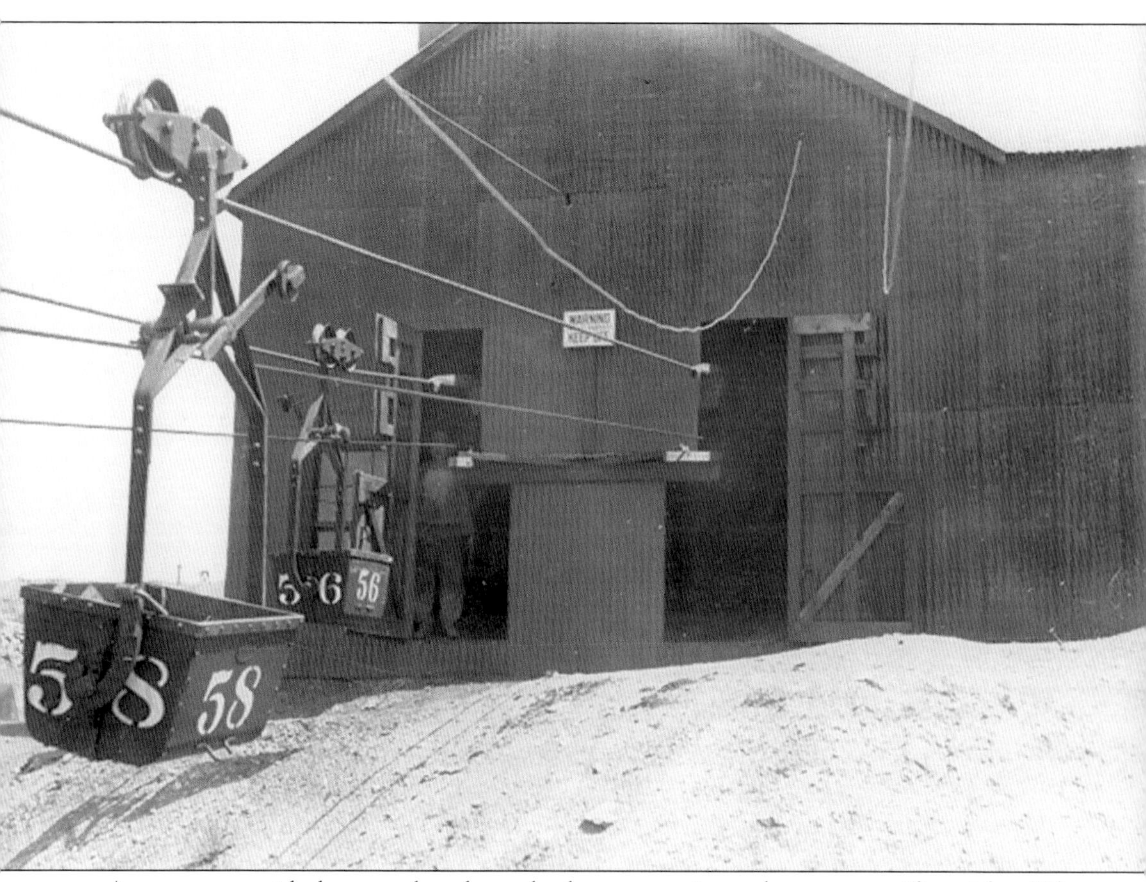

A tram system with these numbered tram buckets was engineered to carry specific weights. When design parameters were exceeded, the results were usually equipment failure, including excess cable wear and stretching, runaway buckets, broken cables, or burned out braking systems. A broken tram system not only presented a danger to the workers, it meant an important link in the mining operation was not available. If material could not be shipped, the mine owners did not make money and the workers could not be paid. At Cerro Gordo, the buckets carried various rock loads, from silver-lead ores to furnace slag to zinc ores. According to information from Herbert Hoover's 1909 *Principles of Mining*, a mining reference book that would have been available to L.D. Gordon, galena, or lead, ores weighed about 4.5 cubic feet per ton, zinc ores between 8 and 9 cubic feet per ton, and quartz rock and granites about 12 cubic feet per ton. The tram buckets used at Cerro Gordo had a volume of approximately 9 cubic feet (1 cubic yard). When the tram buckets were used to haul supplies and equipment up to Cerro Gordo, that weight and volume had to be taken into consideration. (L.D. Gordon Collection.)

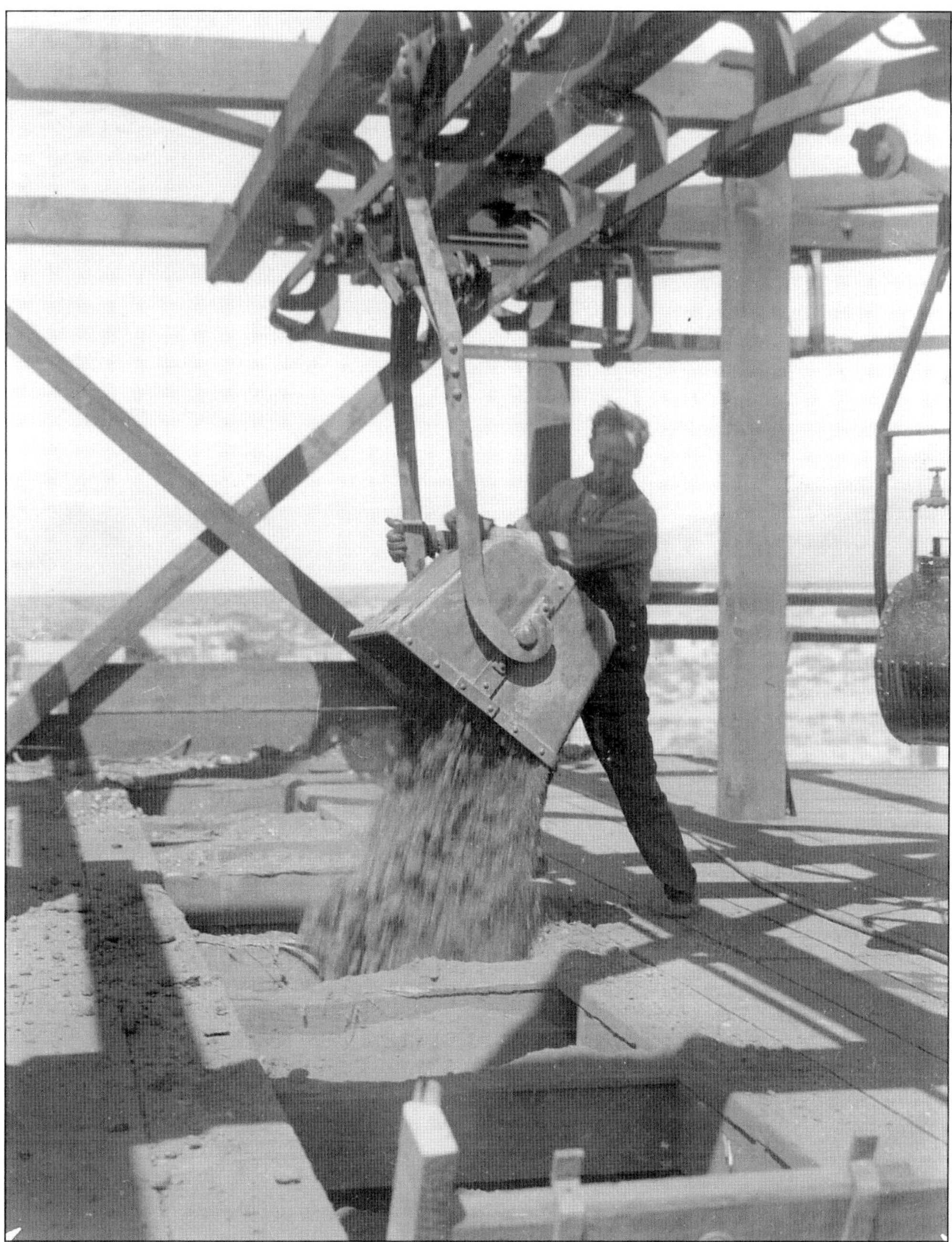

A workman empties a loaded tram bucket at the Keeler terminal. The ore was then loaded on to narrow gauge railcars and shipped to a smelter for refining. Safety equipment for the worker in this case consisted of overalls, boots, and gloves. In spite of the danger from moving machinery, workers were not seen wearing head or eye protection. This photograph was taken before the top floor of the tram terminal was enclosed. (L.D. Gordon Collection.)

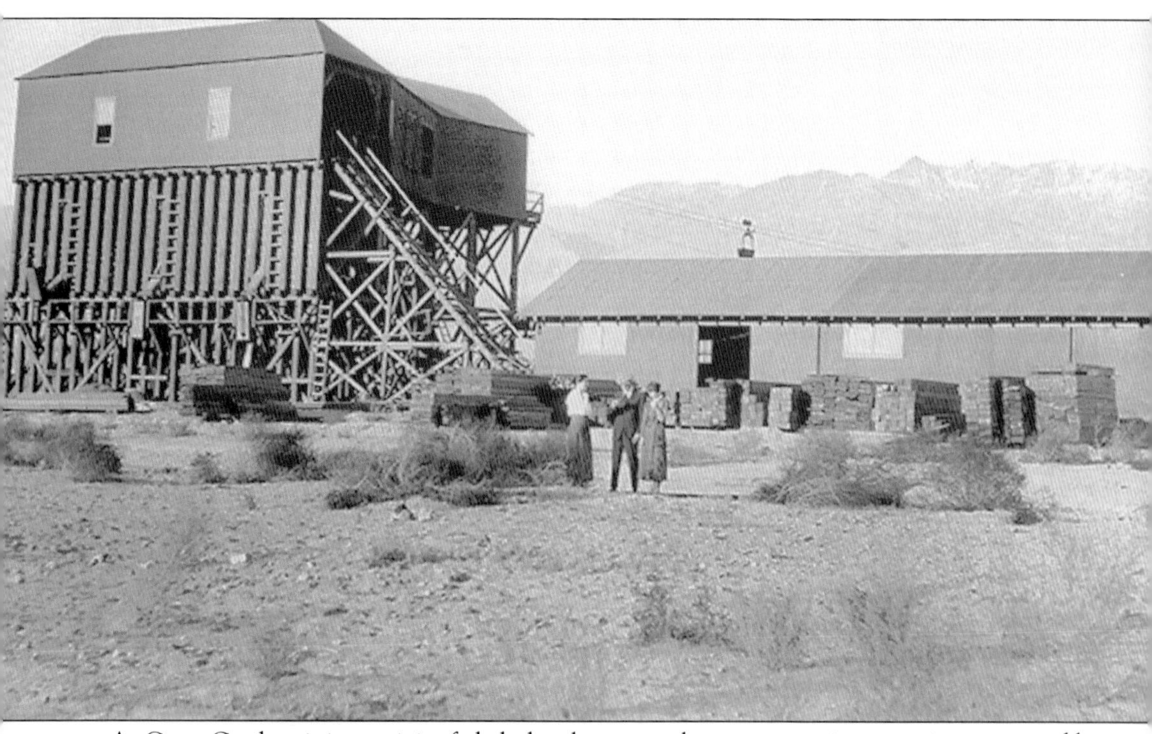

As Cerro Gordo mining activity faded, the ghost town became a tourist attraction, managed by a series of caretakers and owners. While idle for more than a quarter century, the tram towers, buckets, cable, and terminus at Keeler were also local landmarks. In April 1960, a *Desert Magazine* reader noted, "I was astounded, flabbergasted and greatly disgruntled to find that the tram terminal building and the tram, which at one time carried ore down to Keeler from the Cerro Gordo Mines have disappeared! The sturdy terminal building was not merely torn down; it has vanished. I am indeed sorry that the old landmark had to go." Two months later, *Desert* published a response from a representative of Argentum Mines Co. in Nevada. "I should like to assure Mr. Kanagy that the tram has neither vanished nor disappeared . . . The Cerro Gordo tram was purchased recently by the Argentum Mines Co., which has just placed in operation Nevada's largest precious metals mining and milling project on the north side of Columbus Flat in Esmeralda County . . . Plans call for placing the Cerro Gordo tram into operation as soon as possible to transport additional supplies of silver ore from the Alpha T Mine or from the Candeleria dumps. The sturdy terminal building, which M. Kanagy says has vanished, is also at the edge of Columbus Flat very much in evidence and looking forward to a new and interesting career still very much in the desert." Mike Patterson later elaborated, "Roughly around 1958 the tram was 'parted out' for salvage. Apparently quite a bit of the hardware was purchased by a mining company who intended to put it back into service in Candelaria, Nevada. Those plans never came to fruition. Quite a few large tram tower timbers were purchased by a former test pilot who was remodeling his home near Genoa, Nevada. He stacked the timbers 'log cabin' style, for 'the look' as well as the R-value. This writer believes he could have rivaled Scotty's Castle had he opted for the post and beam style construction." (L.D. Gordon Collection.)

Four

Of Mines, Men, Mules, and Machinery

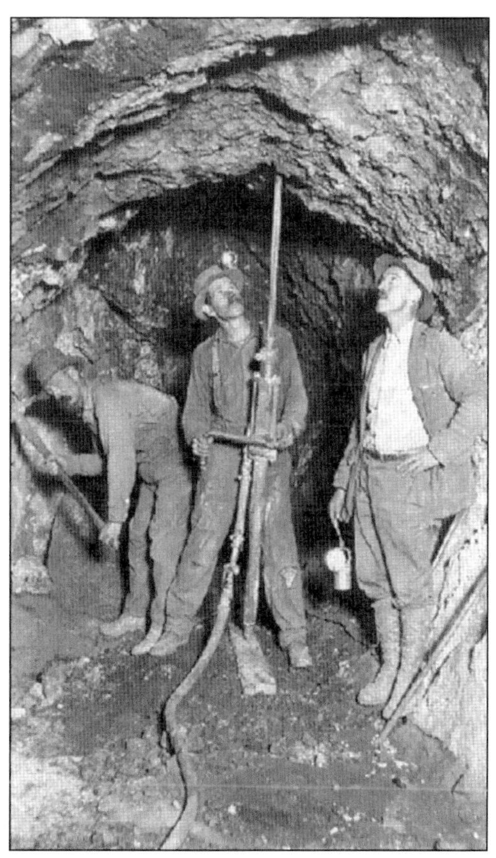

Underground mining is tough, dirty work. The miner in the center uses a pneumatic (air-powered) drill to bore a hole in a tunnel ceiling while the miner on the left works with a pickaxe. Early miners used a sledgehammer to power a chisel-like drill. A good worker could drill about one inch per hour in hard rock. Pneumatic drills sped things up considerably but also caused many deaths from inhalation of rock dust kicked up by the drill. Later modifications used water along with air to cut the dust, but the resulting liquid made many mines damp and muddy. Note the "soft" head covering worn by all three men. (L.D. Gordon Collection.)

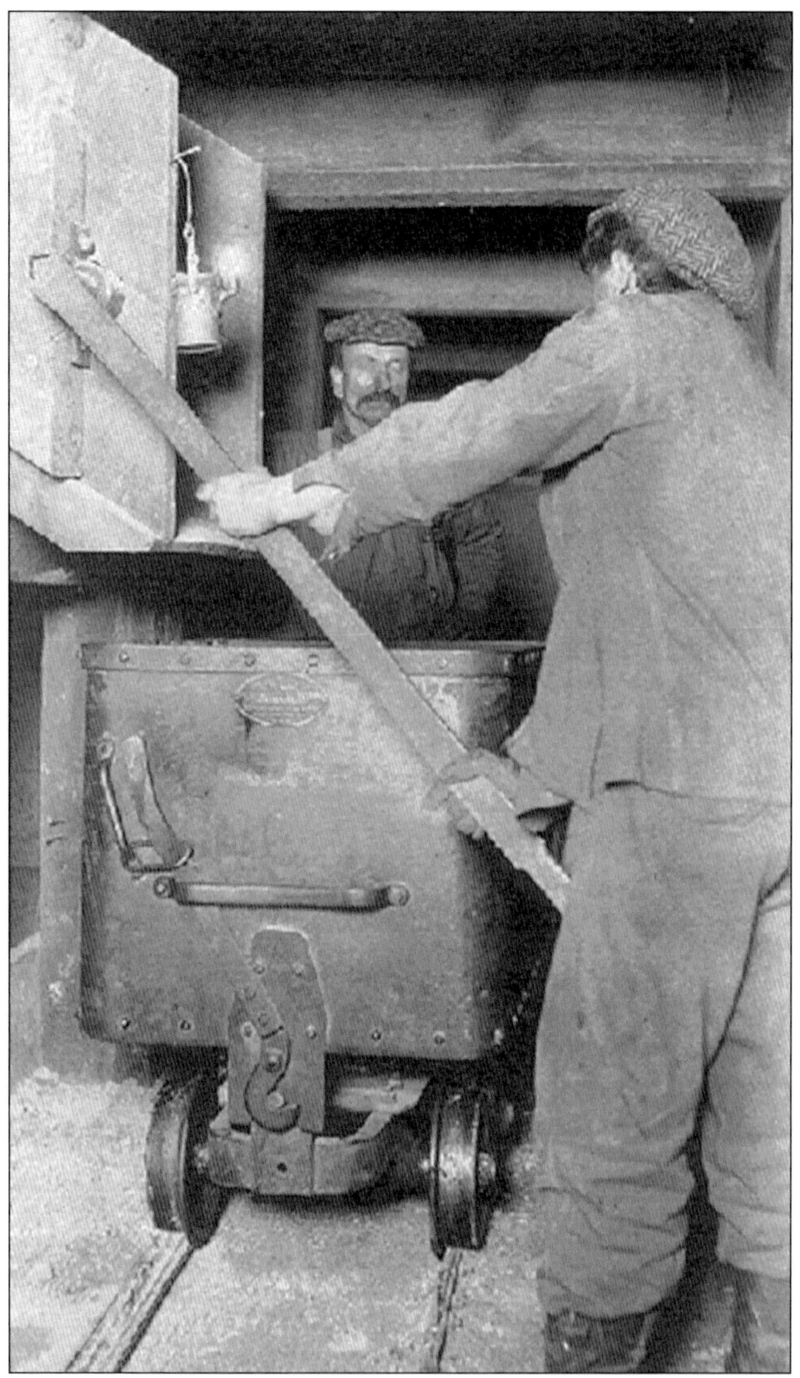

A miner pushes an ore car made of iron while another operates a loading chute underground. When fully loaded, the carts held between 1,000 and 2,000 pounds of rock. Some cars were pushed along the tracks with manpower, while in other areas of the mine the cars were pulled with mules. Eventually, the cars were loaded onto the hoist and lifted hundreds of feet to the surface. The contents would then be either sent to the dump if it was waste rock or to the tram for shipment to Keeler and the smelter. (L.D. Gordon Collection.)

This miner poses inside a hoist cage. The hoist, originally operated by steam and converted to electric power after 1916, raised and lowered men and equipment in the Union Mine. The original shaft was built in the 1800s under the reign of Mortimer Belshaw and Victor Beaudry and was damaged by fire to the 200-foot level in the late 1870s. It was later repaired by then-owner Thomas Boland and used for the rest of Cerro Gordo's operational life. (L.D. Gordon Collection.)

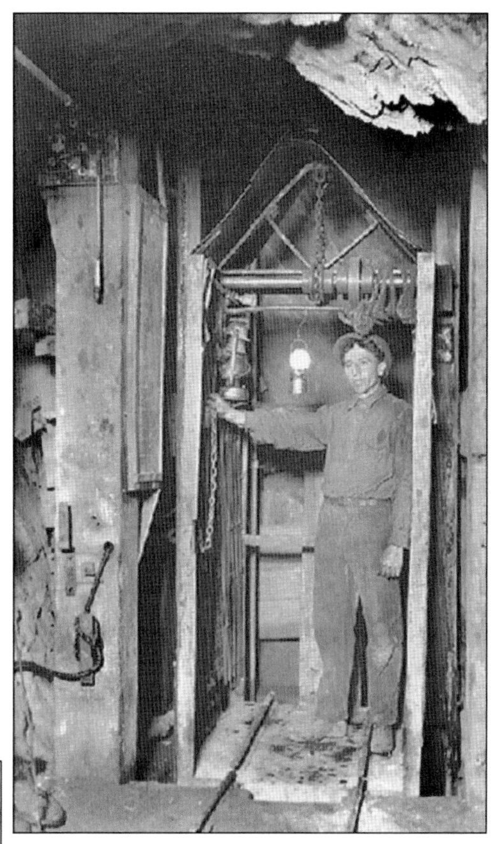

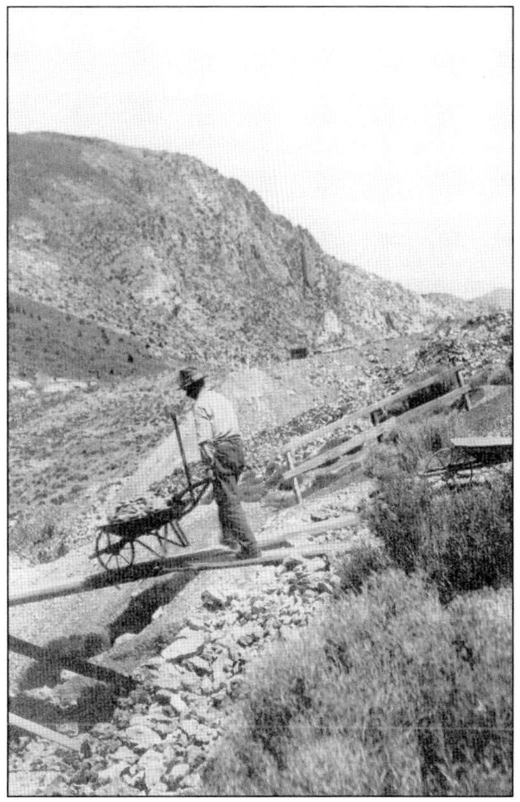

A workman hauls a load of rocks across a rickety plank. It took skill and balance to maneuver a steel-wheeled wheelbarrow with more than 100 pounds of rocks across a narrow plank. Not everyone who worked at the mine was a miner; in fact, large operations like Cerro Gordo employed carpenters, boiler men or steamfitters, and later, electricians. Women were not allowed to work in the mining area, but were employed as cooks, housekeepers, and laundry workers. (L.D. Gordon Collection.)

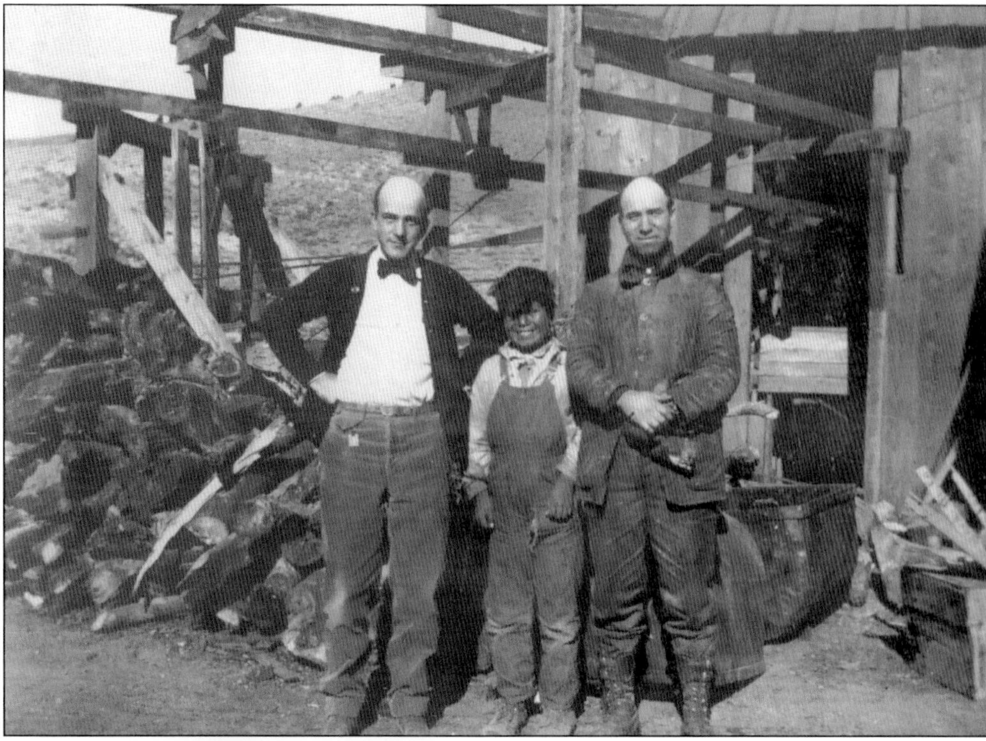

A Native American boy smiles for the camera as he poses with white adults outside the tram station. (L.D. Gordon Collection.)

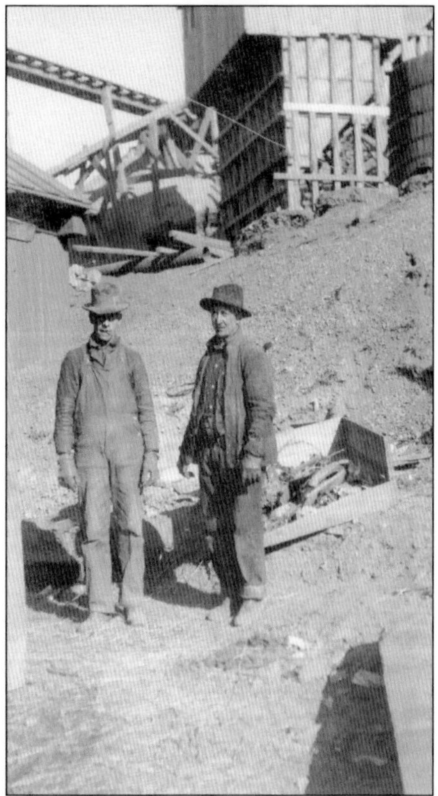

Two workmen pose near the Leschen tram terminal. Mining is rough, dirty work; even those who did not work underground wore sturdy clothing and heavy boots for protection. (L.D. Gordon Collection.)

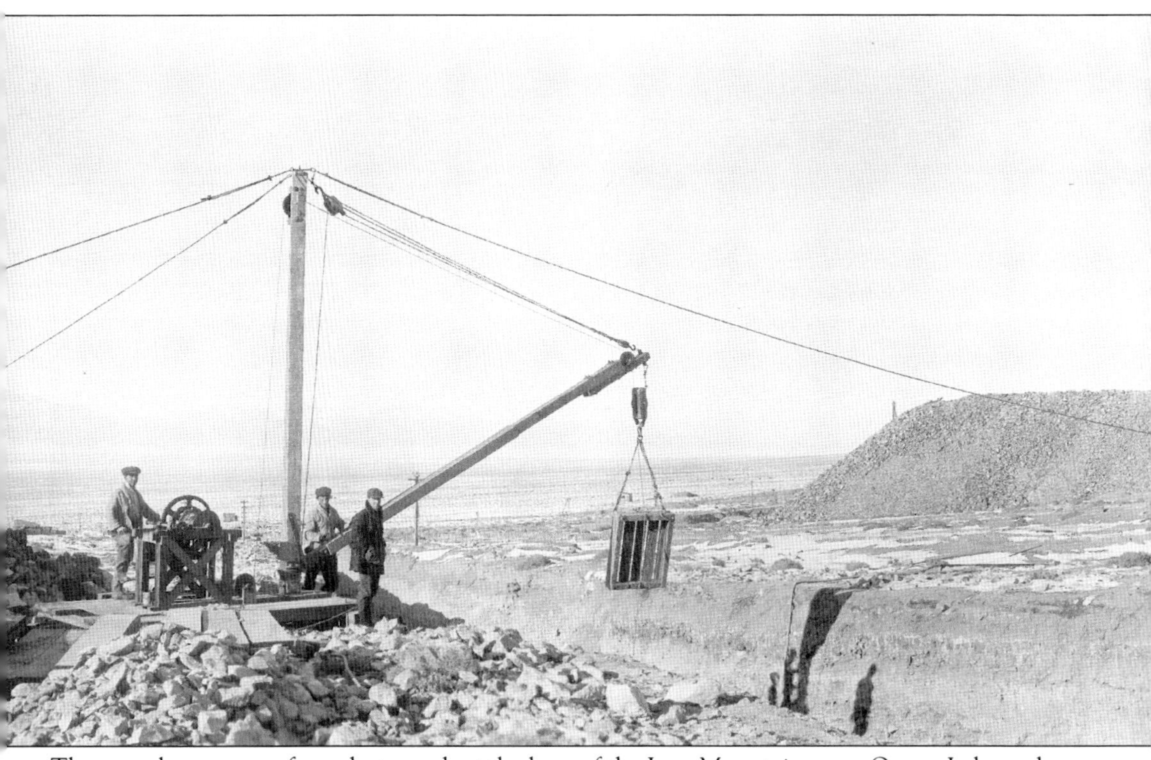

Three workmen pause for a photograph at the base of the Inyo Mountains near Owens Lake and Keeler. They are using a hand-cranked winch to lift a metal base pedestal out of a ditch. Tram towers can be seen crossing the hill in the distance. Internal combustion engines were occasionally used to power portable equipment, but the difficulty of obtaining fuel and replacement parts in remote areas made muscle power a more practical alternative whenever possible. (L.D. Gordon Collection.)

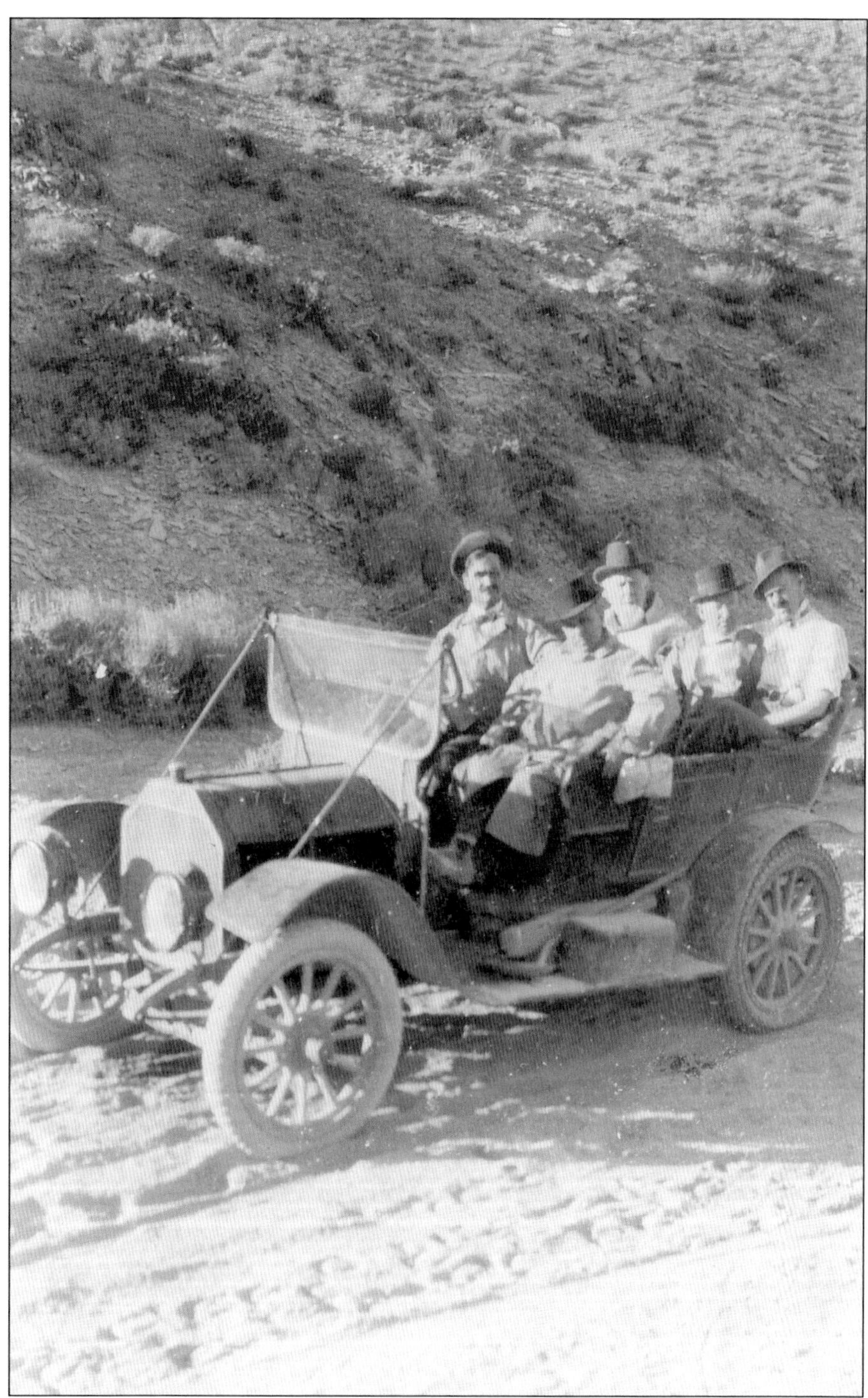

Men pose in an automobile on a relatively flat, sandy part of the road. Automobiles had a difficult time navigating the backcountry roads during Cerro Gordo's zinc era. Mechanical failures and blown out tires were common misfortunes. Even though it was the early part of the 20th century, most of the transportation was still handled as it had been in the 19th century, as mules and horses were deemed more reliable in the harsh environment. (L.D. Gordon Collection.)

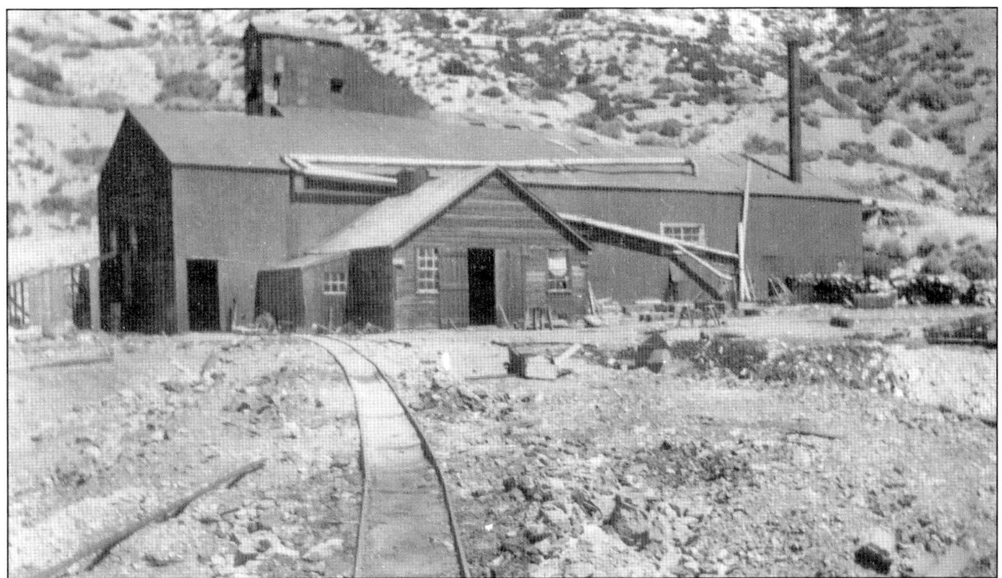

Tracks lead from Cerro Gordo's hoist house (the dark structure in both photographs), which housed the Belshaw shaft extending 900 feet into the ground. The original structure was built during the silver and lead mining days of the 1870s and was rebuilt by then-owner Thomas Boland after a fire in the 1890s. The hoist house is seen above before expansion and after the post-1916 expansion below. The original hoist and compressor equipment were steam powered—the boiler smokestack is visible in both photographs. The tracks could be relocated, as seen in both photographs, to accommodate changes in the surrounding landscape. The operation was converted to electric power after 1916 but the boiler was still kept on standby in case of power failure. (Both, L.D. Gordon Collection.)

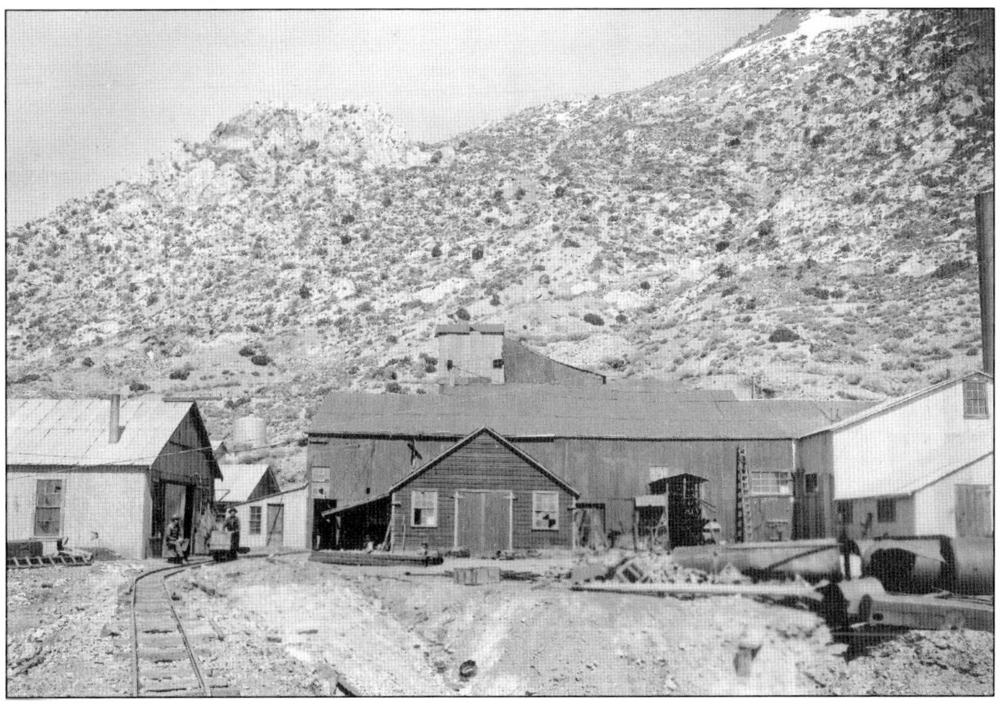

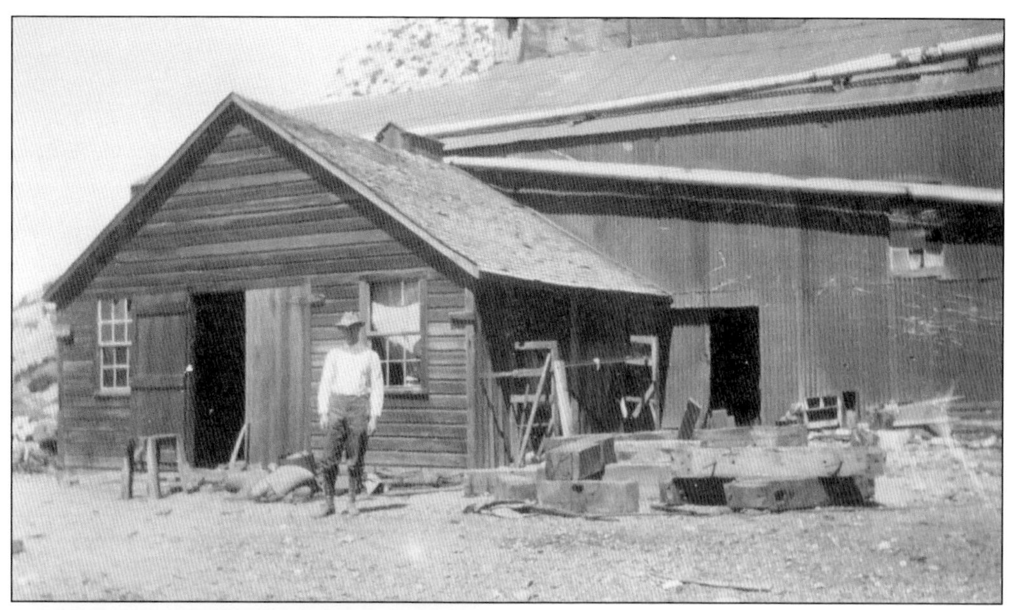

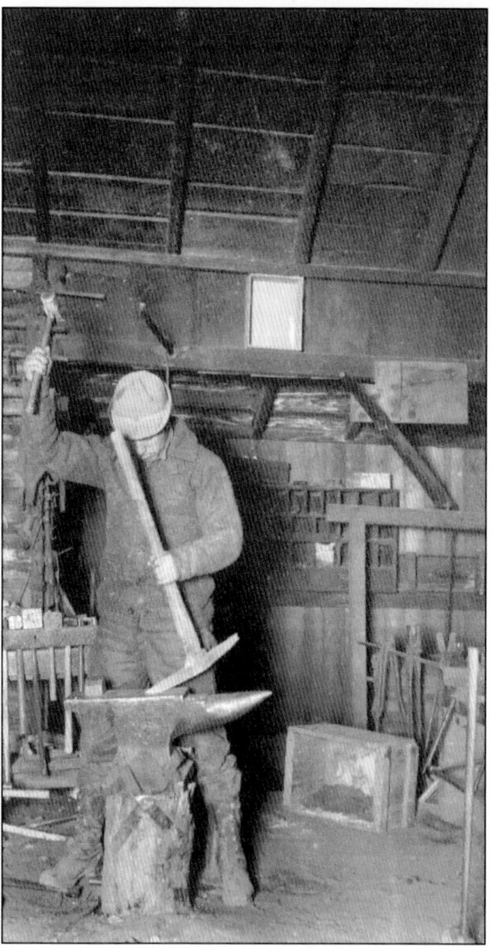

An unidentified man poses in front of the blacksmith shop at the Union Mine hoist house. The blacksmith repaired broken equipment and sharpened drill bits. An assistant, called a tool nipper, delivered sharpened equipment to the working area of the mine before each shift and picked up dull and broken equipment at the end of the shift and returned them to the blacksmith. (L.D. Gordon Collection.)

A Cerro Gordo blacksmith reshapes a pickaxe with a sledgehammer and anvil inside the blacksmith shop. Because of Cerro Gordo's distance from the nearest town, Keeler, it was necessary to do as much equipment repair on site as possible. Broken equipment presented a safety hazard to the miners and the potential for lost profits to the mine owners. In addition to repairs, the blacksmith also fabricated iron and steel equipment. A farrier, sometimes mistakenly called a blacksmith, handled the duties of shoeing the numerous mules and horses. (L.D. Gordon Collection.)

A man dressed in work clothes poses in the doorway of a Cerro Gordo office building. Like many of Cerro Gordo's buildings, this one has disappeared over time. (L.D. Gordon Collection.)

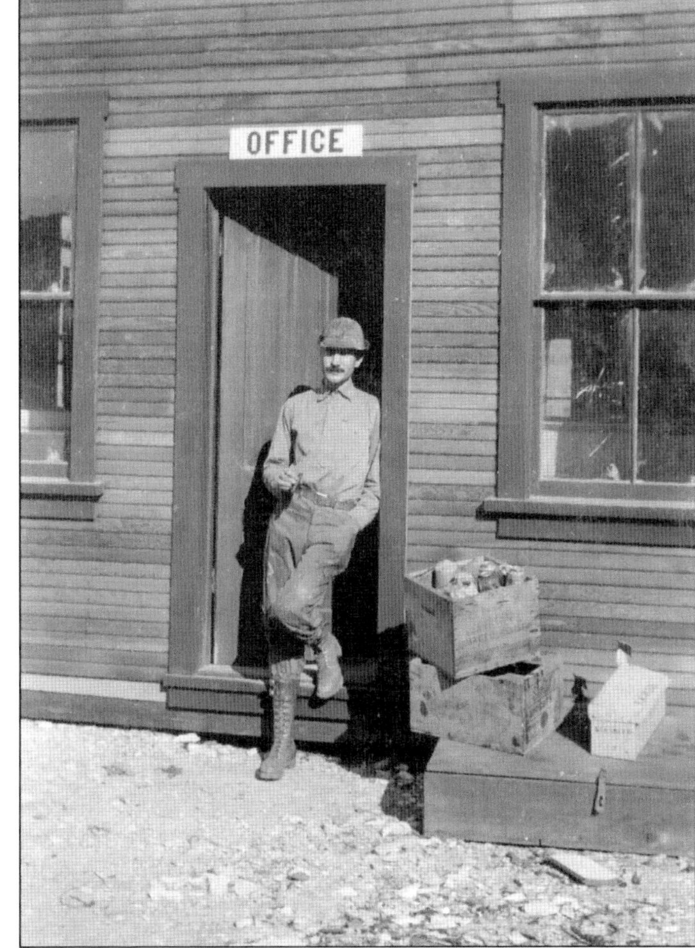

An office worker, cigar in hand and wearing a visor, poses at his desk in one of the offices at Cerro Gordo. While their work was overshadowed by physical laborers who worked above and below ground, office workers tended to the logistics of ordering the equipment, supplies, and food that kept a large-scale mining operation running. (L.D. Gordon Collection.)

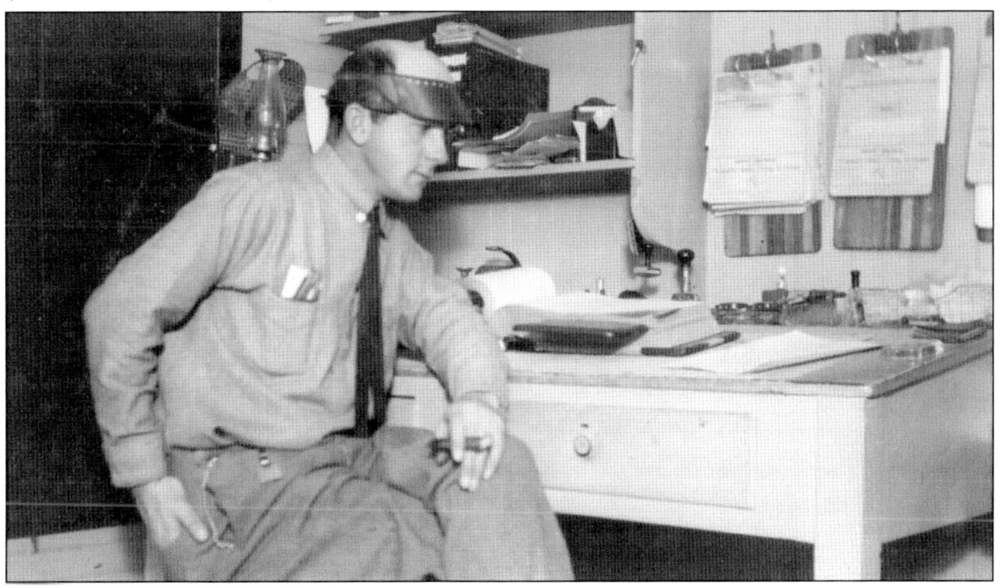

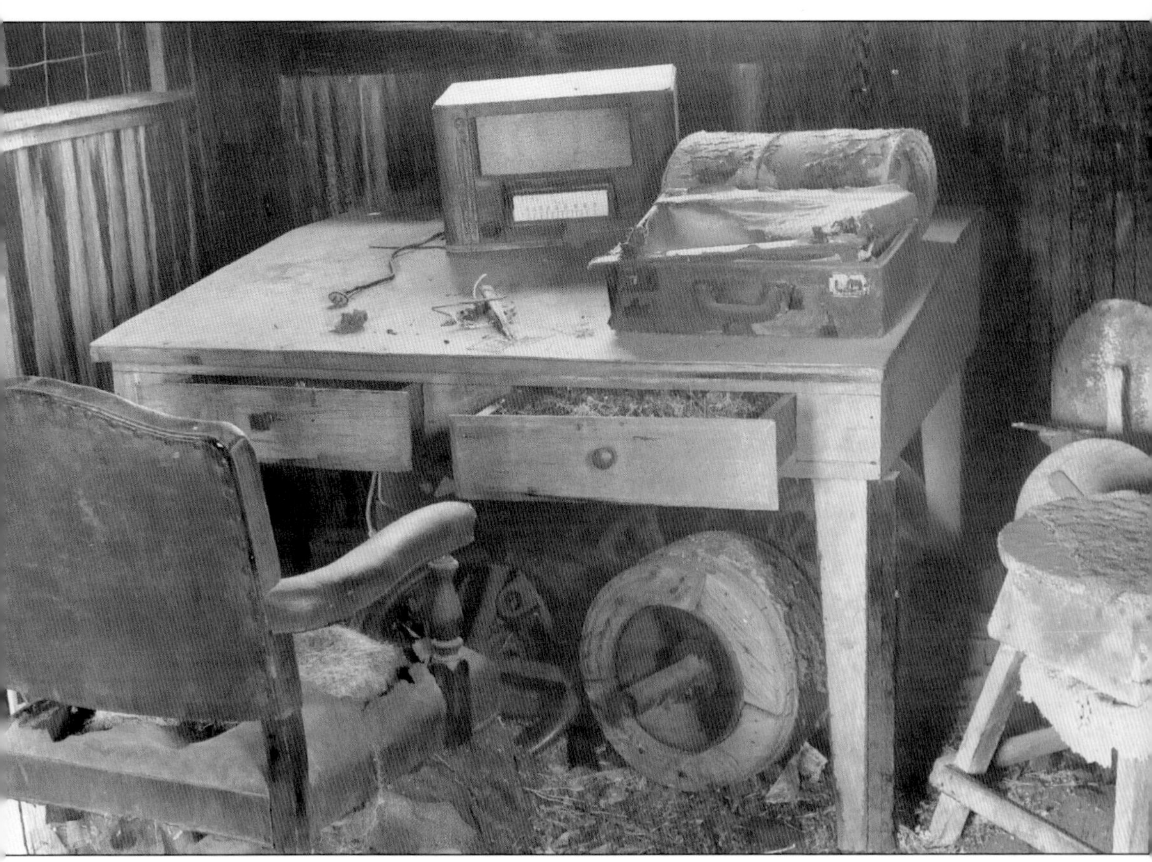

This desk, still with some of its original paint intact, sits in a building at Cerro Gordo today along with other relics of more bountiful days. (Explore Historic California Collection.)

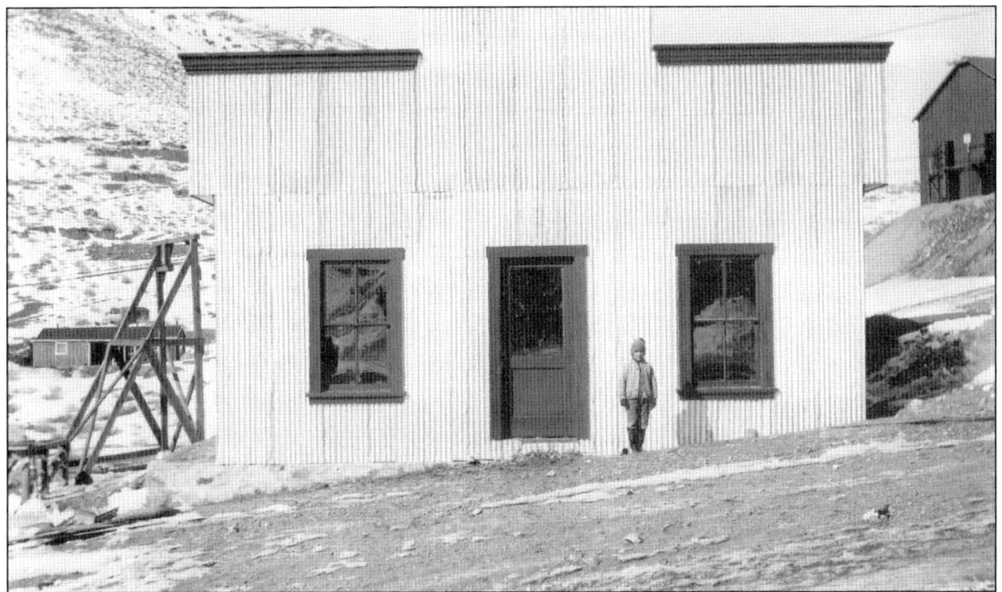

A youngster poses in front of a newly constructed building with galvanized metal siding, which may have housed a shop or recreation hall. The Leschen tram terminal is at far right. (L.D. Gordon Collection.)

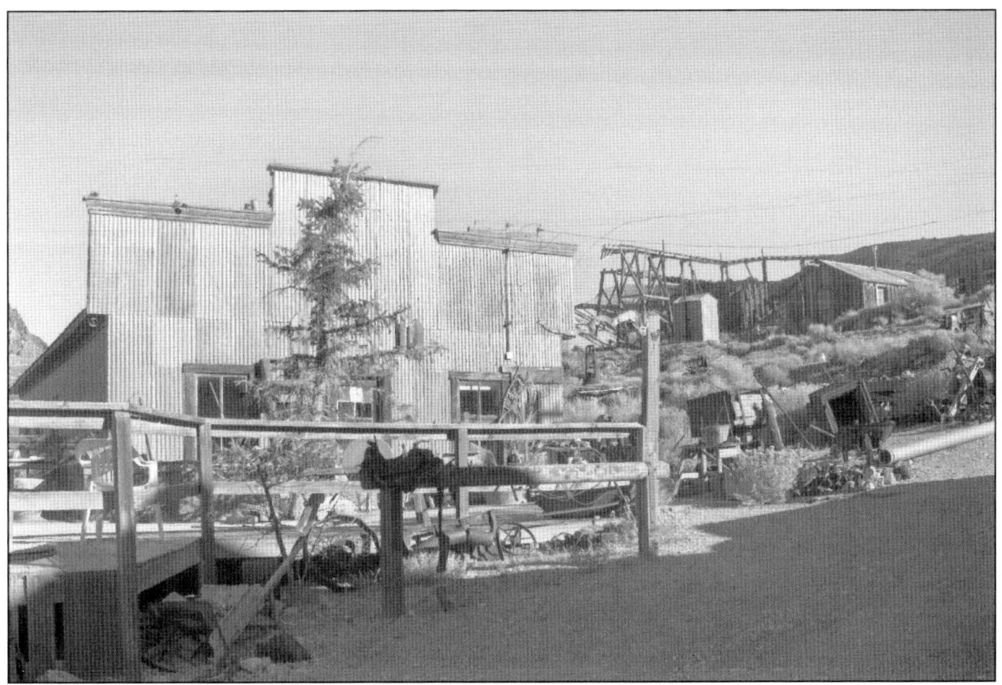

Today, that same building houses the museum. Although sometimes referred to as Beaudry's store, older photographs do not show this structure and the corrugated metal siding was not used in the 1860s or 1870s. (Explore Historic California Collection.)

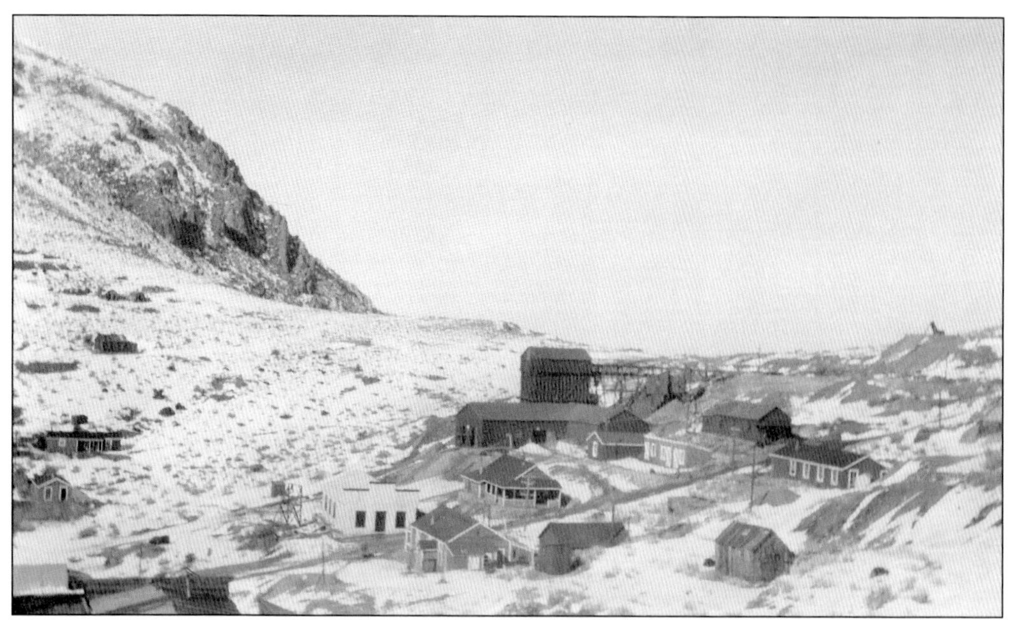

This is an overall view of upper Cerro Gordo looking northeast. The metal-sided building shown on the previous pages is on the lower left, as is the house shown in the background of the photograph below. (L.D. Gordon Collection.)

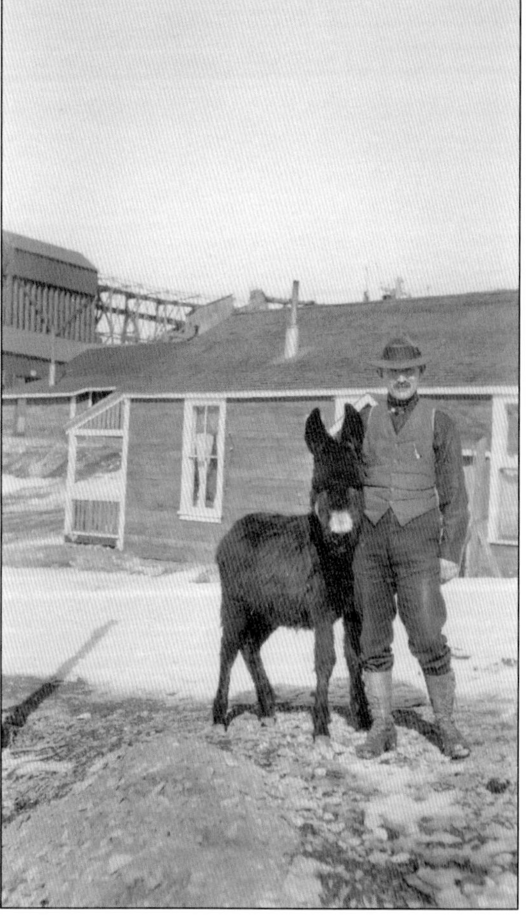

A man and his big-eared donkey pose on the snow-covered ground. The building behind him is known today as the Belshaw House and was reportedly the home of 19th-century silver baron Mortimer Belshaw and his family. (L.D. Gordon Collection.)

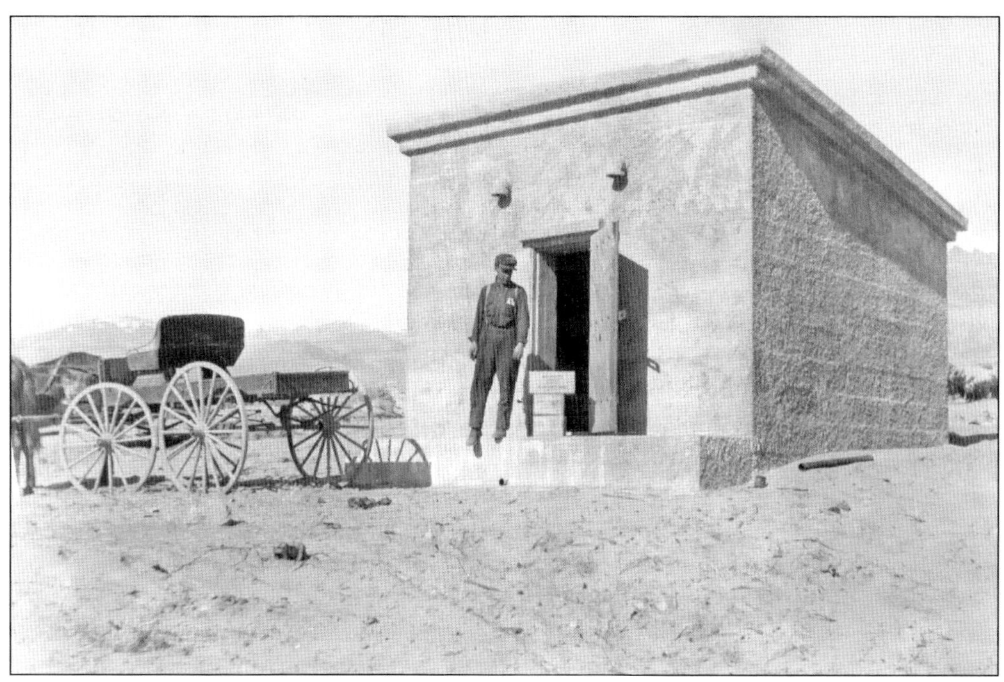

Using a buggy and an early truck, workmen handle boxes of explosives at Cerro Gordo's powder magazine near Keeler. Explosives were used in Cerro Gordo's underground workings as well as in construction of the wire rope tramways. In the early days, blasting powder, or black powder, was the explosive of choice. Dynamite, a much more powerful explosive, was invented by Alfred Nobel and first patented in 1867, but it was slow to gain acceptance. By the 1900s, dynamite, or giant powder, had replaced earlier products in the mining industry. (Both, L.D. Gordon Collection.)

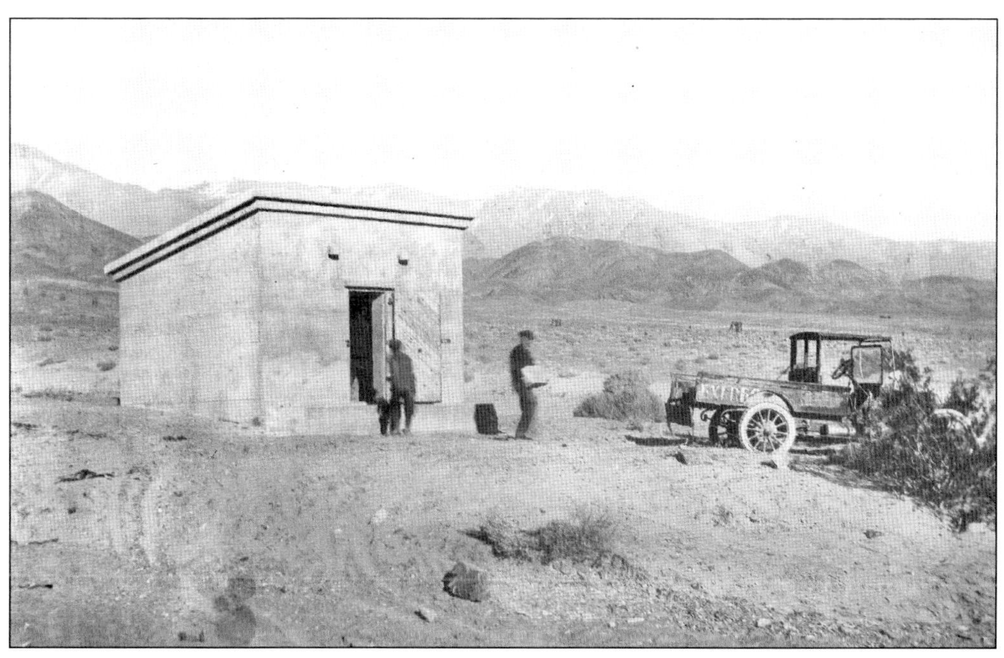

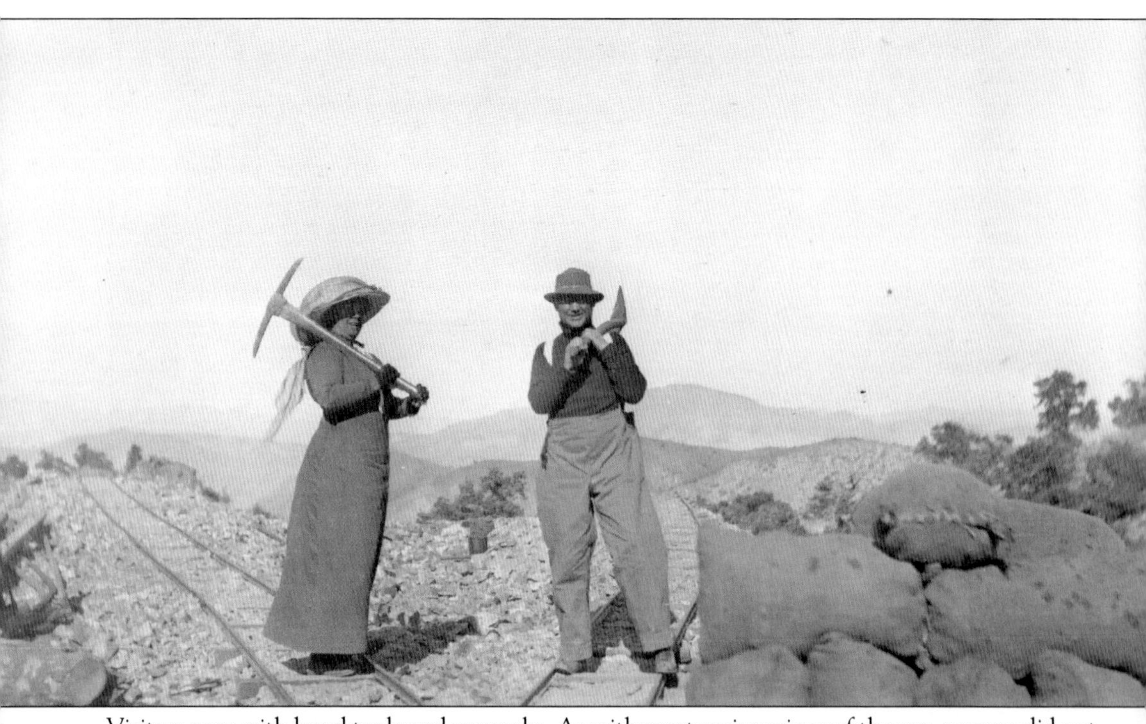

Visitors pose with hand tools and ore sacks. As with most major mines of the era, women did not work directly in the mining operation.

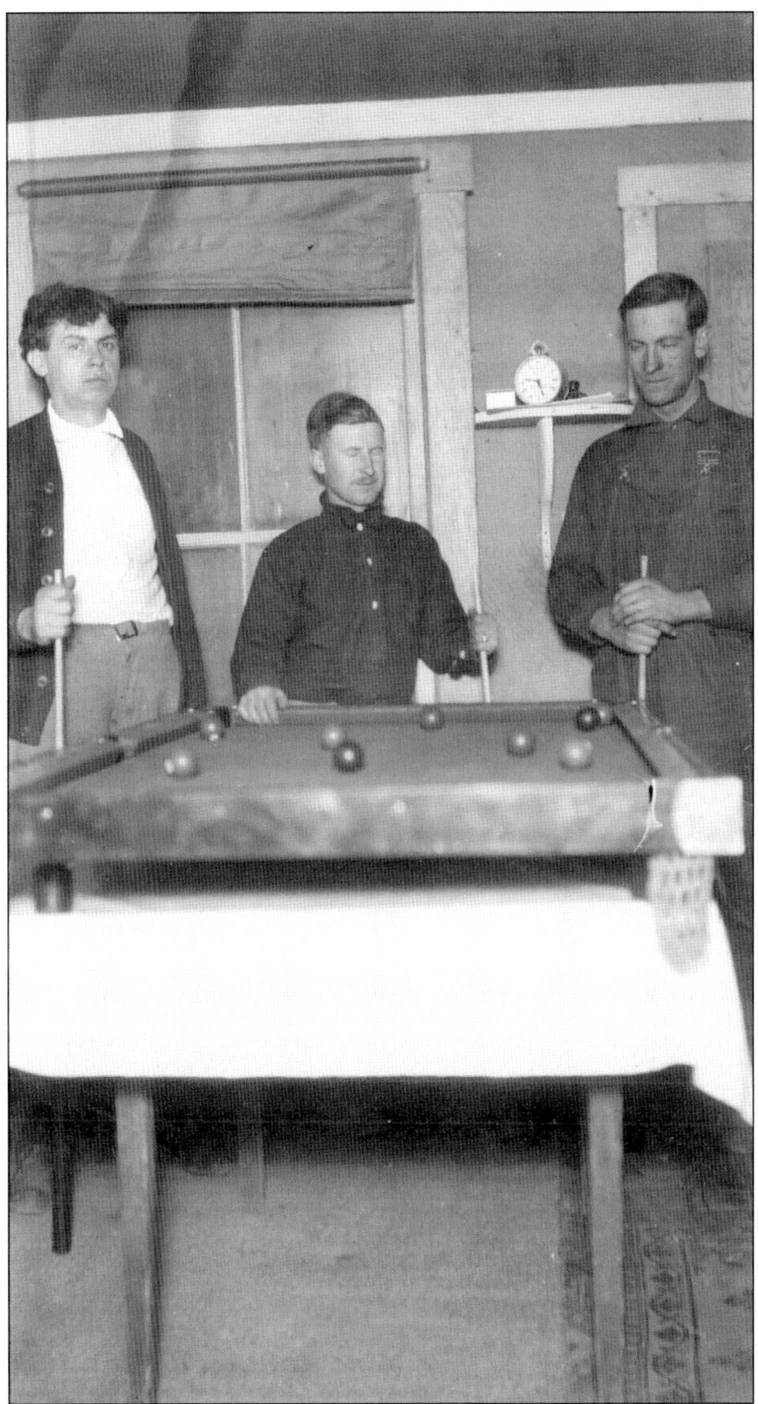

While respectable recreational opportunities were limited, billiard games were a popular way to spend off-hours time. Other leisure activities included reading, listening to early radio broadcasts, and corresponding with friends and relatives. Unlike its 19th-century incarnation, early-20th-century Cerro Gordo was relatively free of excess rowdiness, which was saved for excursions downhill to Keeler and Lone Pine. (L.D. Gordon Collection.)

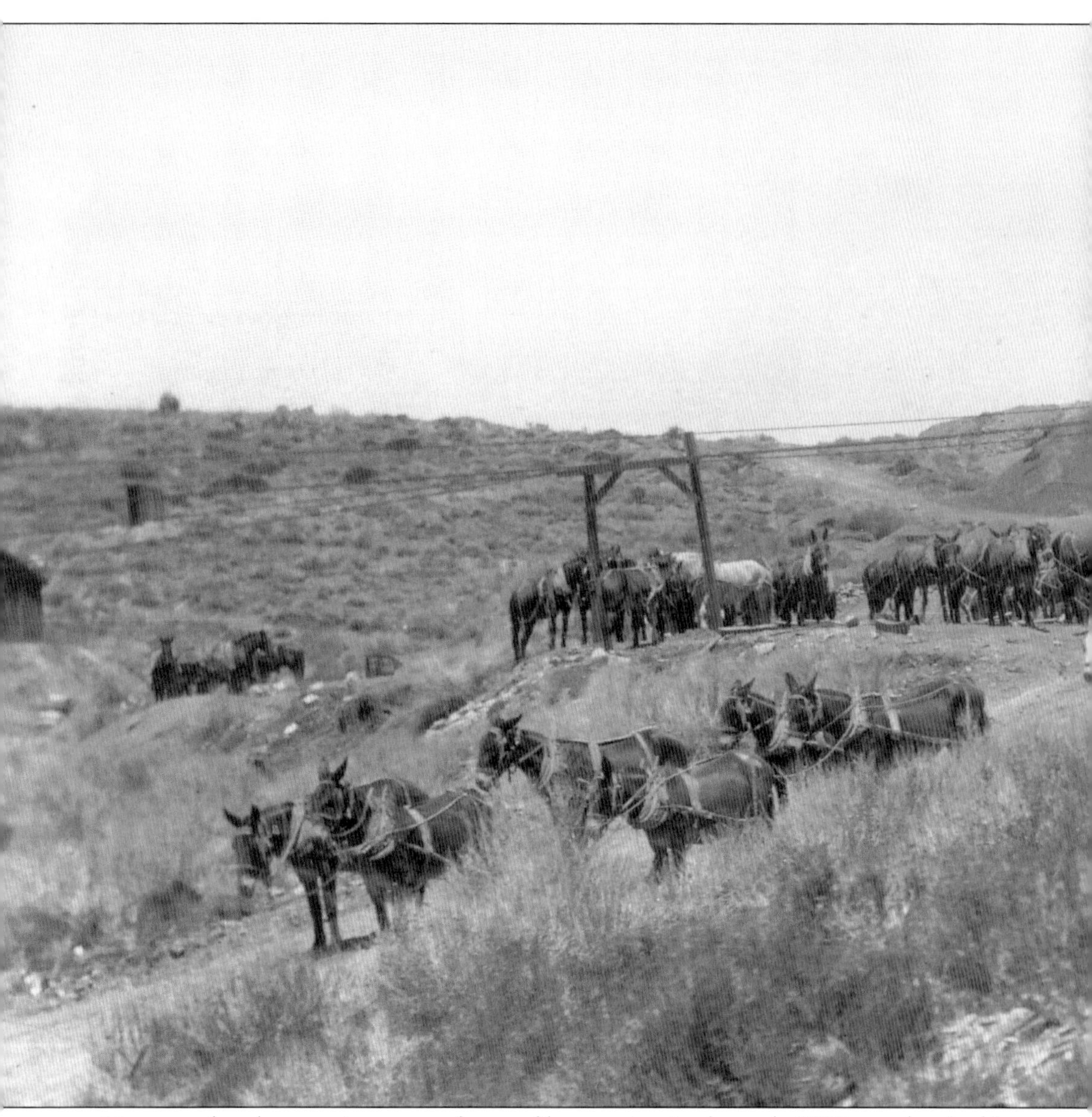

Horses and mules were important forms of locomotion in the early 1900s, as they had been some 40 years earlier in the silver era. The mule barn is the A-frame structure to right of center. Cerro Gordo's high elevation, steep terrain, and rocky ground were all challenges for the internal

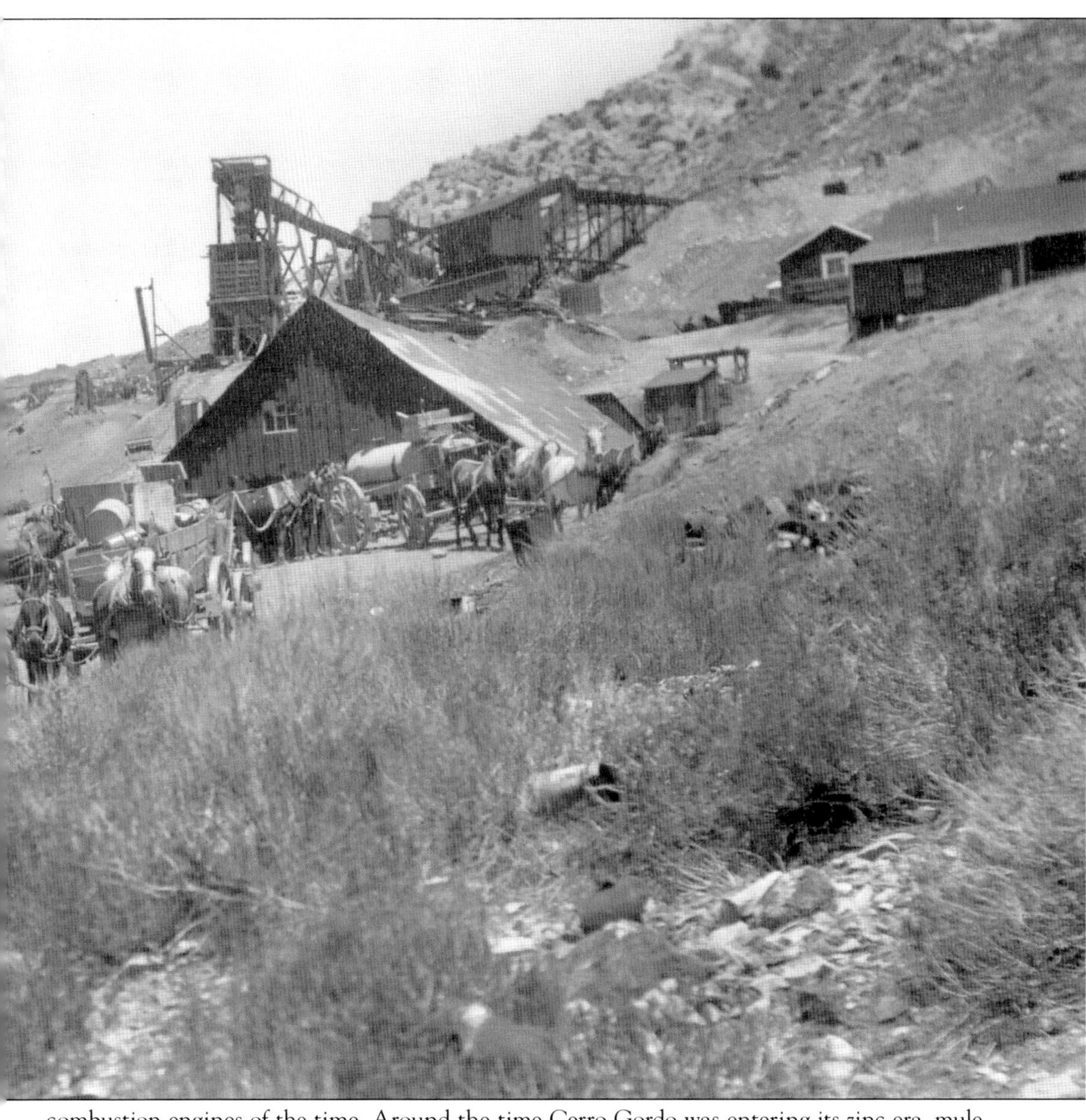

combustion engines of the time. Around the time Cerro Gordo was entering its zinc era, mule power was also used extensively during construction of the Los Angeles Aqueduct from Owens Valley to Los Angeles from 1908 to 1913. (L.D. Gordon Collection.)

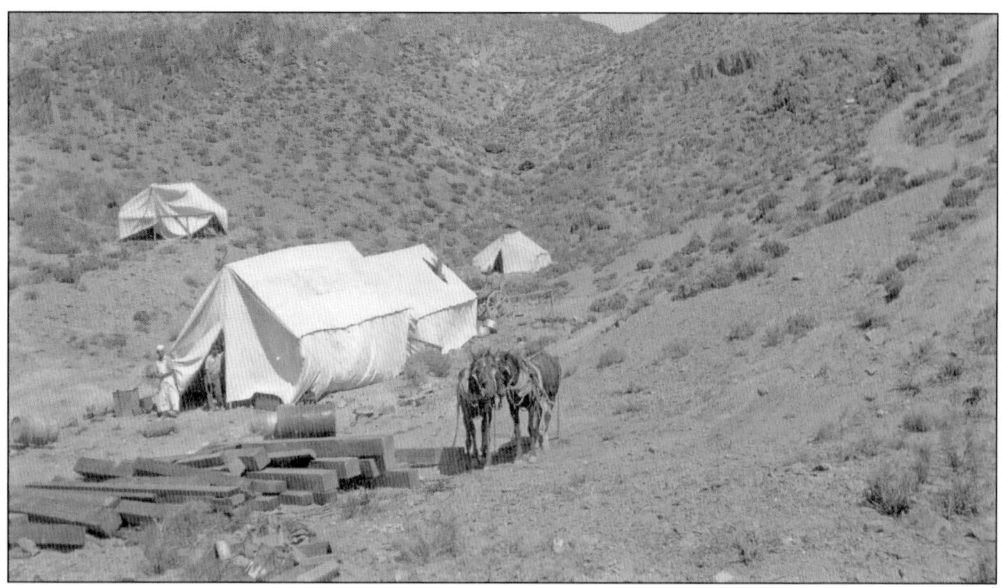

As a cook and young boy look on, a pair of horses nuzzle near the tram construction cook tent above. Horses, mules, and burros did a majority of hauling during the construction of Cerro Gordo's two wire-rope tramways. Below, a team of four mules pulls a water wagon into camp. Water was always scarce and had to be hauled considerable distances. (Both, L.D. Gordon Collection.)

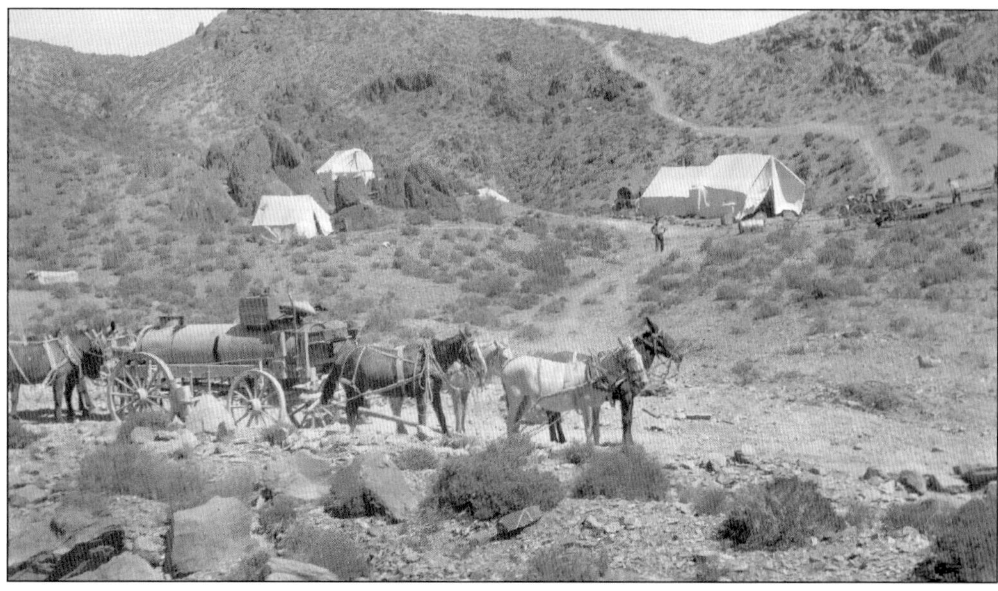

With Owens Lake and the Sierra Nevada Mountains as a backdrop, a team of mules hauls a steam boiler up the steep Yellow Grade Road into Cerro Gordo. The team navigates a narrow section on the eight-mile uphill stretch from Keeler. Electricity replaced steam after 1916 when power lines from hydroelectric generators in the Sierra foothills reached Cerro Gordo. However, the Westinghouse, Church, Kerr steam plant was maintained as a backup because power failures were frequent. (Both, L.D. Gordon Collection.)

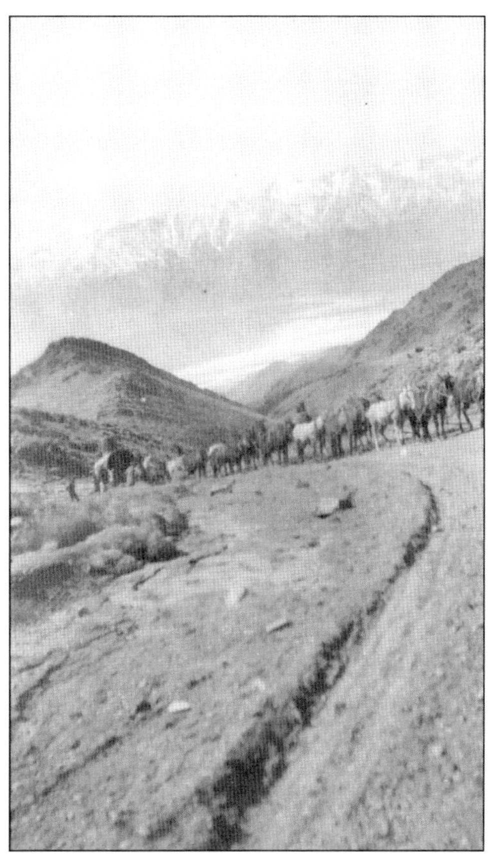

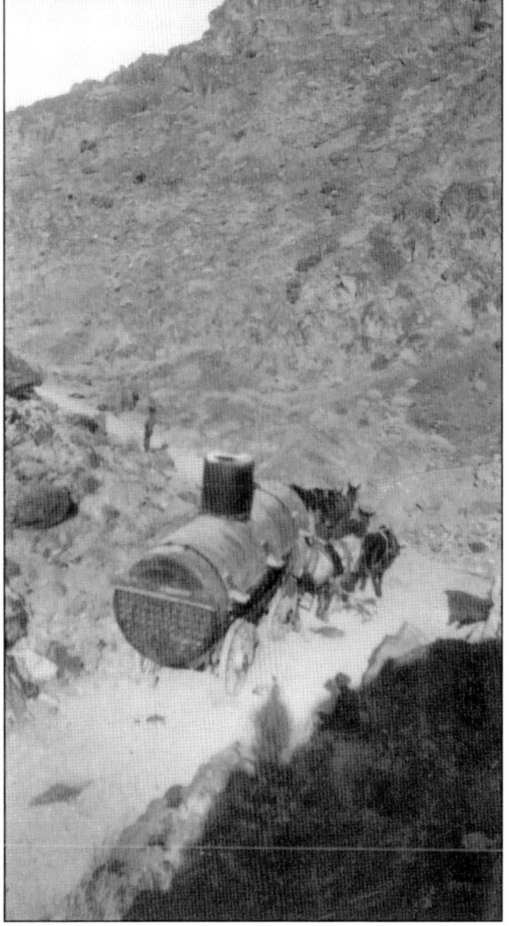

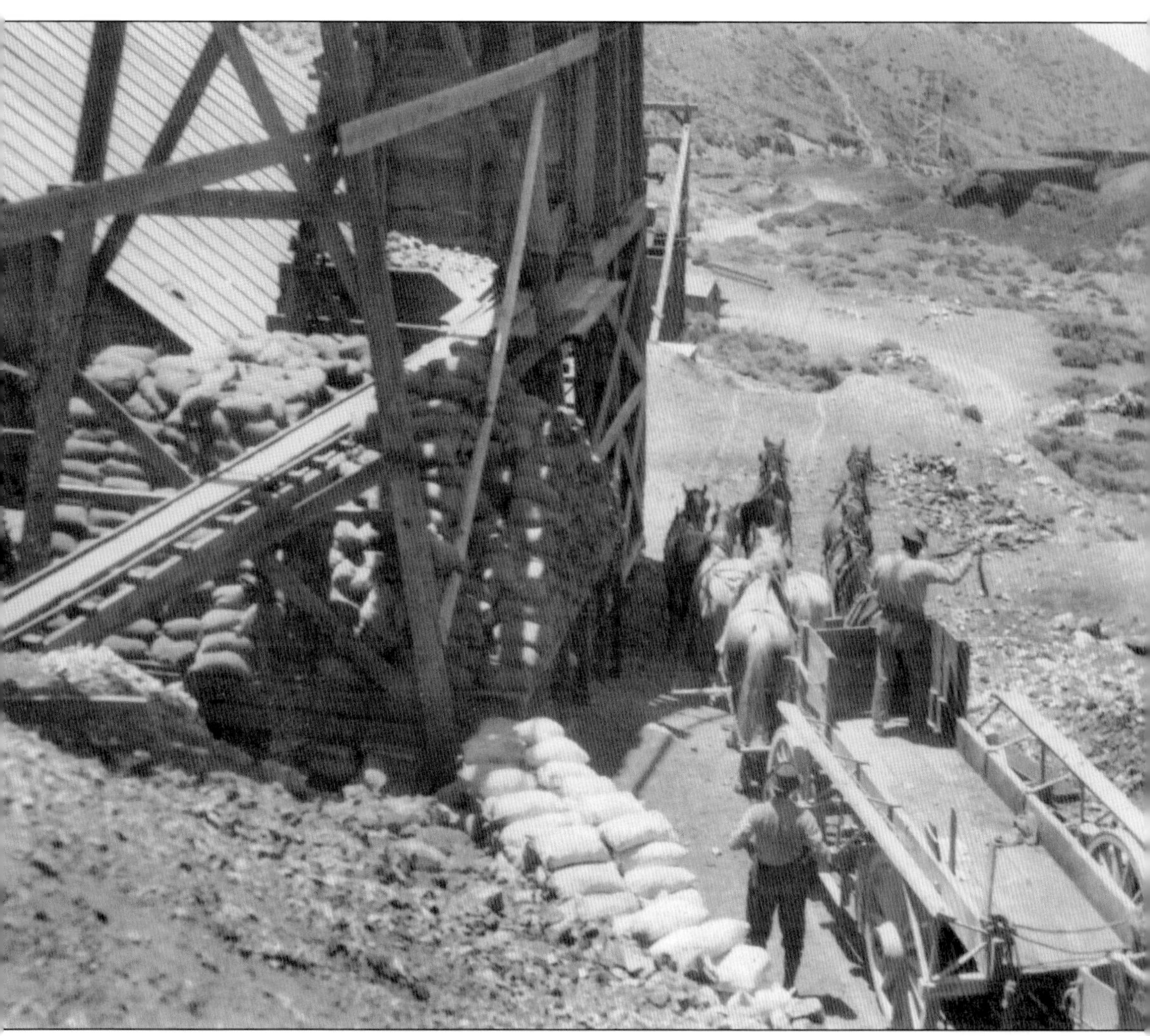

A horse-drawn wagon unloads at the base of the tram terminal structure in Cerro Gordo. Supplies could be shipped into Cerro Gordo on the tram cars or laboriously hauled eight miles up the Yellow Grade Road from Keeler, which was served by the Southern Pacific Railroad. Supply logistics on the mountaintop relied on muscle power and wagon teams. (L.D. Gordon Collection.)

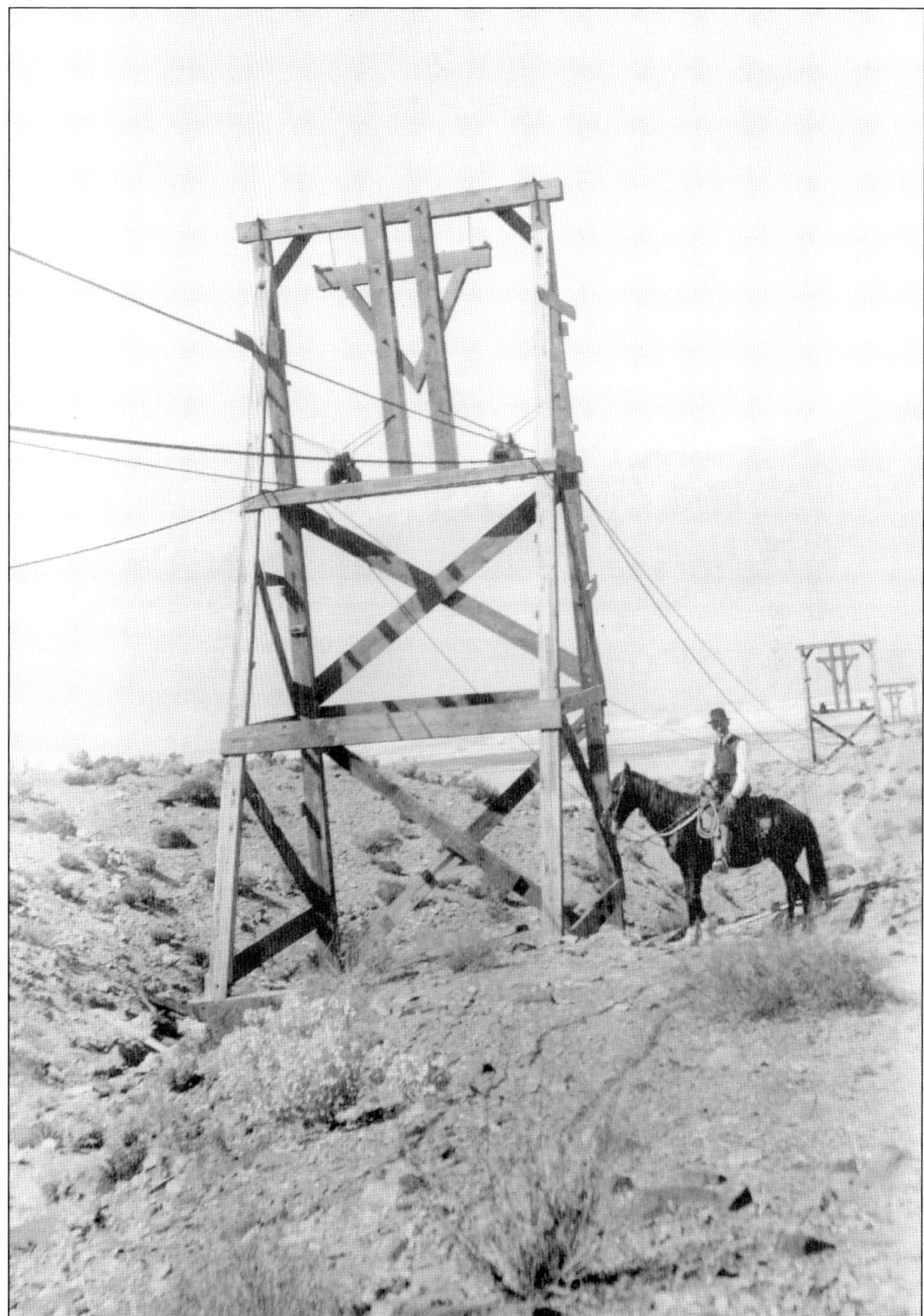

L.D. Gordon poses on horseback by a tram tower at the base of the Inyo Mountains near the Keeler end of the tram. Horses and mules provided reliable transportation in areas where access roads were nonexistent or too rough for vehicles. When she was living on the mountain, Gordon's wife, Cornelia, took pleasure rides on horseback during the warm-weather months. (L.D. Gordon Collection.)

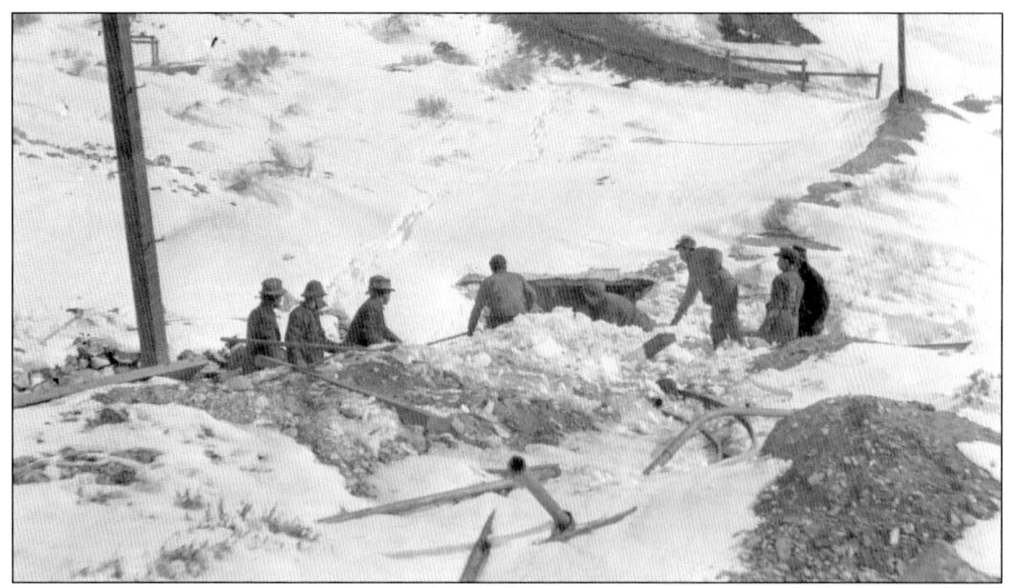

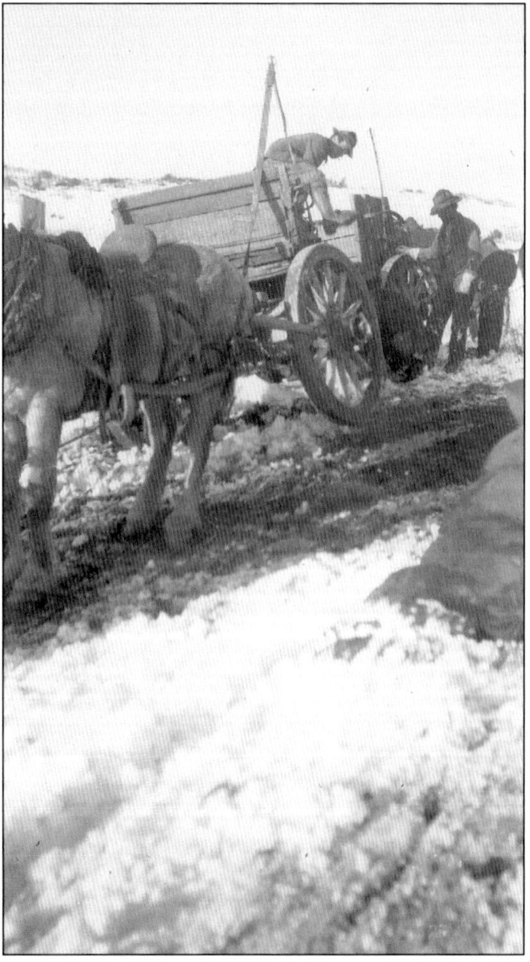

Equipment breakdowns were common under the harsh working conditions of the time, and Cerro Gordo's long winters and high elevation did not make the work any easier. The men pictured above repair a pipeline. At left, two men repair a broken wagon on snow-covered ground. Cerro Gordo had its own blacksmith shop allowing the local repair and fabrication of some equipment. Replacement parts ordered from the outside took days or weeks to arrive by freight wagon or rail. (Both, L.D. Gordon Collection.)

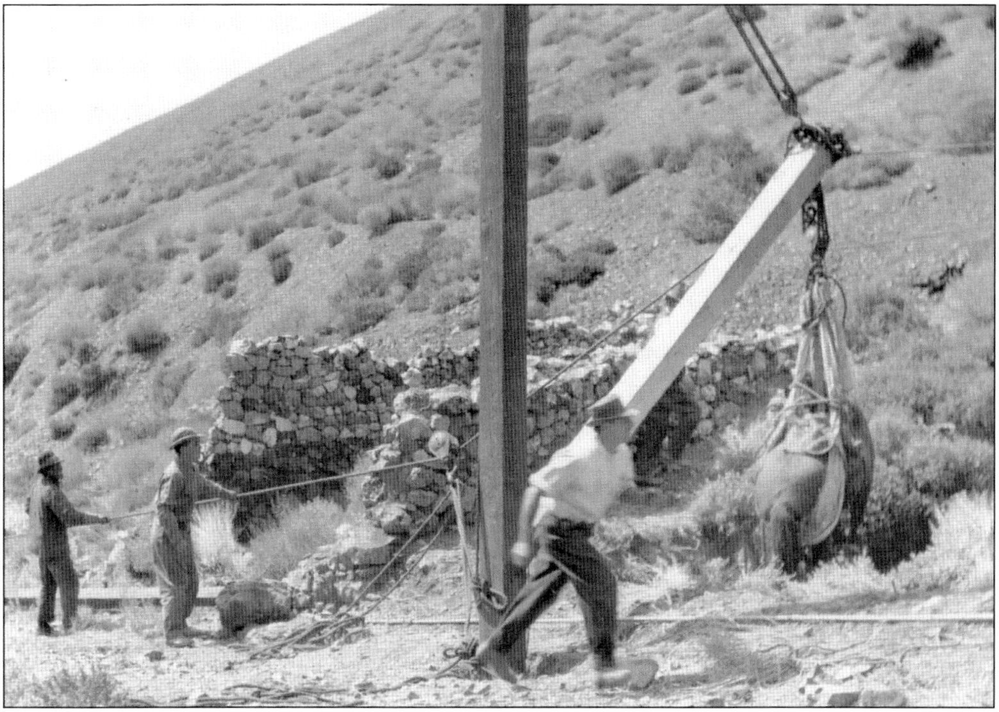

Using a gin pole and block and tackle, a mule is lowered into a vertical mine shaft. Mules were used inside the mines to pull trains of ore cars. Many mules lived out their entire lives in the mines, as it was too difficult and dangerous to bring them to the surface. Mistreatment of mules was a fireable offense at many mines. (L.D. Gordon Collection.)

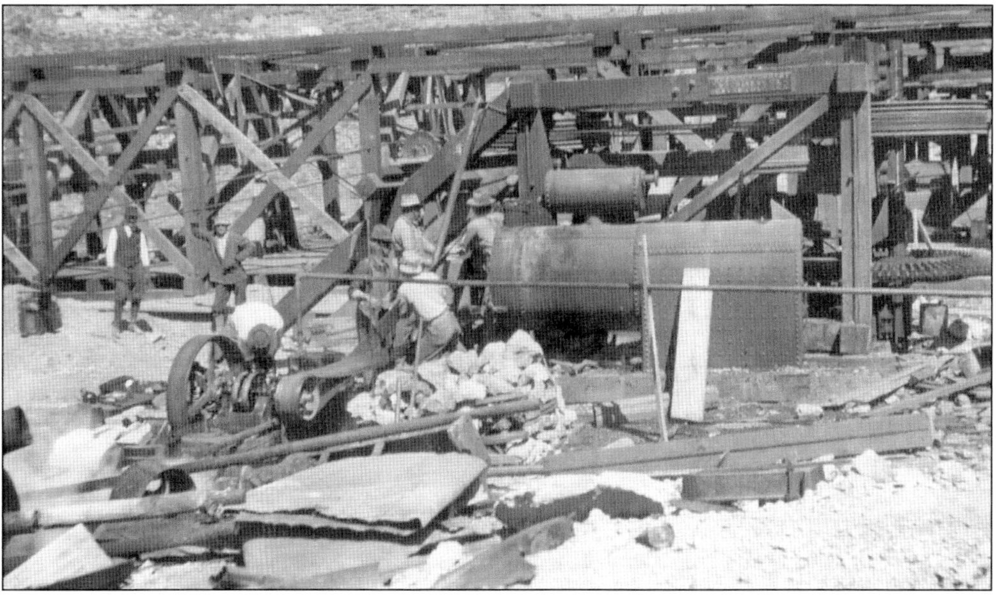

Men work on a boiler and steam engine at the base of the tram terminal. As it had been done in the 19th century, early-20th-century Cerro Gordo relied on steam power until 1916. Boilers were always an inconvenience on the mountain as both the fuel and the water had to be hauled in. (L.D. Gordon Collection.)

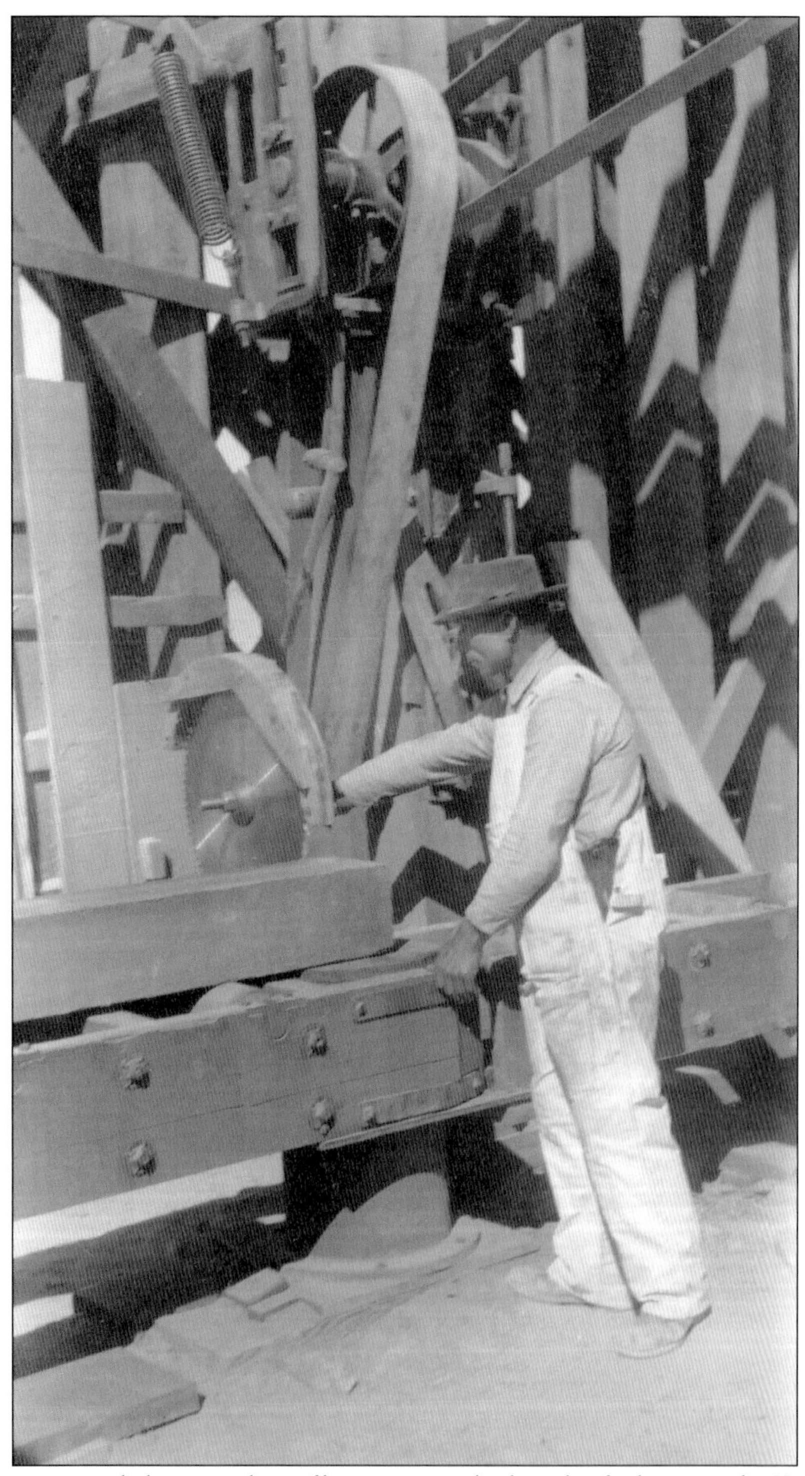

A carpenter uses a belt-powered cutoff saw to trim the length of a beam at the Keeler tram terminal. The saw, as well as other equipment, was powered by a single belt driven by an electric motor. (L.D. Gordon Collection.)

A blacksmith pounds a steel bar on an anvil underneath a sheet-metal awning at the Keeler tram terminal construction site. A large grinding wheel is behind him. Other workers can be seen in the background using the cutoff saw. Workers at Keeler had the luxury of being close to the amenities of an established town while their associates up the hill needed to travel eight miles down the mountain to reach city lights. (L.D. Gordon Collection.)

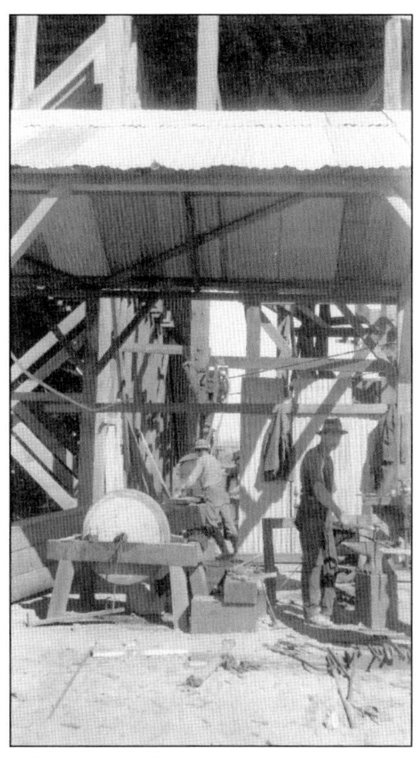

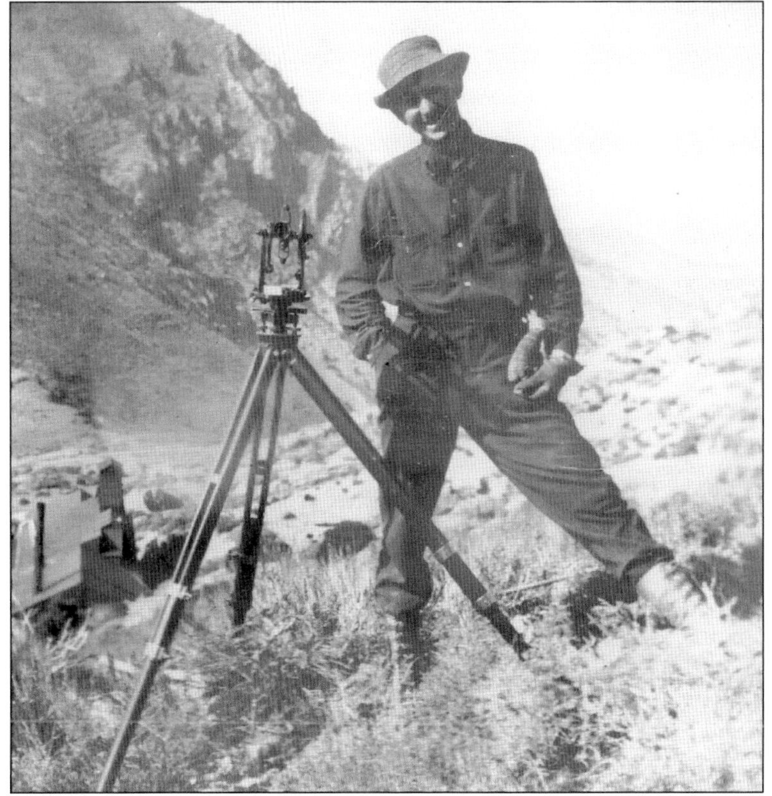

A surveyor poses with his instrument on a hillside at Cerro Gordo. Surveyors were skilled workers, providing accurate alignments for the tram and building construction. (L.D. Gordon Collection.)

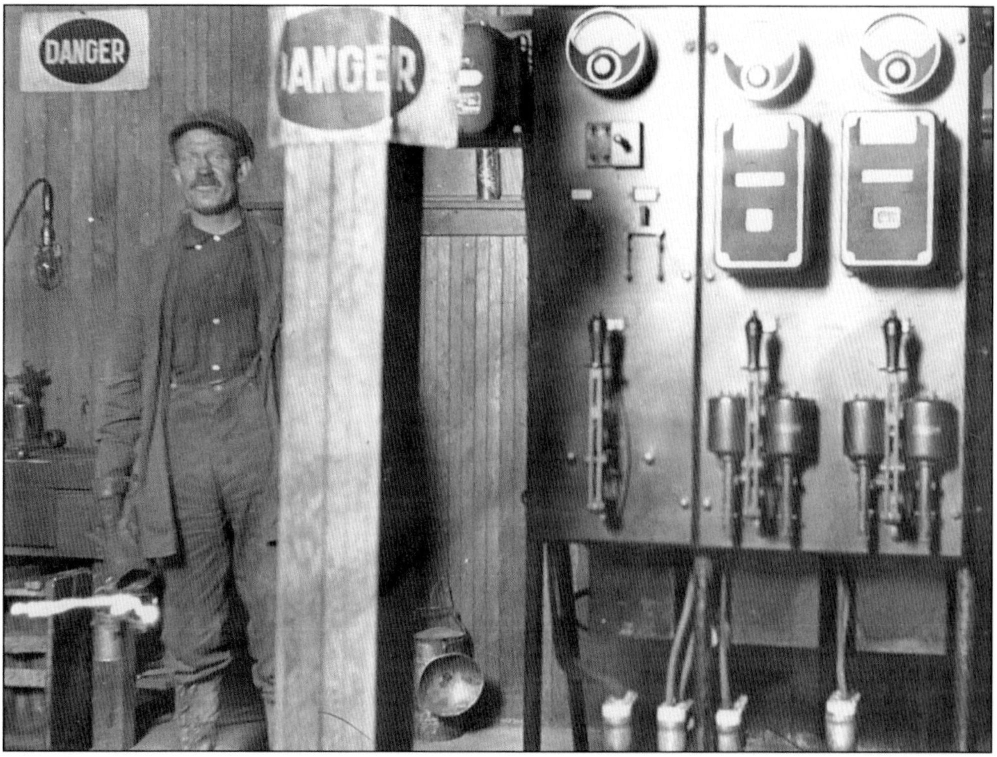

A worker poses next to an electrical switch panel inside Cerro Gordo's hoist house. This panel was operational at 440 volts AC and controlled equipment above and below ground. (L.D. Gordon Collection.)

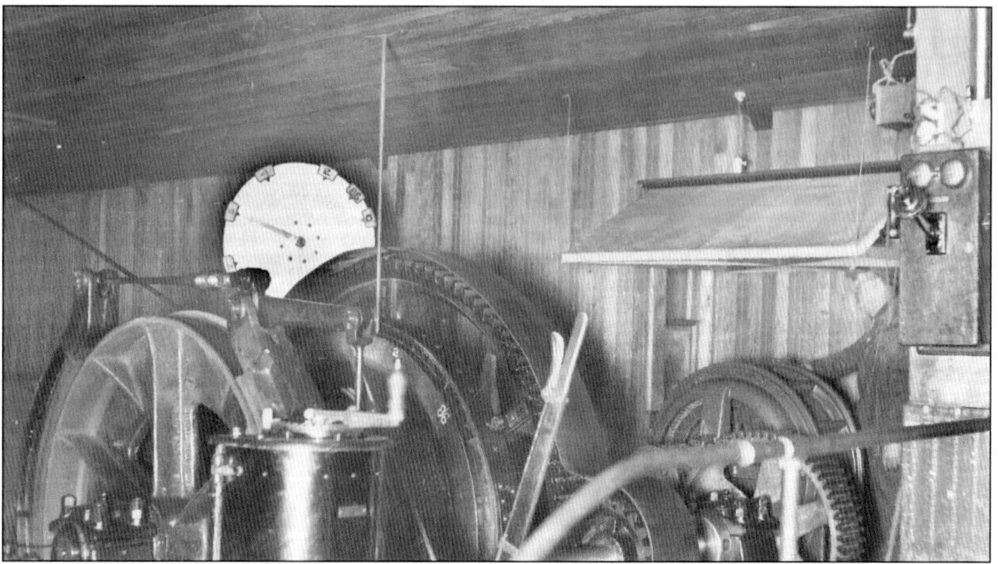

The hoist operator services the hoist's electric motor. The depth gauge reads "Cerro Gordo Mines 1915." The hoist operator was a highly responsible position, as the hoist lifted and lowered men and equipment on an elevator in the mine. A hoist accident or failure would shut down production and sometimes injure or kill miners (L.D. Gordon Collection.)

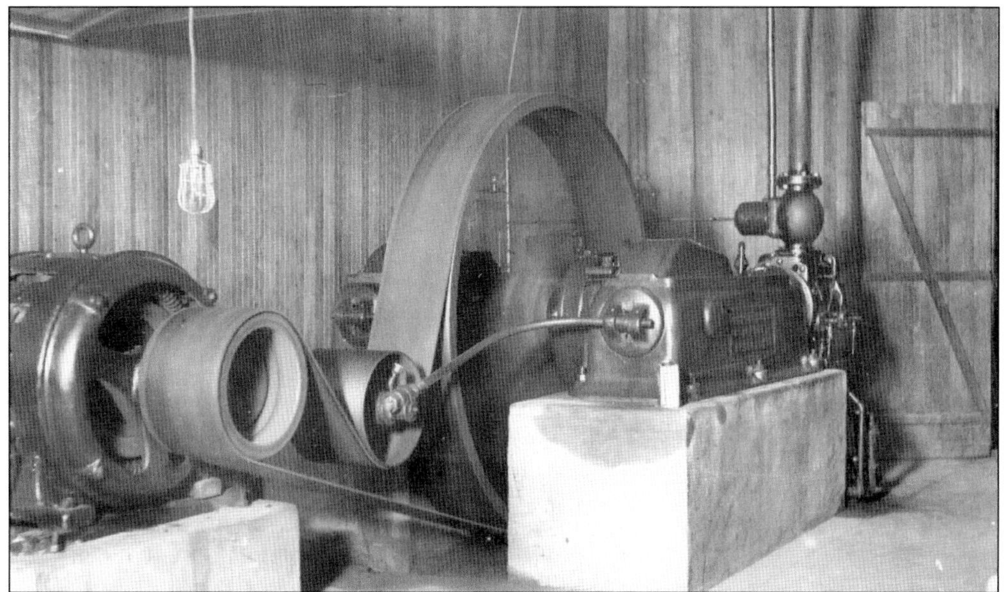

Cerro Gordo's air compressor, manufactured by Ingersoll-Rand, is shown here in operation around 1915. The compressor pumped air to power rock drills, small hoists, and pumps underground. Because they discharged only air and some oil, pneumatic equipment was favored for underground work. The compressor provided the air at high volumes and relatively low pressures. Ventilation in the mines was handled by natural drafting and supplemented by fans and duct work. (L.D. Gordon Collection.)

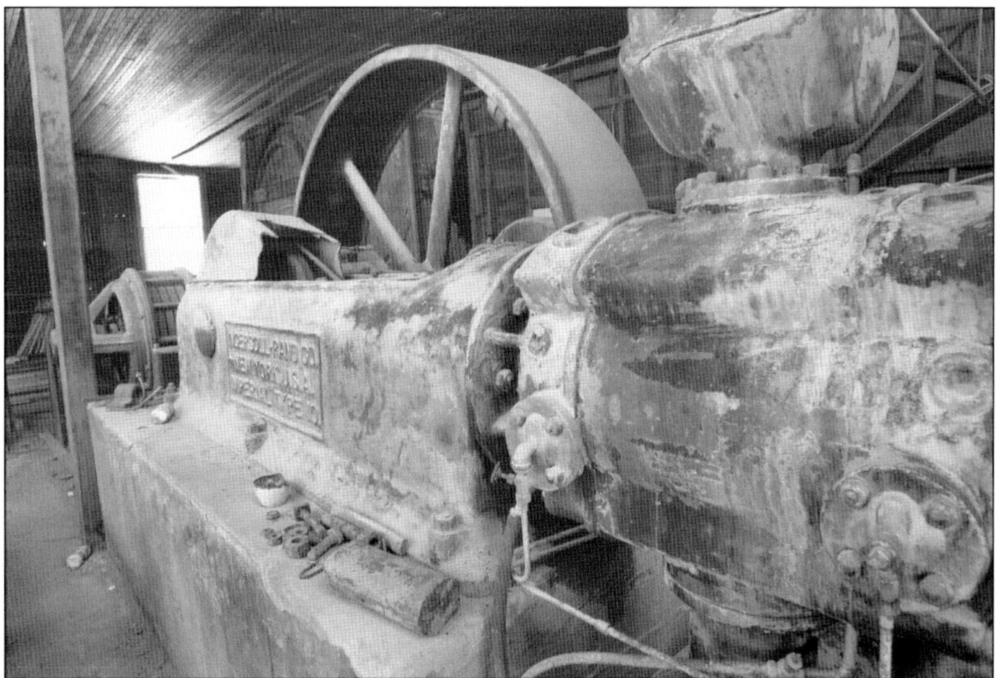

This 2005 photograph shows the Ingersoll-Rand Imperial Type 10 compressor now idle in the hoist house. It was a two-stage, double-acting compressor with an intercooler. (Explore Historic California Collection.)

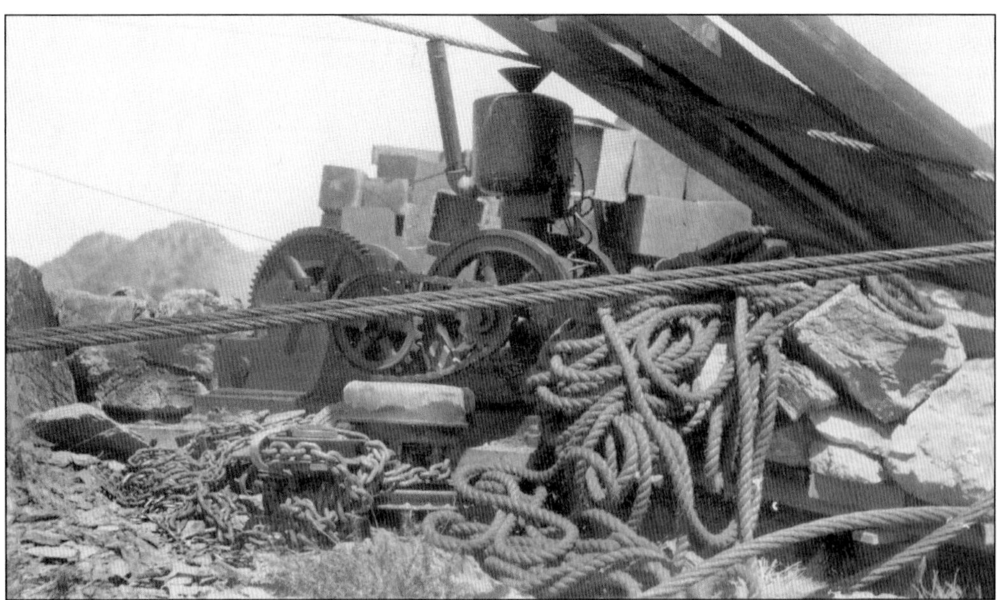

A "hit and miss" internal combustion engine connected to a hoist drum is almost lost among the twisting rope and steel cables at a tram construction site. Portable equipment was usually powered by muscles, as internal combustion engines were used infrequently. (L.D. Gordon Collection.)

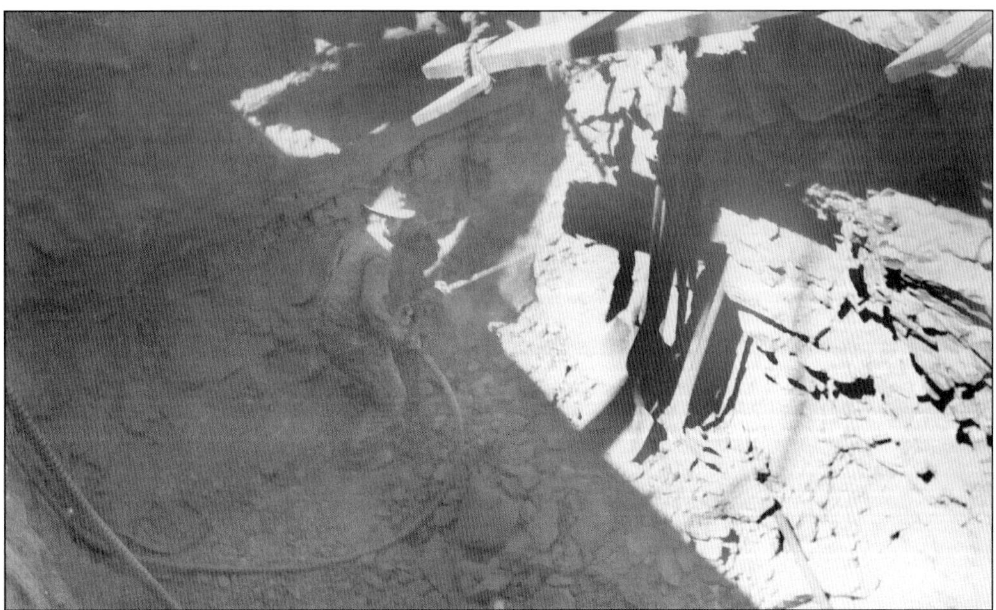

A worker uses a pneumatic drill inside an excavation hole. In spite of the boards suspended by ropes and being surrounded by loose rock, the only safety equipment he wears are gloves and a wide-brimmed hat. Pneumatic drills were hazardous in their own right, as they could buck and kick back into the operator. The Occupational Safety and Health Administration, which administers work safety rules, would not appear for almost another 60 years. (L.D. Gordon Collection.)

Five

Gone to the Ghosts

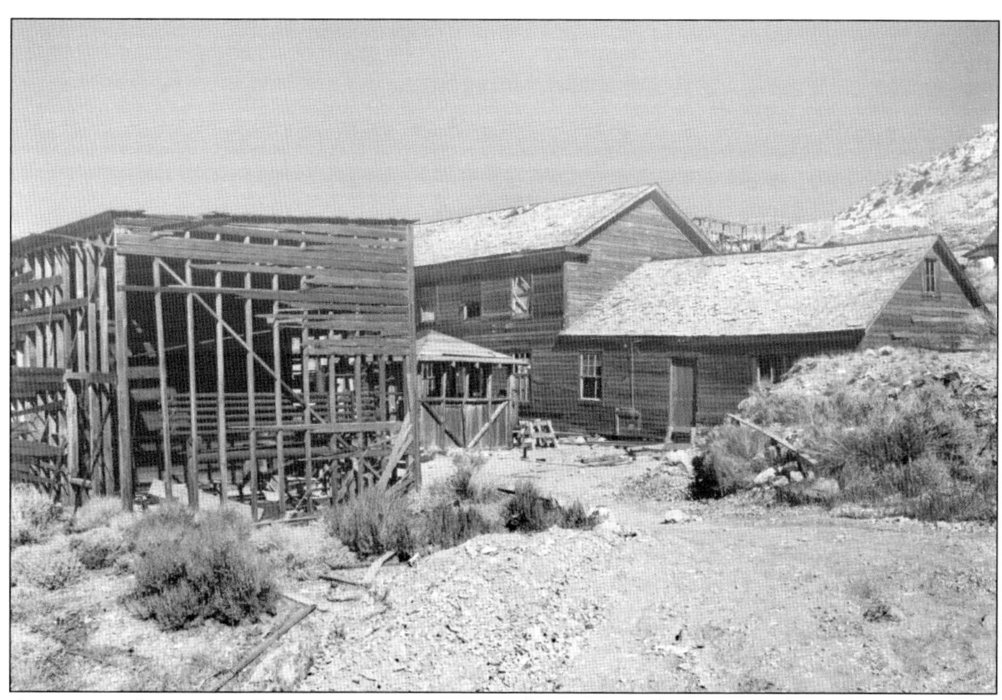

A century after its first boom, the mining town of Cerro Gordo was a shadow of its former self. Only a few buildings struggled to survive on the harsh desert mountaintop. This image from November 1991 shows the icehouse and the back of the American Hotel in the early stages of "restorative reuse" by Jody Stewart and Mike Patterson. The hotel was built in 1871 and the icehouse, built about 1916, was the first commercial icehouse in Inyo County. (Explore Historic California Collection.)

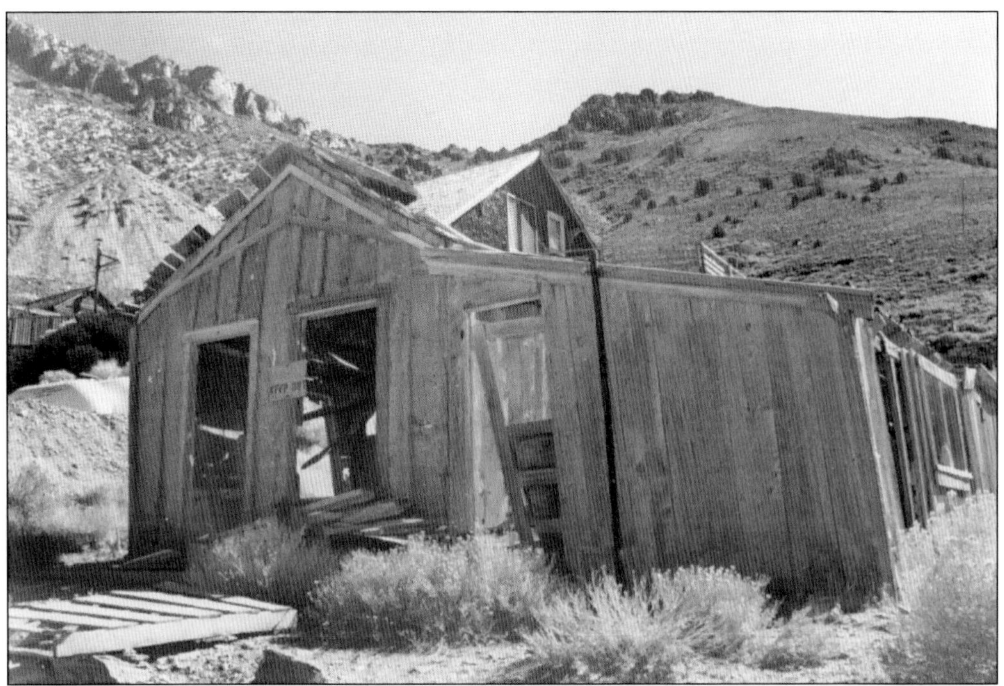

The Crapo House, next door to the American Hotel, was equally rundown when it was photographed in November 1991. It was the scene of the last shootout in Cerro Gordo, on December 29, 1892. (Explore Historic California Collection.)

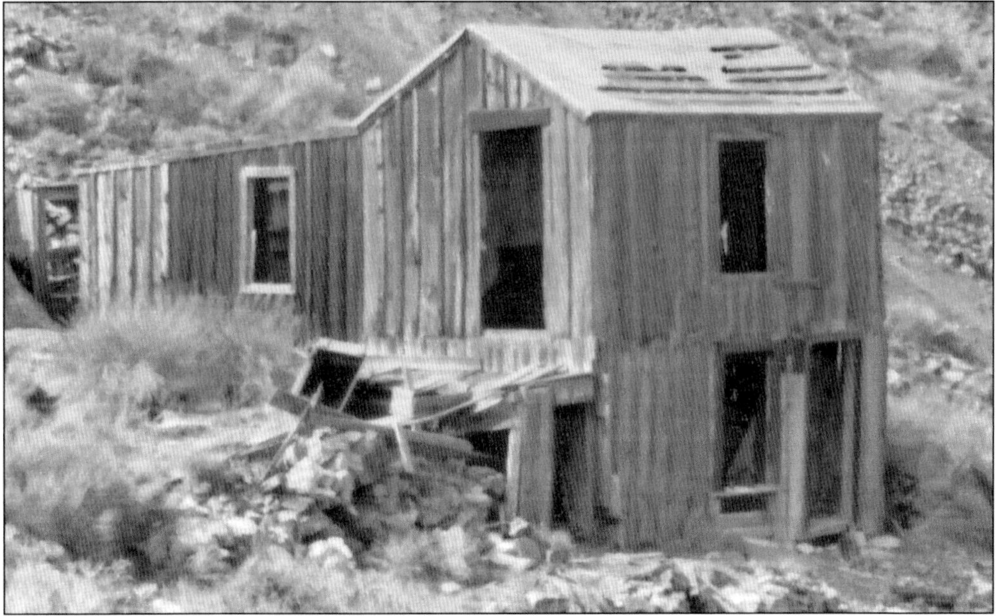

Photographer Jack Freer captured the remains of the Hunter House in this 1970s photograph. The dwelling was once the home of William Lyle Hunter, the Owens Valley miner and rancher who developed the Belmont silver mines east of Cerro Gordo. Hunter also located copper deposits in Death Valley and served as supervisor and clerk of Inyo County. Hunter Mountain, an area he once ranched, is named for him. (Jack Freer Collection.)

Robert C. Likes sits on the porch of the American Hotel waiting for the early-morning cloud cover to clear. During his employment at North American Rockwell in Canoga Park, he became field trip chairman and cartographer of the company's Ghost Town Club, eventually becoming president. From 1969 to 1971, he wrote for *Desert Magazine*. His adventures took him and Glenn R. Day to Cerro Gordo, where they met town owner Barbara Smith and, with her permission, researched and wrote *From This Mountain Cerro Gordo*. (Robert C. Likes Collection.)

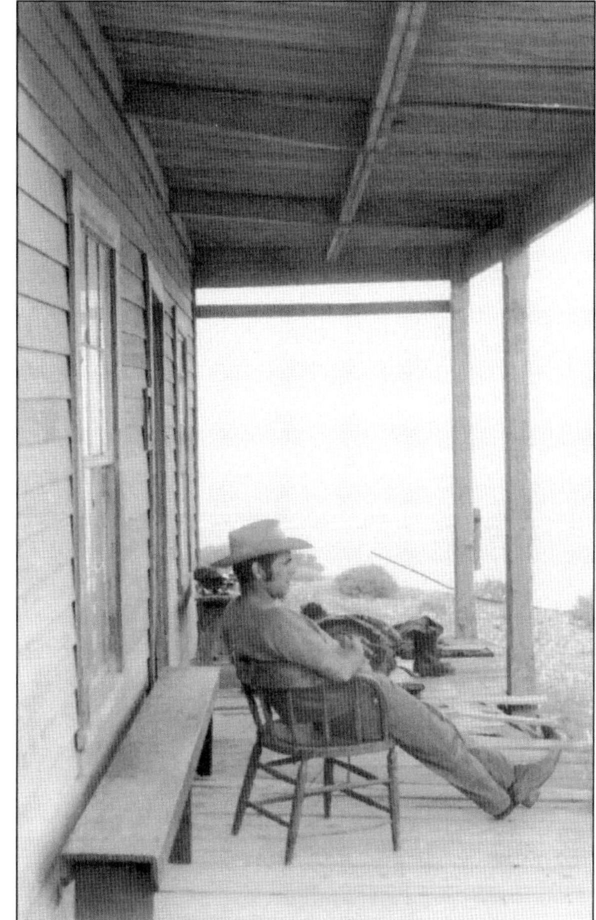

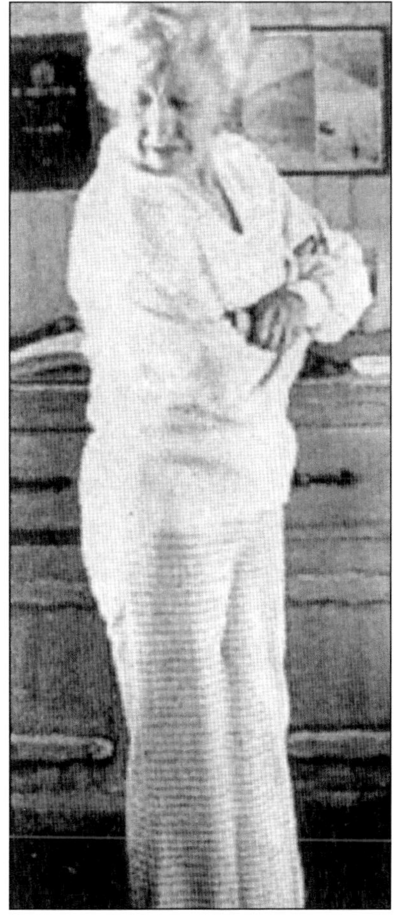

Barbara Smith is shown here in the 1960s. A local Owens Valley girl, she wandered up Lee Flat and married Wally Wilson after a fight and a divorce from her husband, a Hollywood assistant director. Barbara and Wally eventually came to own the old mining camp in lieu of back wages for caretaking. Barbara outlived Wally and two more husbands and struggled to keep the ghost camp alive for tourists who would wander up the mountain. (Robert C. Likes Collection.)

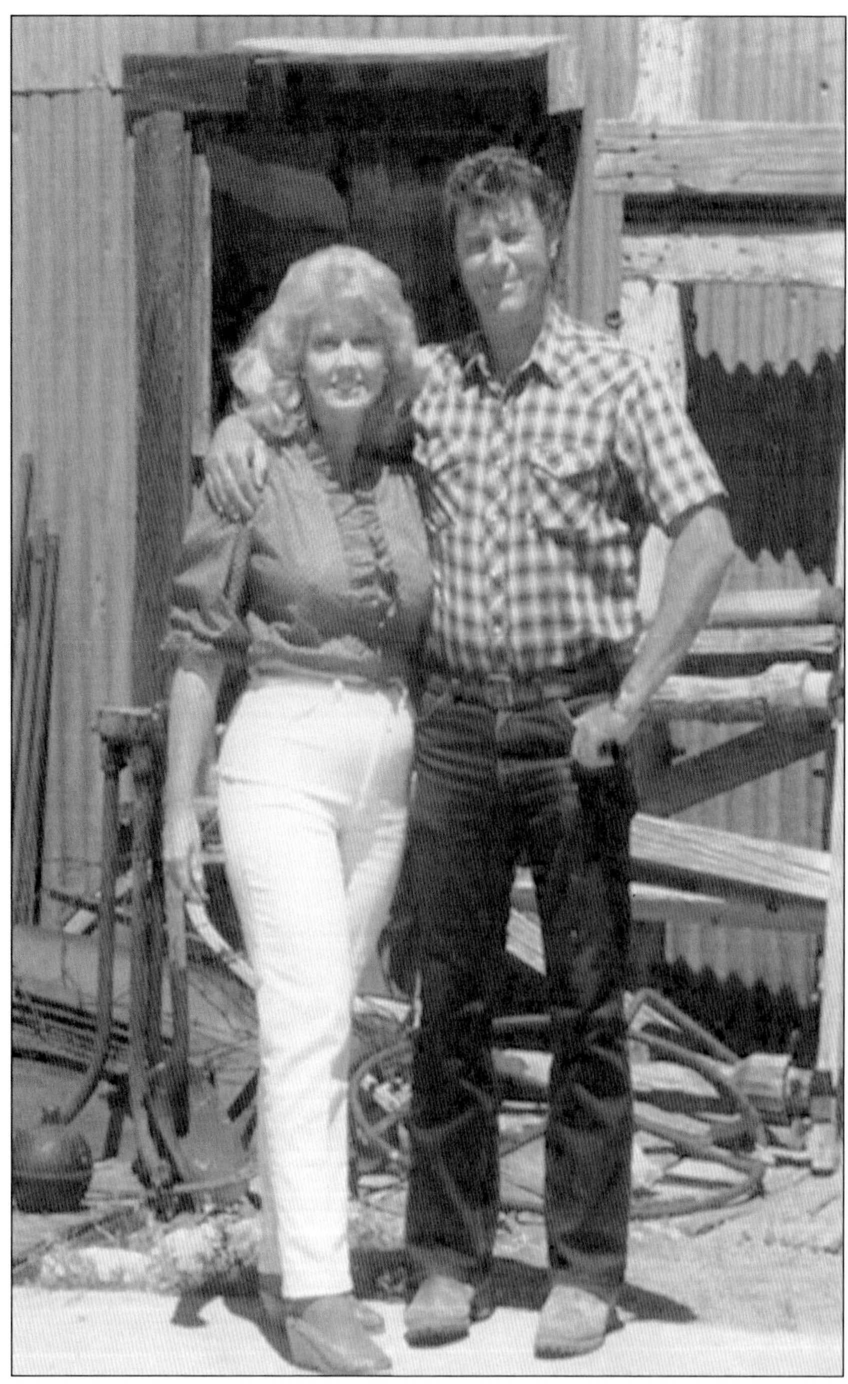

Jody Stewart and Mike Patterson pose in front of the museum building around 1985. Stewart, the niece of Barbara Smith's last husband, Jack Smith, was an Owens Valley girl who moved to the big city. The Smiths, needing money to help keep Cerro Gordo open, convinced Jody to visit and make an investment. Through repeated investments, Jody acquired full ownership and eventually moved to the mountain ghost town and began a program of "restorative reuse" with town manager Mike Patterson, who eventually became her husband. (Mary Grimsley Collection.)

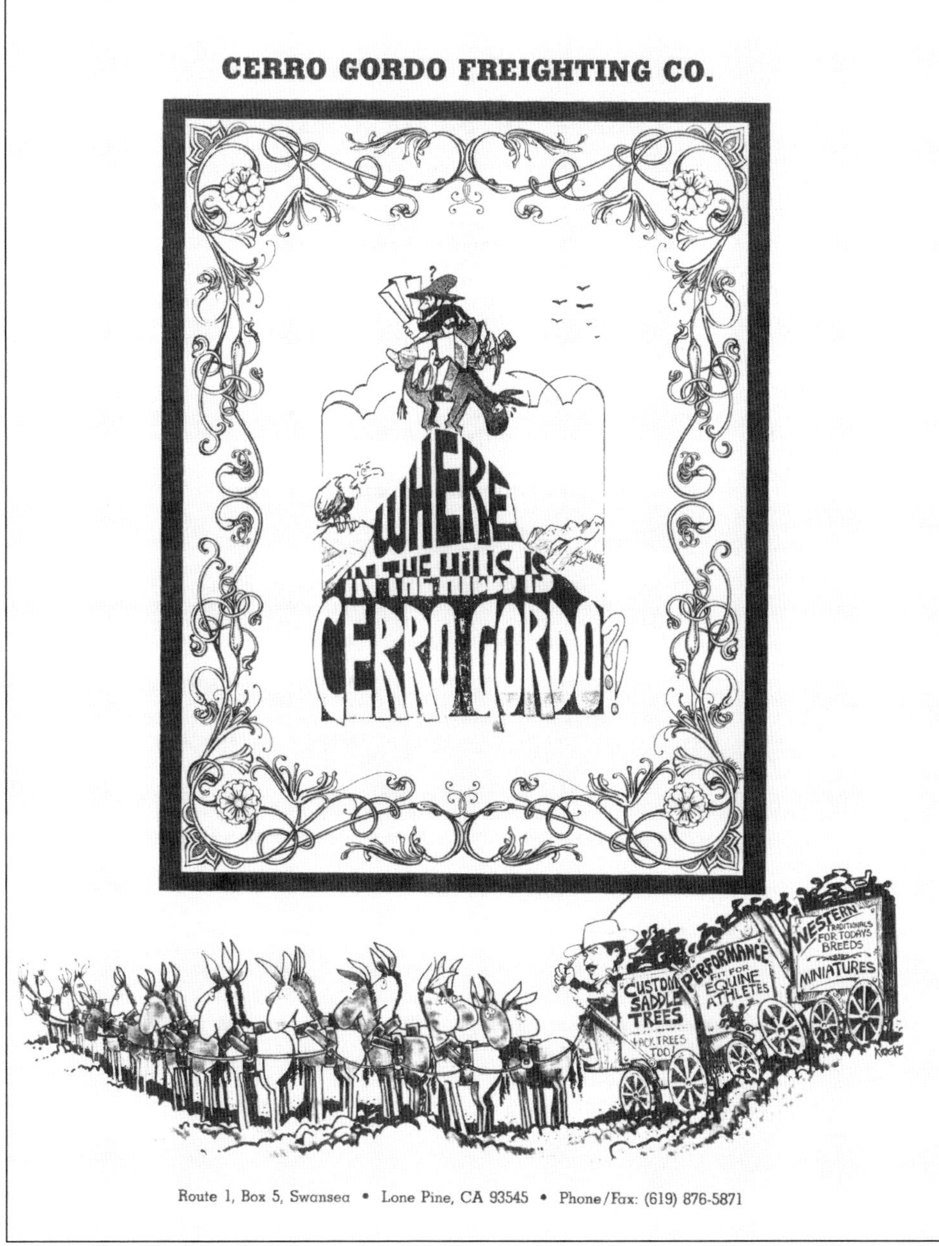

Mike Patterson and Jody Stewart had several enterprises to help fund their restorations. Mike purchased a 1940s E.H. Bohlin "form-fitter" and a sore-backed horse, which led to state-of-the-art "wood butcher" equipment and a saddle shop where he made and sold saddle trees. This pamphlet explains the history of Cerro Gordo and their personal history with the town as well as the debut of the saddle shop, complete with an order form. Over the years, a portrait parlor was operated on the mountain and several buildings were made available to overnight guests as a "bed and cook your own breakfast" inn. With their ventures in Cerro Gordo, they called themselves the "ghost and ghostess of Fat Hill." This was only one of at least two manifestations of the Cerro Gordo Freighting Company, which was originally coined by Remi Nadeau and his company of freight wagons and mules during Cerro Gordo's first mining boom. (Cerro Gordo Collection.)

Cerro Gordo's Bugle of Freedom

Volume 1 Issue 1 **December 1994**

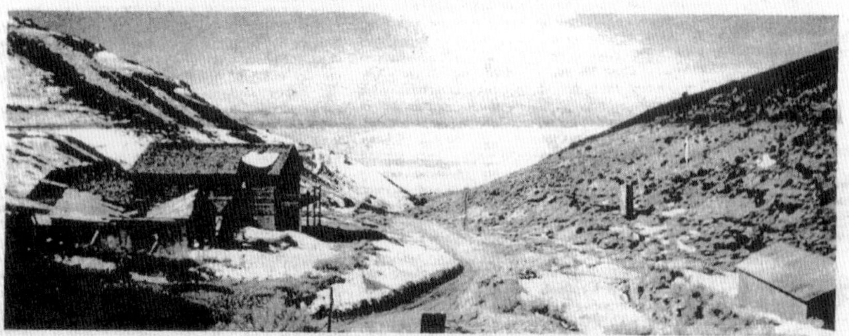

NEWS OF AN INYO COUNTY RESTORATION PROJECT

Do you ever wonder what is new here at

Cerro Gordo?

The snow lies crisp on the ground. The skies are a mild baby blue and the views are truly spectacular! Today, there is not a cloud in the sky.

I slowly permit my eyes to wander out my 126 year old living room window. The vast expanse of the Owen's lakebed 5,000 feet below beckons from this historic 1800's ghost town. I'm a newcommer here, newly transplanted from Boulder, Colorado to do scientific research under contract to NOAA (the National Oceanic and Atmospheric Administration); but I can already imagine the exclamations emanating from the drivers of the mule-drawn wagons as they haul loads of silver ore daily down the tortuous nine mile "Yellow Grade Road" to Swansea. (*I also hear the sighs from present day adventurers who brave the road to ultimately reach the mining town of Cerro Gordo).*

But

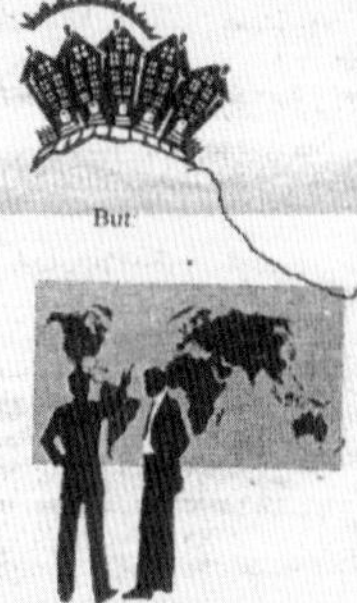

Where is Cerro Gordo?

My mind continues to reminisce while my eyes focus 10 miles distant, across this dry lakebed below, to the majestic snow capped peaks of the Sierra Nevada Mountains some 30 miles distant. How lucky I am to be a part of the Cerro Gordo experience!

From this spectacular vantage point, I would like to take this opportunity to send a message to the Friends of Cerro Gordo. For the imminent holiday seasons:

" *I extend a very warm and special wish of happiness to each of you.*"

'Happy New Year'!

Echoes from the past

By issuing subscriptions to this quarterly newspaper, along with other fundraising efforts, we hope to raise moneys necessary for the restoration of this truly remarkable historic landmark.

Each issue will bring to you excerpts from historic news articles that included mention of Cerro Gordo's life and times. **Don Becker** (consultant historian) has kindly provided references so that I may share all the wonderful stories with you. Below, I present to you a sample of these articles direct from the newspapers archives.

And, now for a few excerpts of the wonderful history of Cerro Gordo!

1) May 14, 1867.
Territorial Enterprise
- Virginia City, NV.

"*We yesterday saw some specimens of ore and silver bullion that were brought to this city by a Mexican named Bernarda Arambula. They came from Kearsarge country and were obtained at a place called Cerro Gordo, about forty miles east of Camp Independence. The ores shown us are of the richest character, and came from veins that range in width from one to four feet. In the camp known as Cerro Gordo there are said to be hundreds of veins of a similar character, and only a few of them have been prospected. The Mexicans have six small furnaces, and extract silver from the ore by smelting. The leads are held in*

By 1994, Jody Stewart and Mike Patterson had an address book of friends, family, and volunteers interested in their ghost town restoration. They published the first edition of the *Cerro Gordo Bugle of Freedom* and at least three more editions followed. The paper was named after an original attempt at a newspaper during the 1800s, which was published solely for the purpose of keeping residents informed on the Prussian War going on at the time. The newer edition kept people informed of restorative efforts and served as a history of the town. (Explore Historic California Collection.)

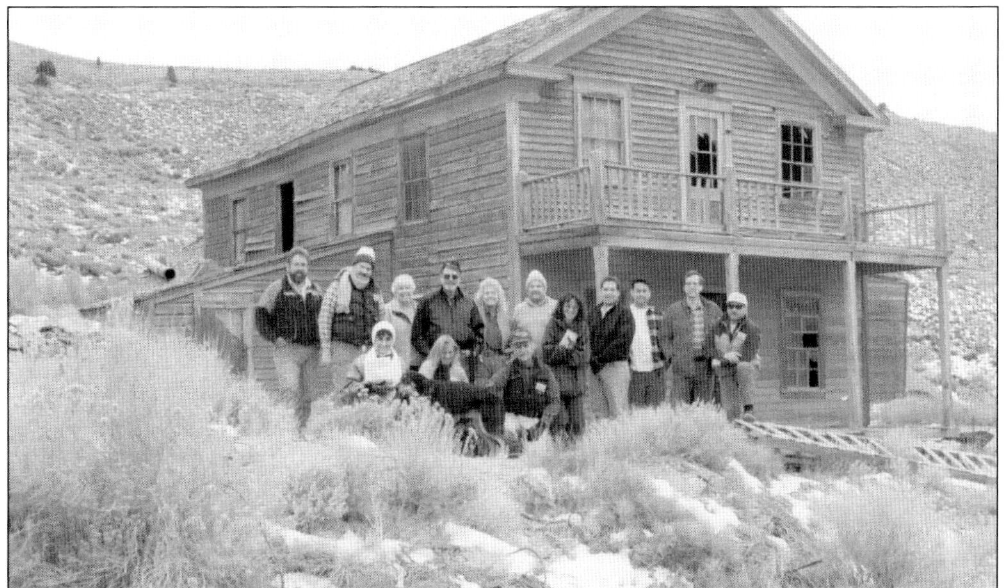

The American Hotel has always been a favorite spot for visitors to pose for a picture. The Explore Historic California four-wheel drive tour group arrived on a brisk day in November 1991 and posed with the ghostess herself—standing in the middle of the group, easily recognizable with her friendly smile and long blonde hair. This is just one of many groups and thousands of visitors who have wandered up the Yellow Grade to visit. (Explore Historic California Collection.)

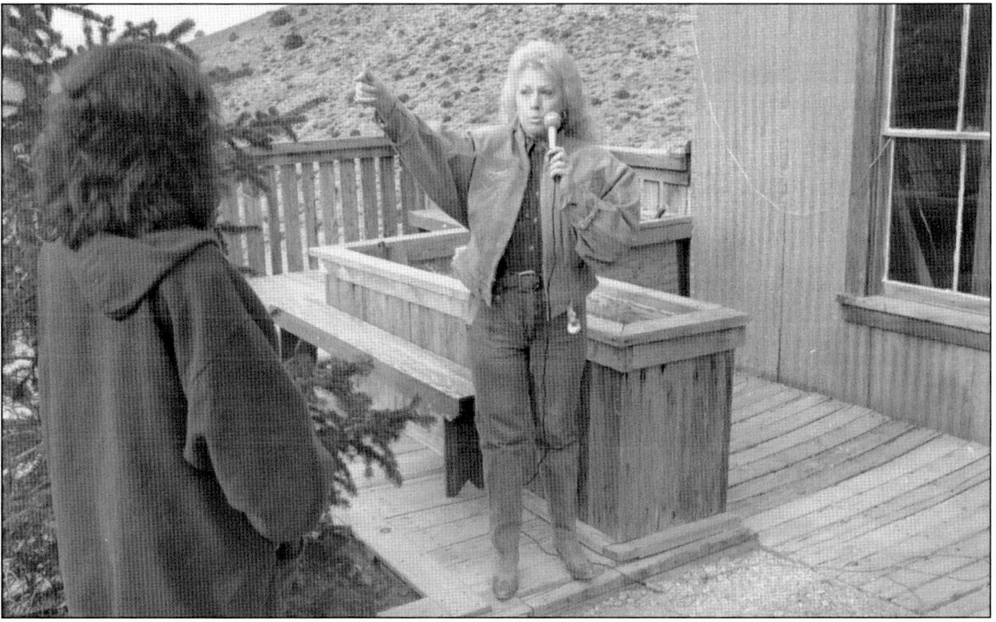

Jody Stewart stands with a microphone before the Explore Historic California four-wheel drive tour group, telling the story of how she wandered up the mountain in her Porsche, dressed in fancy clothes and high heels, and financially rescued her aunt and uncle, Barbara and Jack Smith, so that they could keep Cerro Gordo. Eventually, Jody wound up with full interest in the town—and big plans on how to attract visitors and restore historic buildings. (Explore Historic California Collection.)

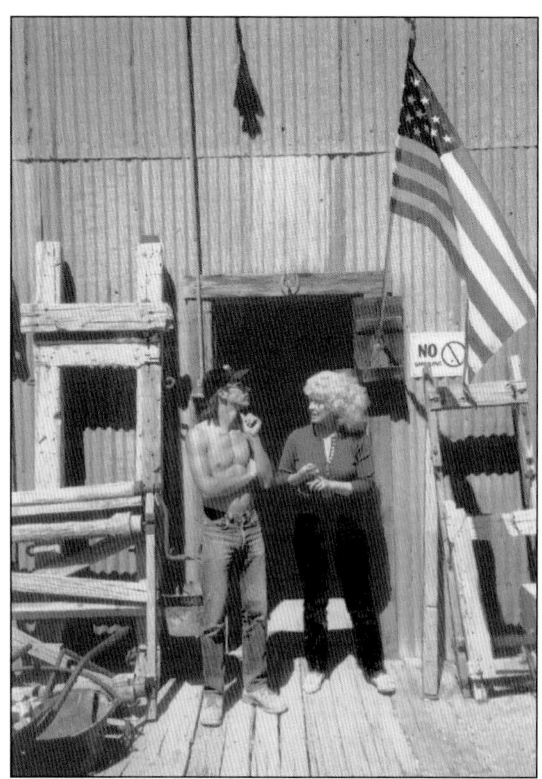

Jody Stewart frequently posed with visitors at Cerro Gordo. Above, she talks with a visitor outside the museum building in the 1980s. Below, she poses with Mary Westervelt of North Vancouver, British Columbia, in 1988. Visitors frequently send Stewart and Patterson thank you cards and photographs. (Both, Cerro Gordo Collection.)

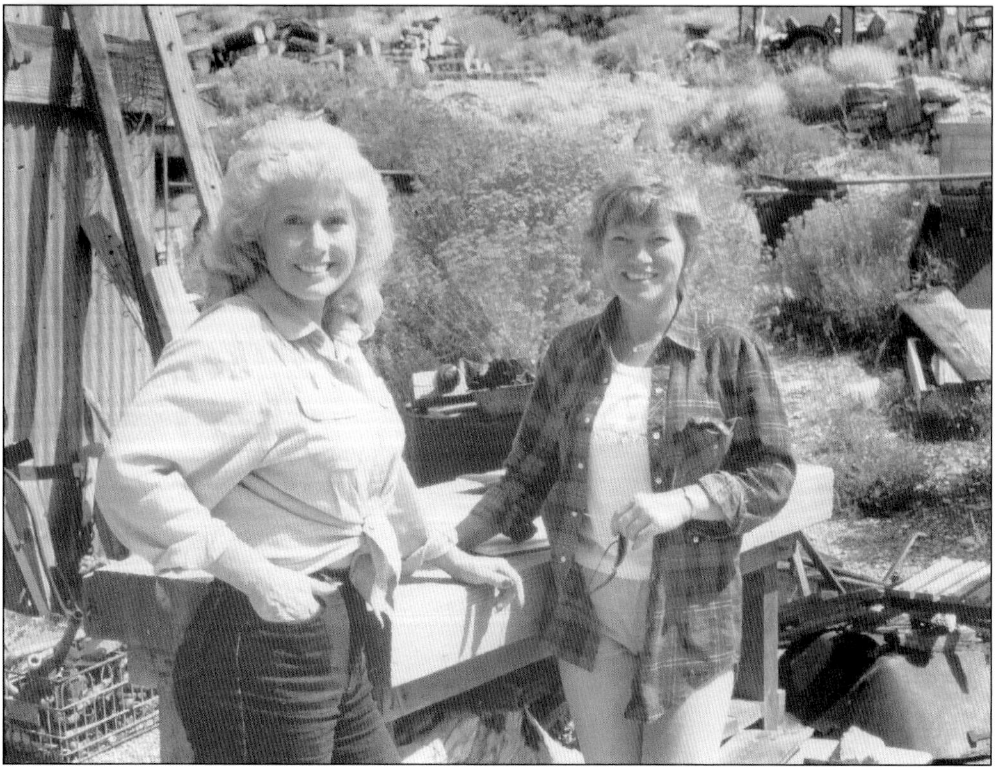

Jody Stewart stands in front of the 1868 Belshaw House, which has gone through many transformations over the years. Originally the home of silver baron Mortimer Belshaw, it has been home to innumerable caretakers as well as Mike Patterson's saddle shop, the photography salon seen here, and an overnight rental for guests who wanted to experience ghost town ambience at its best. During its incarnation as a guest rental, the house featured electricity, gas, wood, and propane heat, running water, a flush toilet, complete cooking facilities, a reading library, and satellite television. Two bedrooms and a couch provided sleeping for four to five guests. Below, Mike Patterson and Jody Stewart take advantage of their own photography salon for a fun shoot. (Both, Mary Grimsley Collection.)

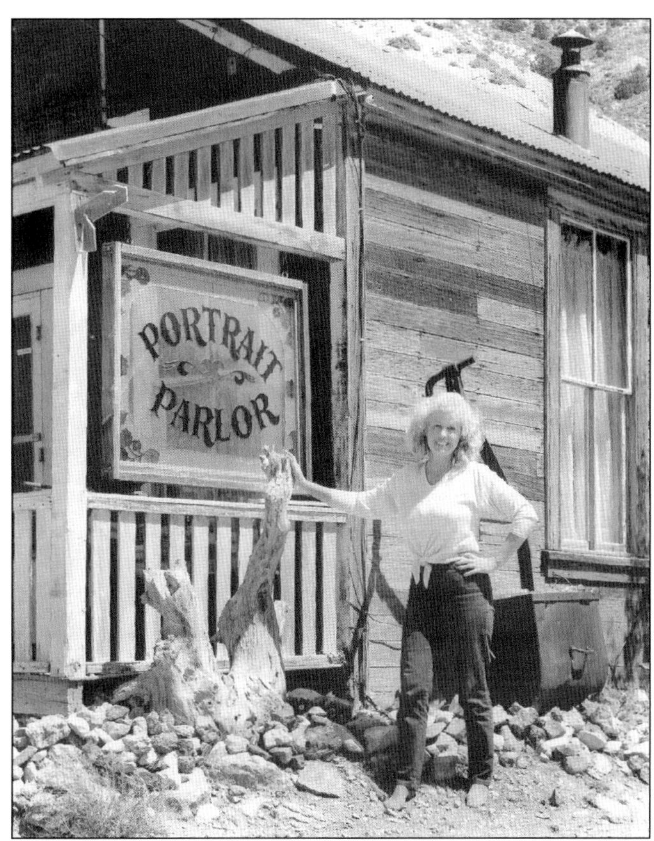

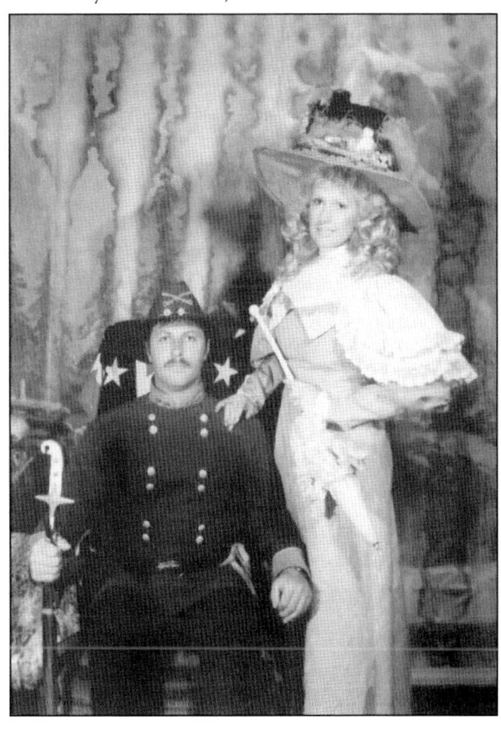

August 15, 1987

Dear Jody Stewart:

Allow me to introduce myself. My name is Douglas Gordon, and my Grandfather was Louis D. Gordon. I came across your name in my continuing search for additional information on the Cerro Gordo mine. If all of our family information is correct, (which is pretty vague, due to the fact that my Grandfather and Father are both deceased), Louis Gordon owned/operated Cerro Gordo in the early part of this century. I have an awful lot of old pictures, etc. of the mine that you may be interested in, as I understand that you are doing something in the way of a museum or history of Cerro Gordo. I am sorry if this may not be making a lot of sense at this point, but I am writing this in hopes that it will reach you with the limited address that I have. I am planning a trip to the Keeler area as well as parts of Nevada sometime in September and very much want to stop at Cerro Gordo to try and gather as much info as possible on my Grandfather's mining operations in Calif. and Nevada.

Please give me a quick telephone call at home [illegible], there is an answering machine on it), or call me at work during the hours of 7:00 a.m. to 4:00 p.m. Mon.-Fri. at [illegible]. I will then call you back, as I think that we could have a very interesting conversation.

I got your name from Jane Fisher of Chalfant Press in Bishop, Ca, when I was ordering the book *From This Mountain, Cerro Gordo*. I have not received it yet, so I don't know of the contents, but I have great expections about it.

Thank you for your time, and I am looking forward to hearing from you.

Sincerely,

Douglas Gordon

In 1987, Douglas Gordon, the grandson of Louis D. Gordon, contacted Jody Stewart to introduce himself. Gordon was going through his grandfather's extensive photography archive and wanted more information about Cerro Gordo. Many of the images in this book come from the L.D. Gordon Collection through the generosity of Doug Gordon. (Cerro Gordo Collection.)

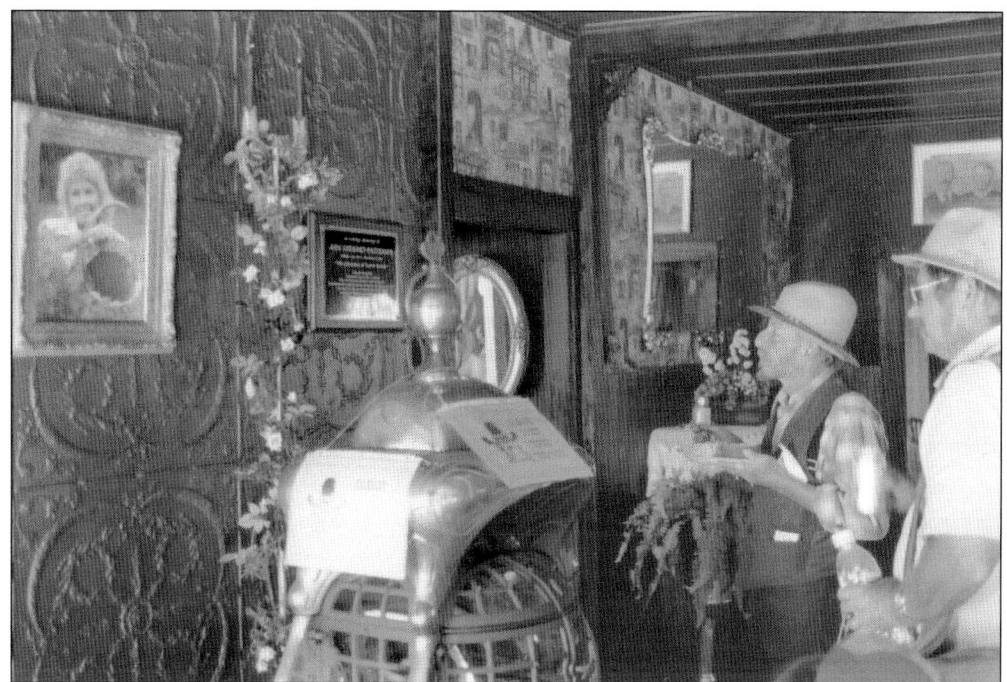

On December 7, 2001, after a 17-year reign as ghostess of Cerro Gordo, Jody Stewart succumbed to lymphoma. A wall in the dining hall of the American Hotel was redone in tribute to her. The image above shows the beautiful antique punched-tin paneling on the wall, the memorial plaque, one of Stewart's last pictures, and a newly installed antique stove. Attendees at her memorial service, held in mid-May 2002, somberly read the plaque and remembered the woman who brought Cerro Gordo into a new millennium. The plaque below describes all of Jody's accomplishments in life and pronounces her not only "ghostess," but "keeper of the keys." (Both, Explore Historic California Collection.)

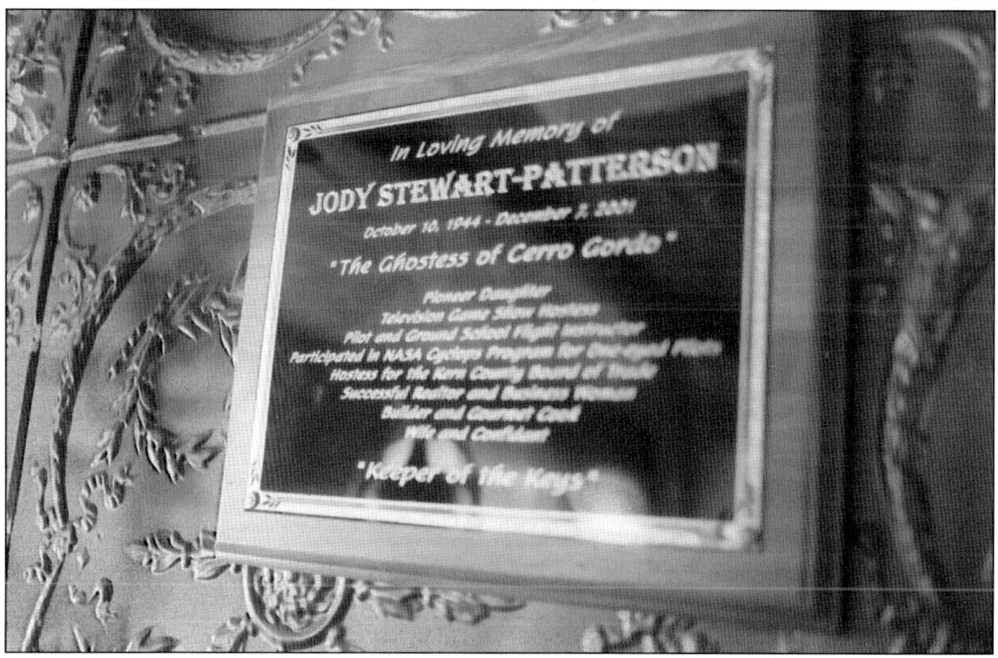

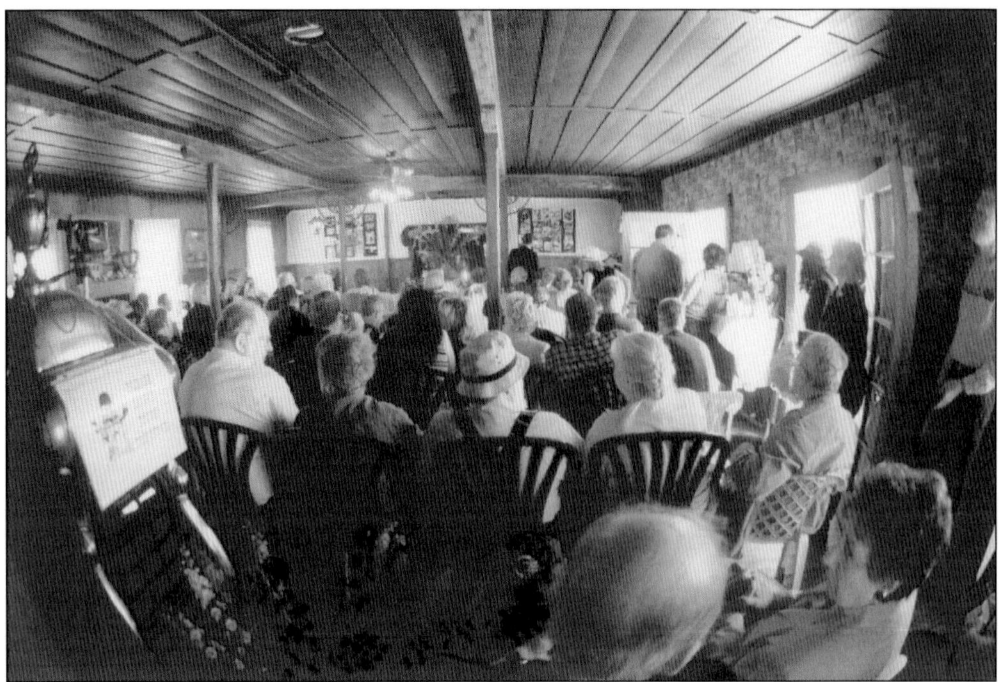

The American Hotel overflowed with friends, family, and visitors who had fallen in love with Jody Stewart and her town. The actual memorial service was held in the dining room of the hotel. The service included the presentation of various plaques, and personal eulogies and remembrances by both close and casual friends. Those who could not be seated outside filled the porch and the deck with the doors open so they could strain to hear and see. There was nary a dry eye in the house for the beloved ghostess of Cerro Gordo. (Both, Explore Historic California Collection.)

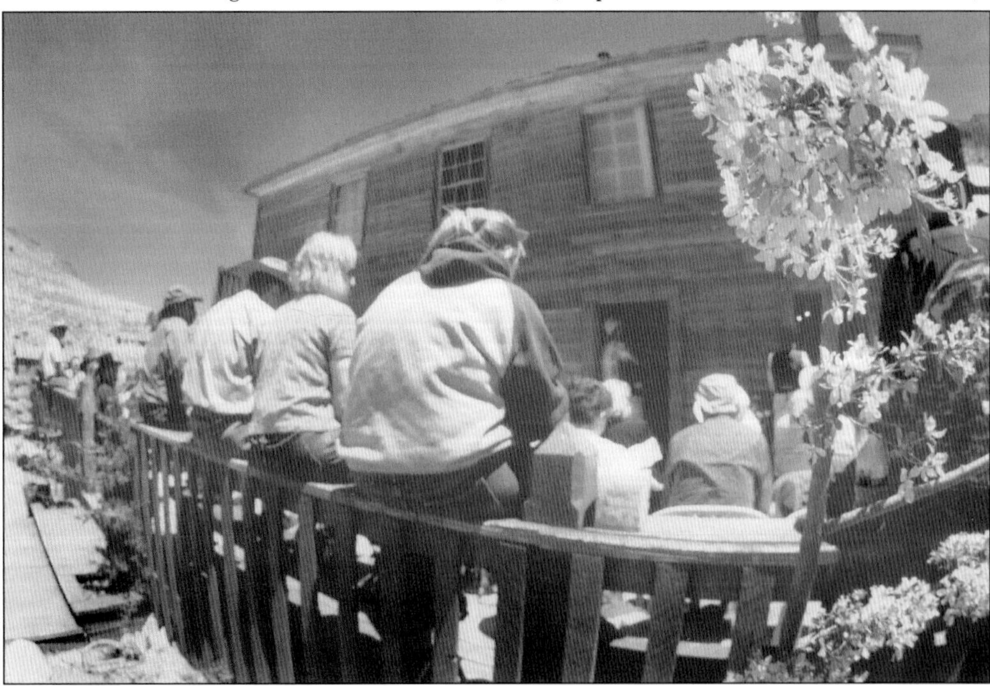

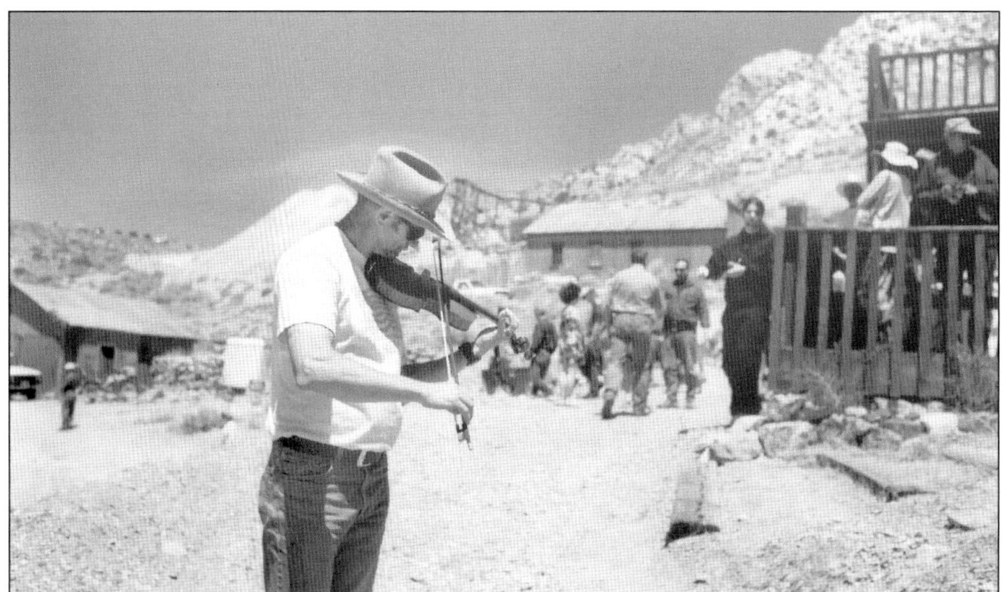

A solemn tune is played by a fiddler as guests mill around the American Hotel and the town. The original estimate of 200 mourners swelled to 500 when all statistics were collected—a Cerro Gordo population not seen since the late 1800s. An old wringer washer contained chrysanthemums and guests were invited to take blossoms and place them on Jody's memorial site. (Explore Historic California Collection.)

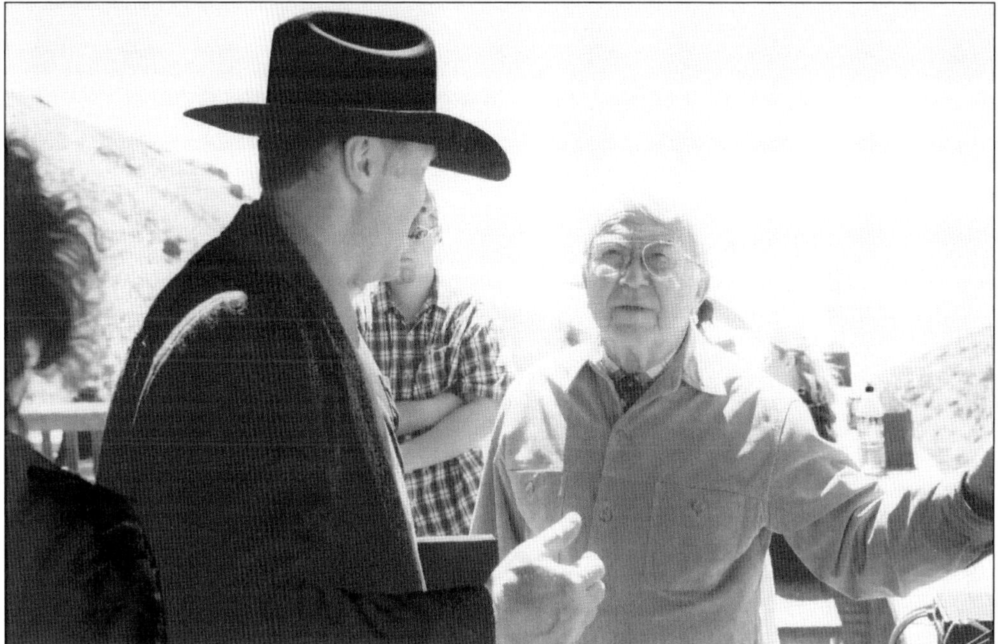

On the left in a black hat and suit, the grieving Mike Patterson talks to one of the distinguished guests, Remi Nadeau, at his wife's memorial service. The great-great-grandson of Cerro Gordo Freighting Company's Remi Nadeau, he extended condolences and swapped memories of Jody and the history of her restored ghost town before hiking to the cemetery to leave a chrysanthemum at her grave. (Explore Historic California Collection.)

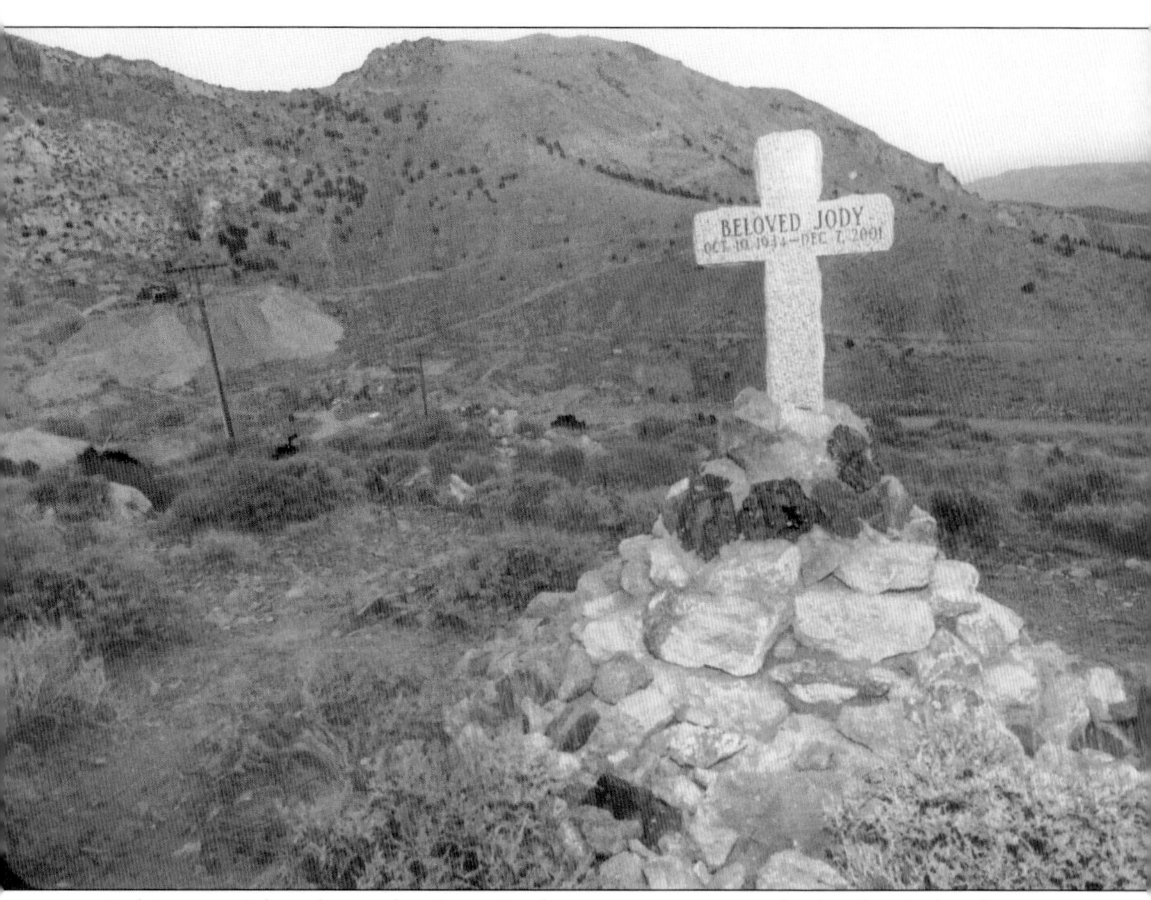

Jody's memorial marker in the Cerro Gordo cemetery was erected a few days before the services by her husband Mike Patterson. The carved stone, reading, "Beloved Jody Oct. 10, 1944 – Dec. 7, 2001," was commissioned by Mike to go atop a cairn of rocks the couple had collected for a dry garden they never got to build. All the mourners walked up to the cemetery and placed flowers on her grave. (Explore Historic California Collection.)

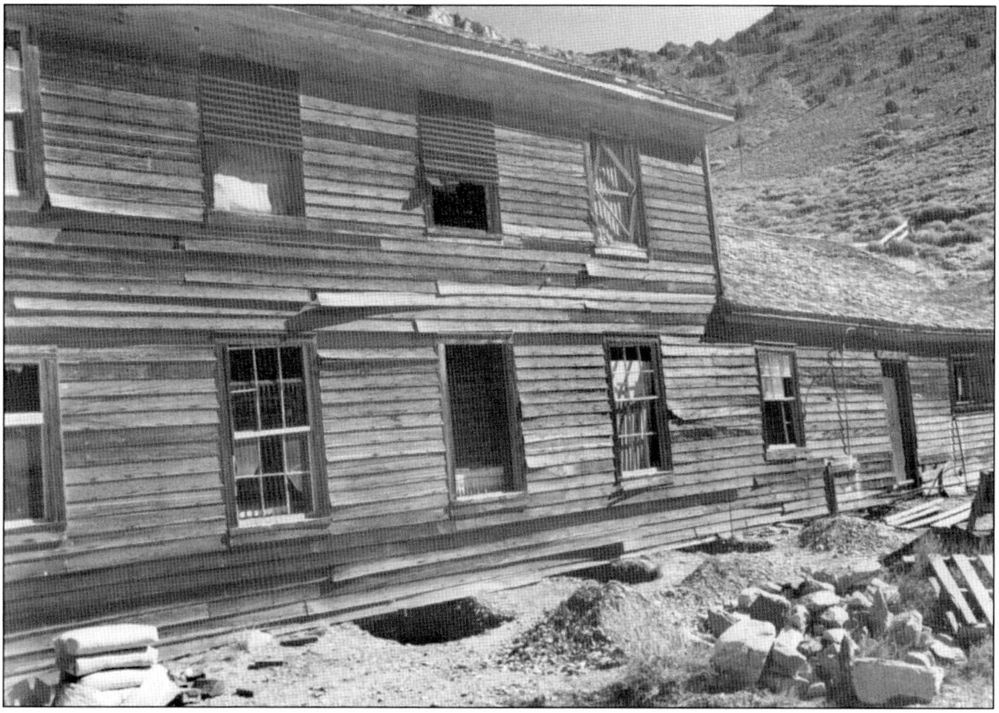

The American Hotel became Jody Stewart's pet project. It is seen above with shattered windows and deteriorating siding in November 1991. Although it was unsafe to go inside, visitors could peer in windows to look at the original cook stove and envision how it was brought up by mules in the 1870s. By 1997, the downstairs of the hotel was restored and volunteers would come up to cook for overnight guests who requested catering. The wood-burning stove was restored to its original glory but was never converted for propane use. Commercial cook stoves were installed and tables lined the dining room, accommodating groups and visitors who needed to sit inside away from the weather. Stewart and Patterson served up as much history as food over the years. The hotel was only for day use and occasional meals, with the kitchen and dining room restored and the upstairs reserved for offices. Below is a photograph of the hotel in 2011. (Both, Explore Historic California Collection.)

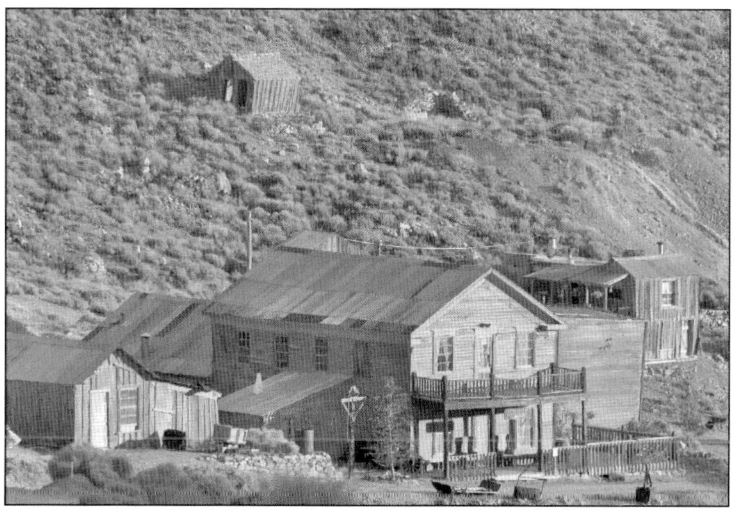

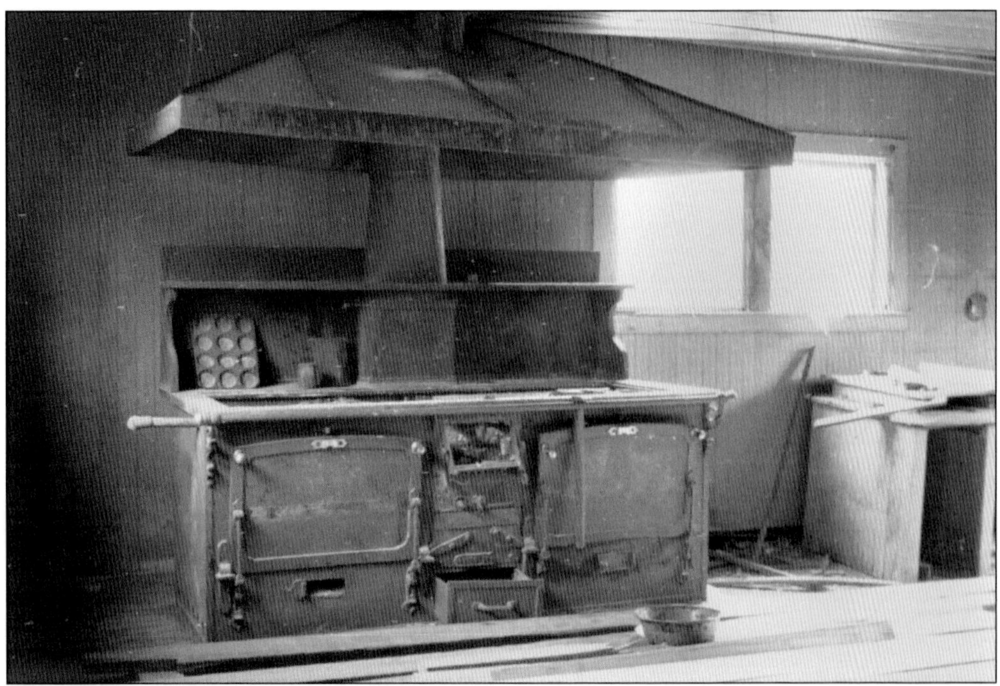

The American Hotel's kitchen and cook stove are shown above in 1993 prior to restoration. While still not operational, it now holds an assortment of Dutch ovens, waffle irons, and molds (below). The original manufacturer's plaque in the center of the stovetop reads "Holbrook Merril & Stetson, San Francisco & Sacramento, Cal. Contractors." While substantial in size and weight, the stove was designed to break down into more manageable components to be hauled by pack animals or wagons. (Both, Explore Historic California Collection.)

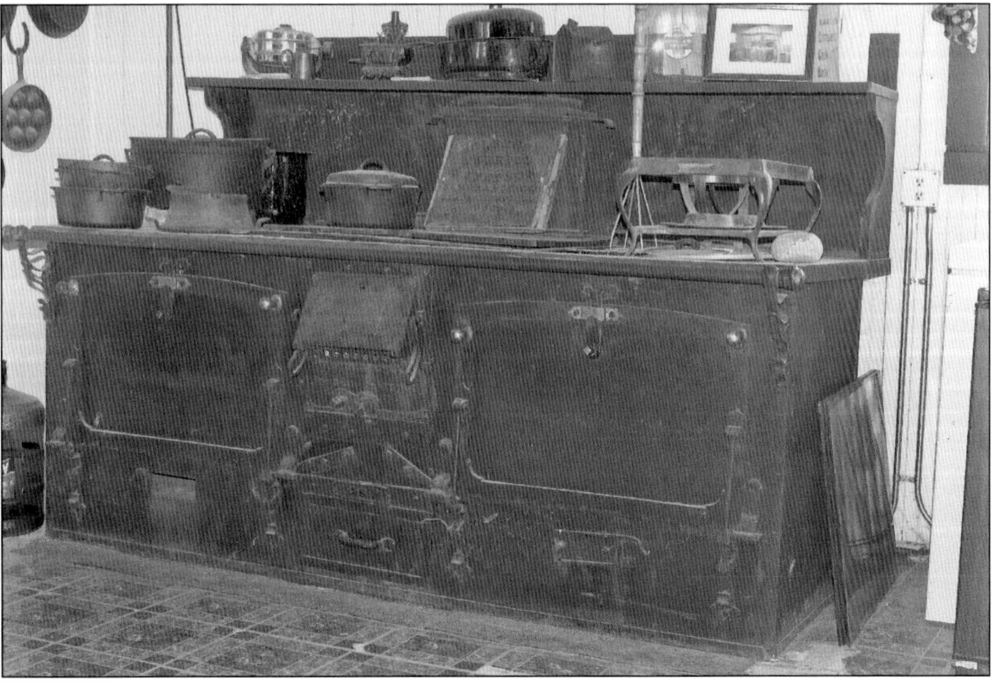

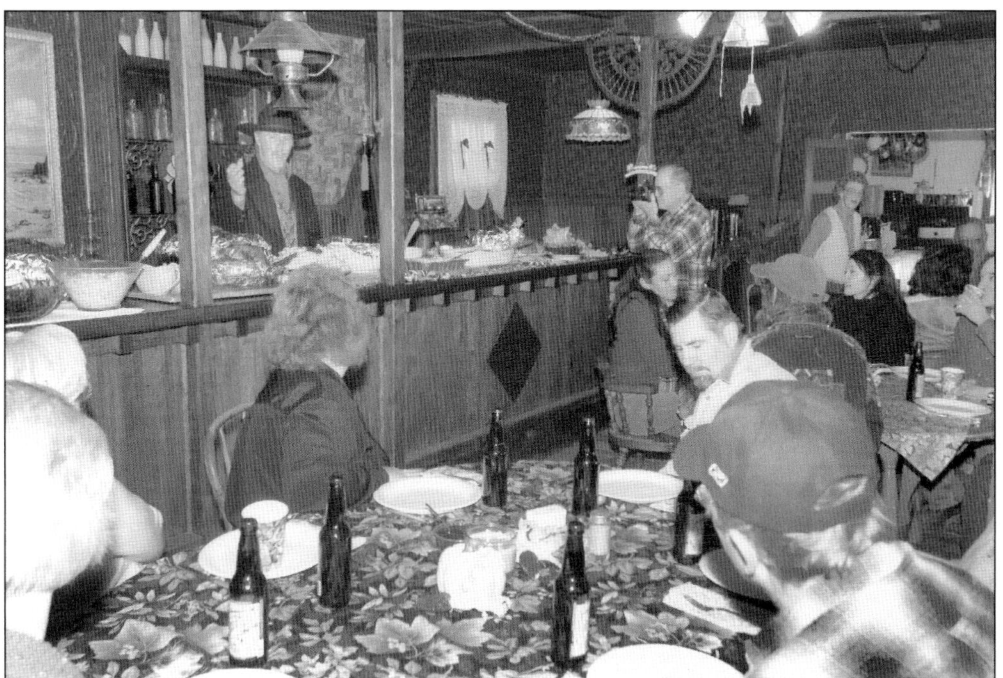

Following Jody Stewart's death, Mike Patterson hosted several Thanksgiving dinners in the American Hotel for friends and volunteers. The meal was potluck-style, with cooking and preparation in the restored kitchen and a buffet on the bar Mike had commissioned. Although the hotel never had a bar, it is typical of the bars seen in mining and cow towns in the 1870s and patterned after an actual bar Patterson had seen. (Explore Historic California Collection.)

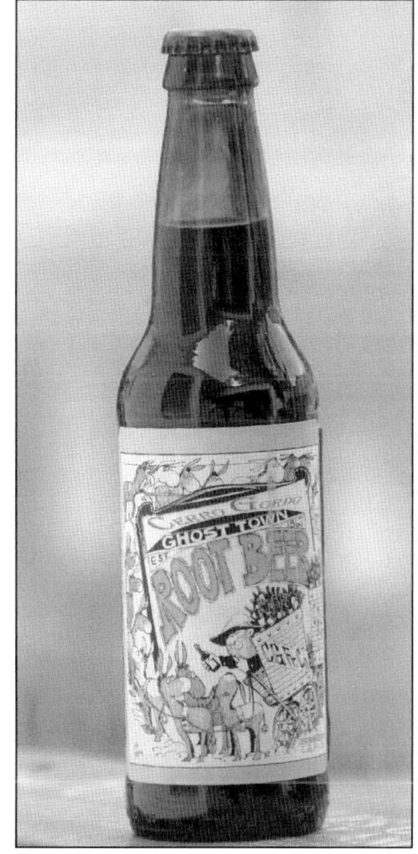

By 2006, Mike Patterson was serving his own label of root beer under the Cerro Gordo Freighting Company name. Much to the delight of visitors, he would slide a bottle down the bar to the thirsty and serve up a good history tale while he did. The root beer was bottled in Ridgecrest at Indian Wells Brewery and the first labels were slapped on by two of Mike's friends in the kitchen of the hotel. Later, when the design was tweaked to his liking, the bottles came from the company with the labels attached. (Explore Historic California Collection.)

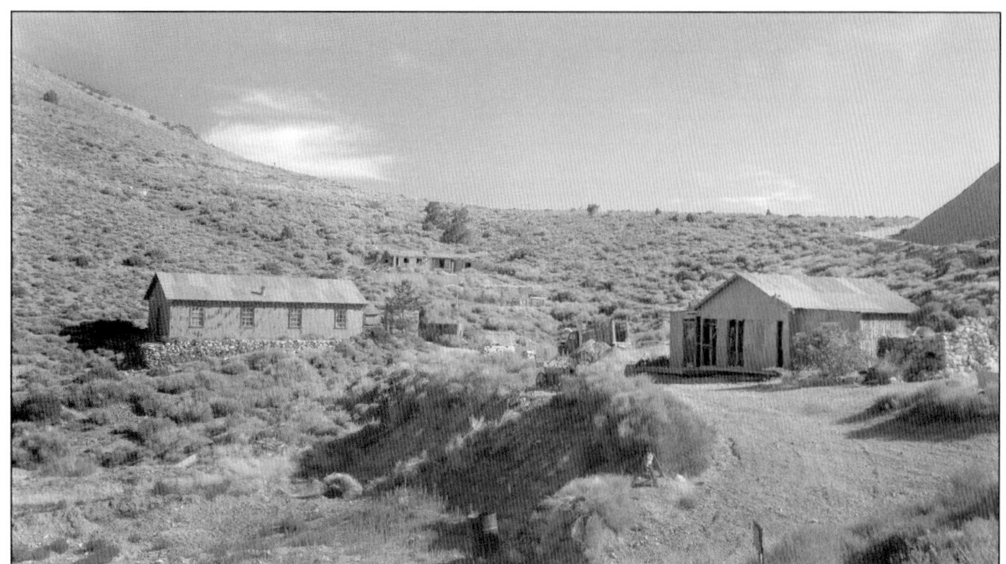

By the early 1990s, the bunkhouse from the Louis D. Gordon zinc era (the grey building on the far left) was restored for overnight stays and "cook your own" meals. Six bedrooms accommodated up to 11 people comfortably, with quilt-covered beds and old dressers. The front door opened up to a kitchen/dining room complete with a propane stove, refrigerator, running water, and woodstove. The woodstove and a propane heater in the hallway kept the rooms toasty in the winter months. The grey building on the right, known as Ned Reddy's garage, was later converted into a chapel and theater. (Explore Historic California Collection.)

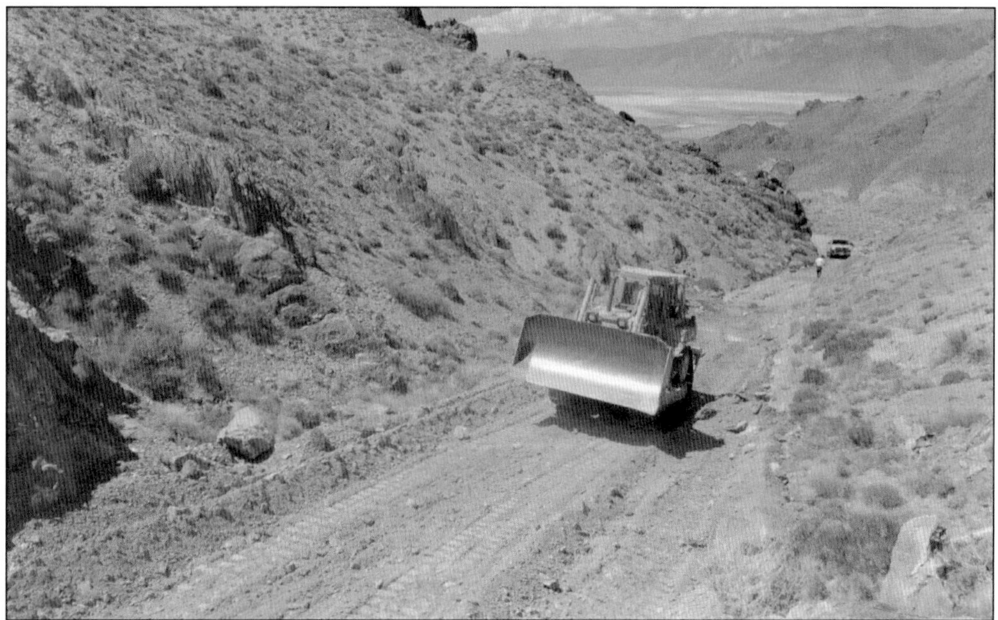

The Yellow Grade Road from Keeler at the shore of Owens Lake to the Cerro Gordo ghost town is usually accessible by high-clearance vehicles, but four-wheel drive is recommended because of its steep grade. In July 2003, flash floods took out a good portion of the road, making it totally impassable for nearly a week before work crews, busy with severe flooding elsewhere in Inyo County, could finally get to it. (Explore Historic California Collection.)

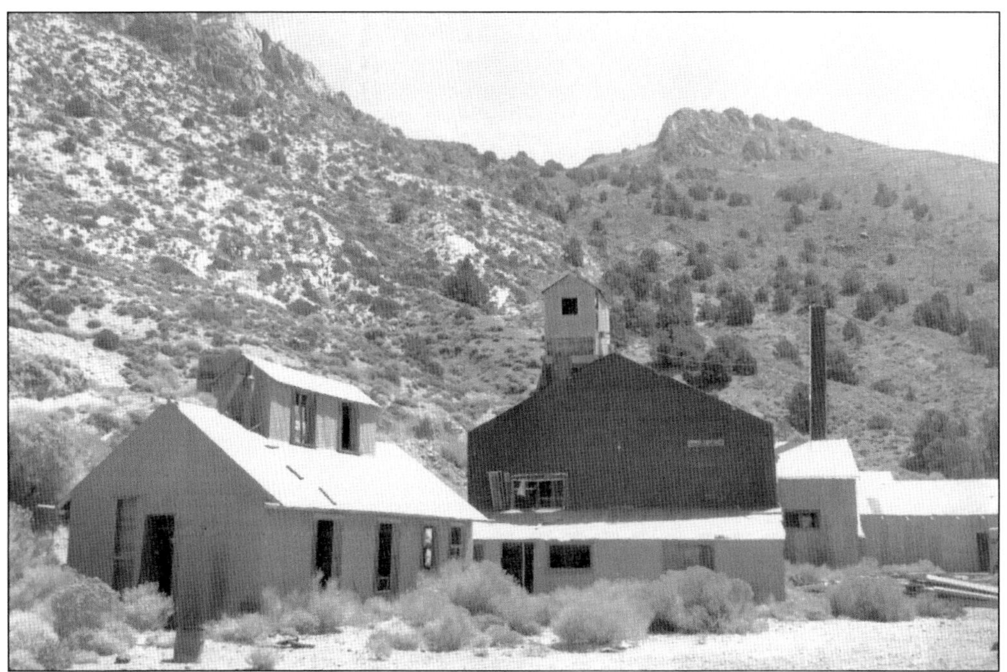

This undated photograph shows the changing room (left) with the hoist house in background. The changing room was a place for the mine workers to change from street clothes to work clothes. The early-1900s building even had washing facilities. (Cerro Gordo Collection.)

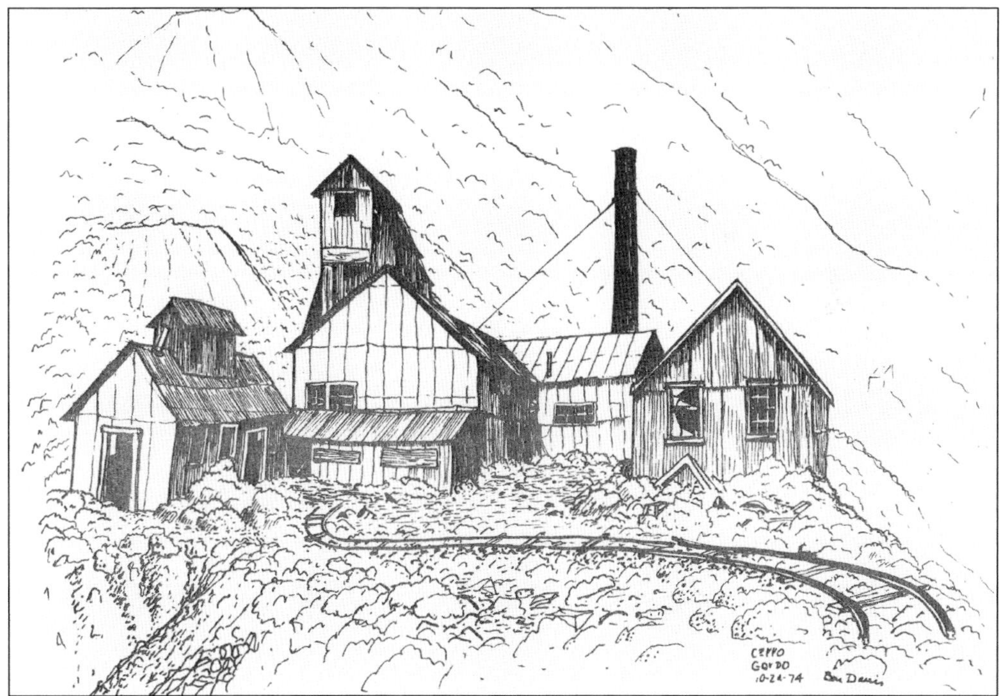

A pen and ink drawing dated October 24, 1974, by Ben Davis also shows the changing room. The drawing was used as part of Cerro Gordo Mines' logo and appeared on business cards and stationery. (Cerro Gordo Collection.)

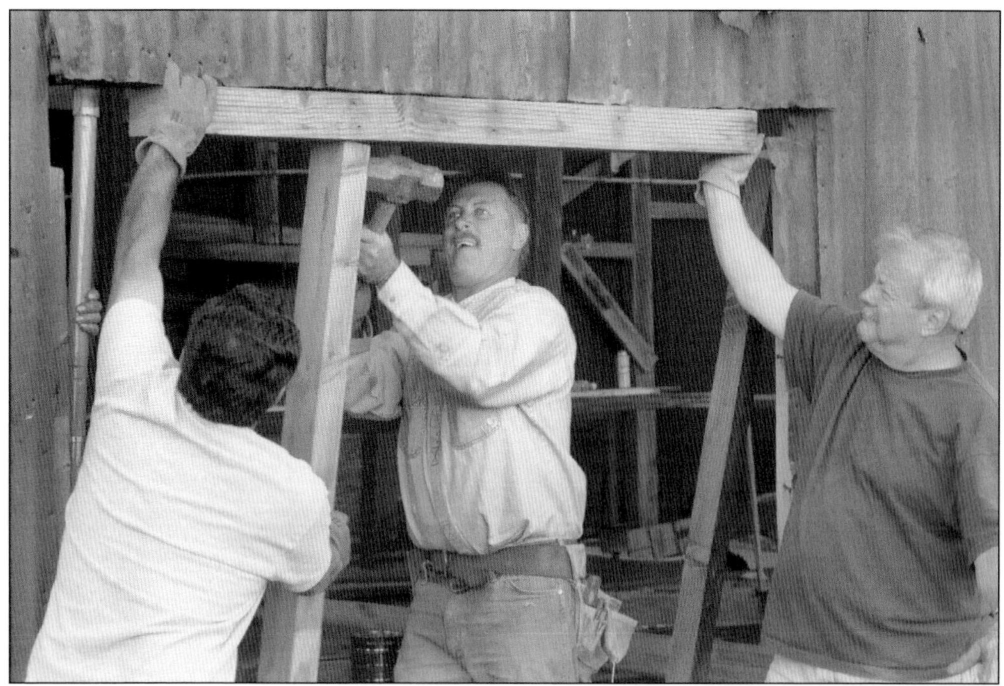

Mike Patterson (center) works with members of a volunteer group called the Cerro Gordo Fire Department to stabilize the Union Mine hoist house in 2005. They replaced timbering and fasteners that had deteriorated over time. The present hoist house was rebuilt in 1877 after it was destroyed by the fire that spread to the 200-foot level of the Union Mine. Old photographs of the hoist house elsewhere in this book show a blacksmith shop attached to the front of the structure. The blacksmith shop would be off to the left of the photograph below. The hoist house contained the opening to the 900-foot-deep shaft along with the elevator and hoist equipment, compressor, motors, and a steam boiler. (Both, Explore Historic California Collection.)

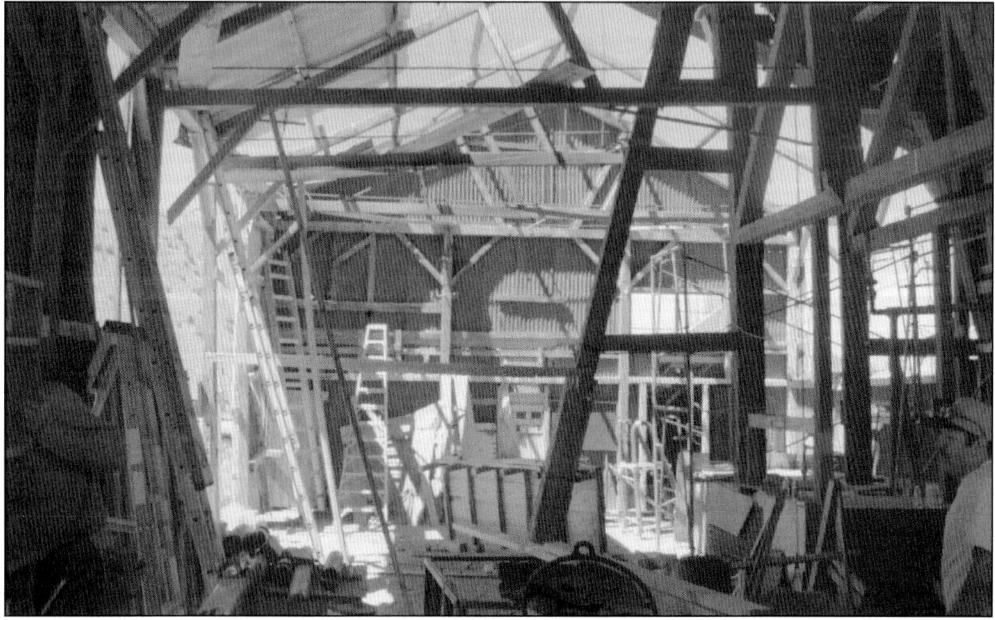

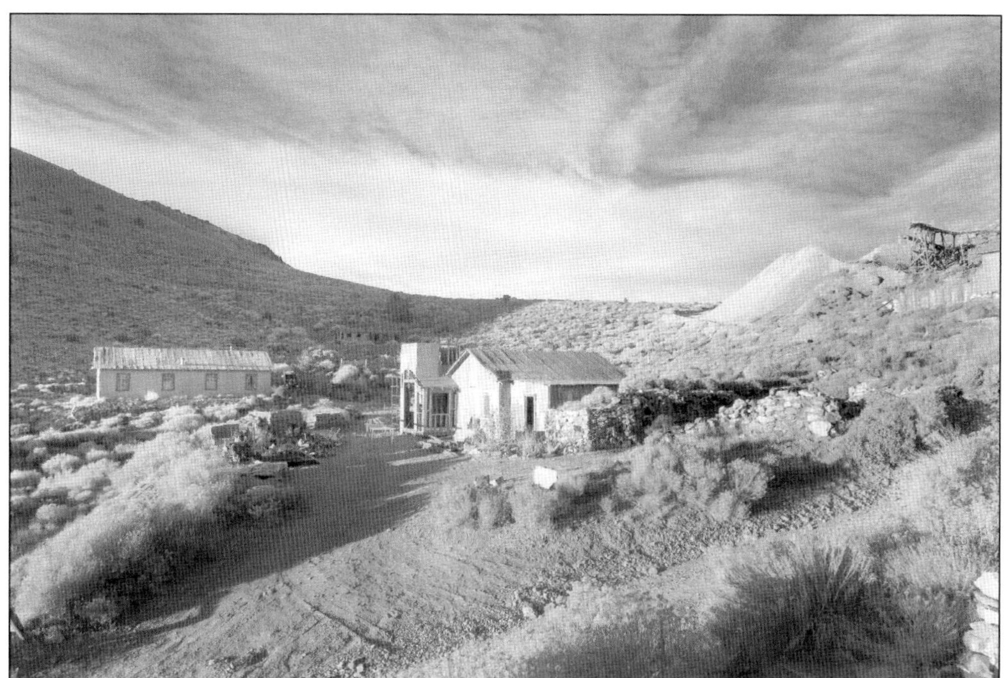

Cerro Gordo was a rough-and-tumble mining town with no church or schools, but Mike Patterson was determined for his town to have a place for weddings, chapel services, and old movie watching. Volunteers helped him turn the tin building (center, with wood construction) into the first church. The building in the left background is the bunkhouse, and beside the chapel to the right is the rock foundation of an original mule stable. (Explore Historic California Collection.)

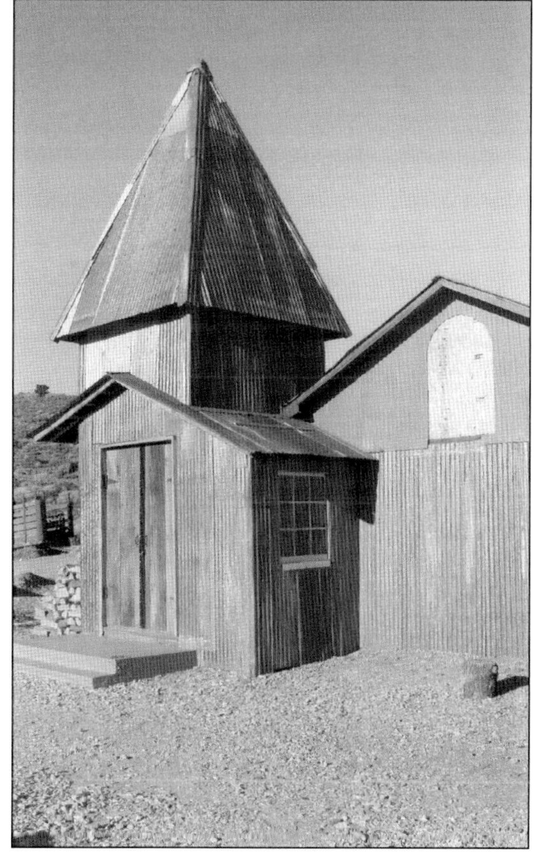

The nearly completed chapel is shown here with the steeple finished, waiting for a stained glass window to be placed in the boarded-up arched window on the right. The inside of the building still needs work, but it contains a partial floor, stabilized walls, a projector box, and theater seats. Mike Patterson's vision was to use the building both as a chapel and a theater where old westerns could be shown. Unfortunately, the project was halted in 2009, not long after this picture was taken, after the death of Mike Patterson. (Explore Historic California Collection.)

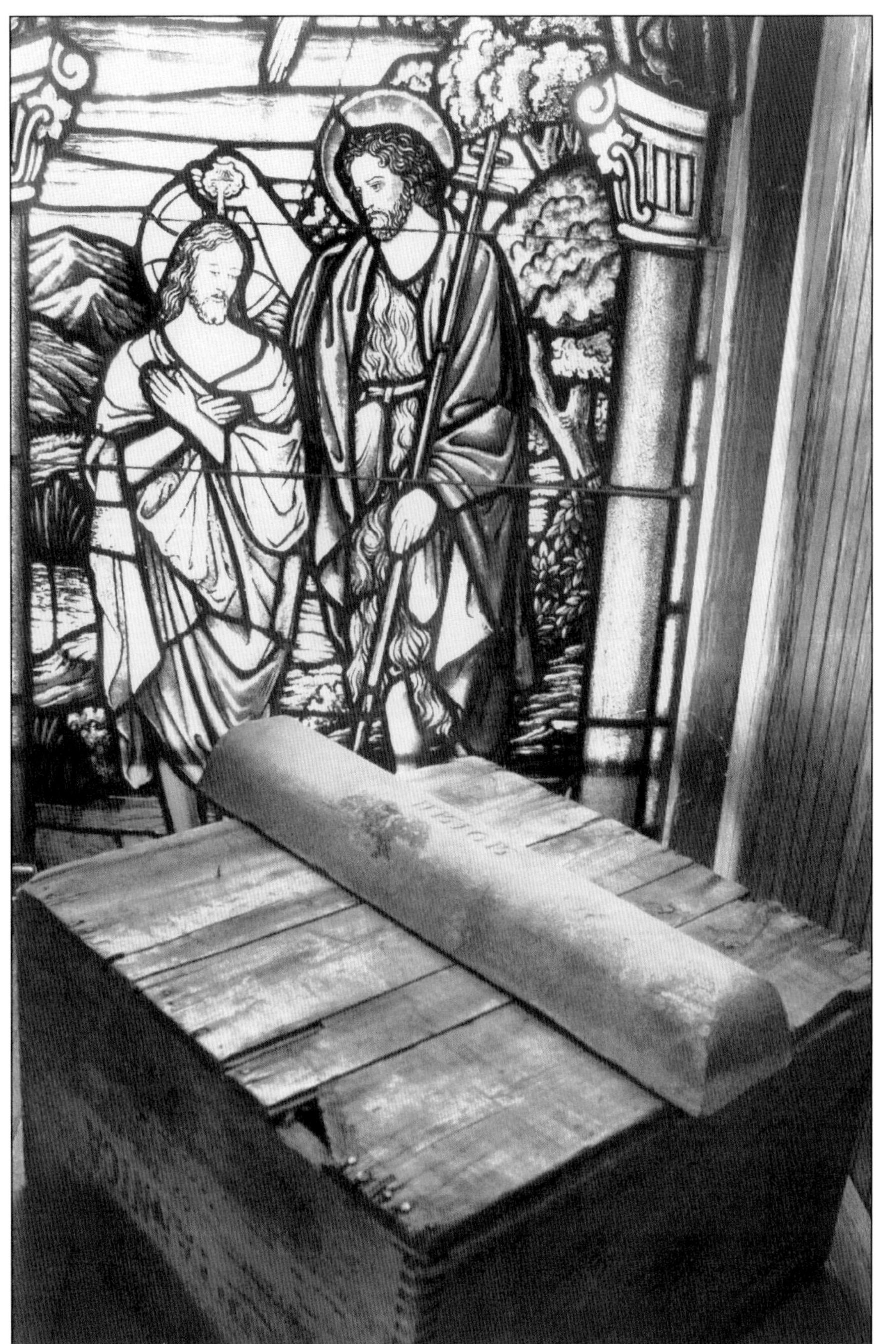

A year before work began on the chapel, a stained glass window was brought in and put on display beside a Cerro Gordo silver bar during the 2005 Thanksgiving celebration. The bar was on loan, but the window still waits to be installed in its rightful place. Silver bars like this are held at the Eastern California Museum in Independence and the Los Angeles Natural History Museum. It weighs approximately 83 pounds, and looks like a loaf of French bread. It was produced by the blast furnaces of Beaudry and Belshaw with ore from the Union Mine, containing at best 25 percent silver. The rest was mostly lead. (Explore Historic California Collection.)

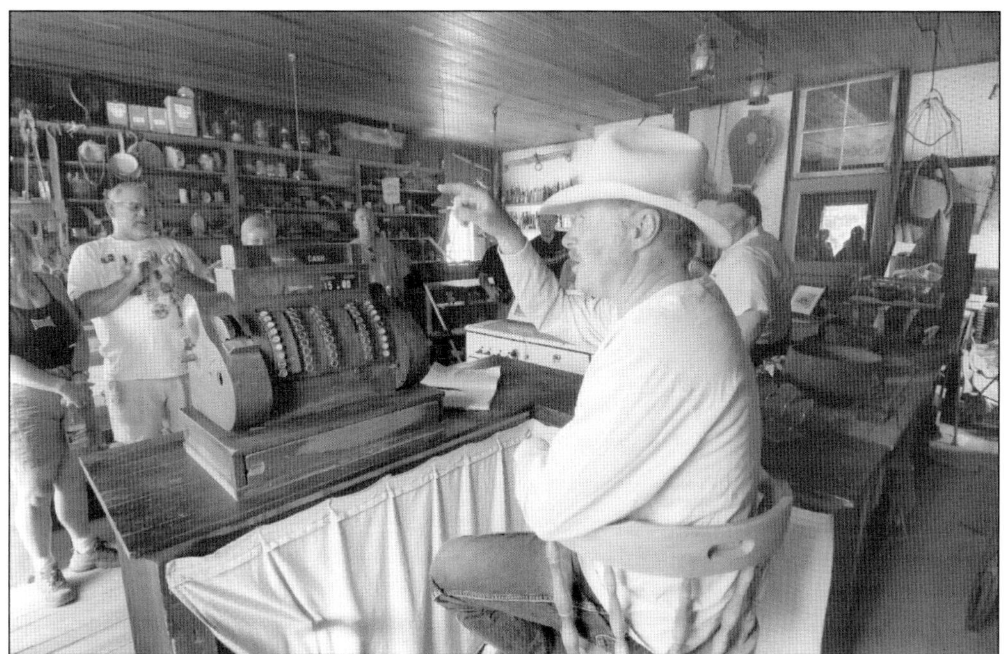

A ghost town owner wears many hats. Above, Mike Patterson is seen in the museum at his finest, telling histories true and farce to a group of visitors. Below, Mike dons an old miner's cap and holds a miner's candle from Cerro Gordo's early days. The soft cap was good for keeping dust off the head in the mines and might protect from a minor scratch, but it did little to prevent real injury. The miner's candleholder would have been stuck in a nearby wall to provide scant light in the darkness of the mine and the hook would hold a miner's lunch pail, keeping the meal warm. (Both, Explore Historic California Collection.)

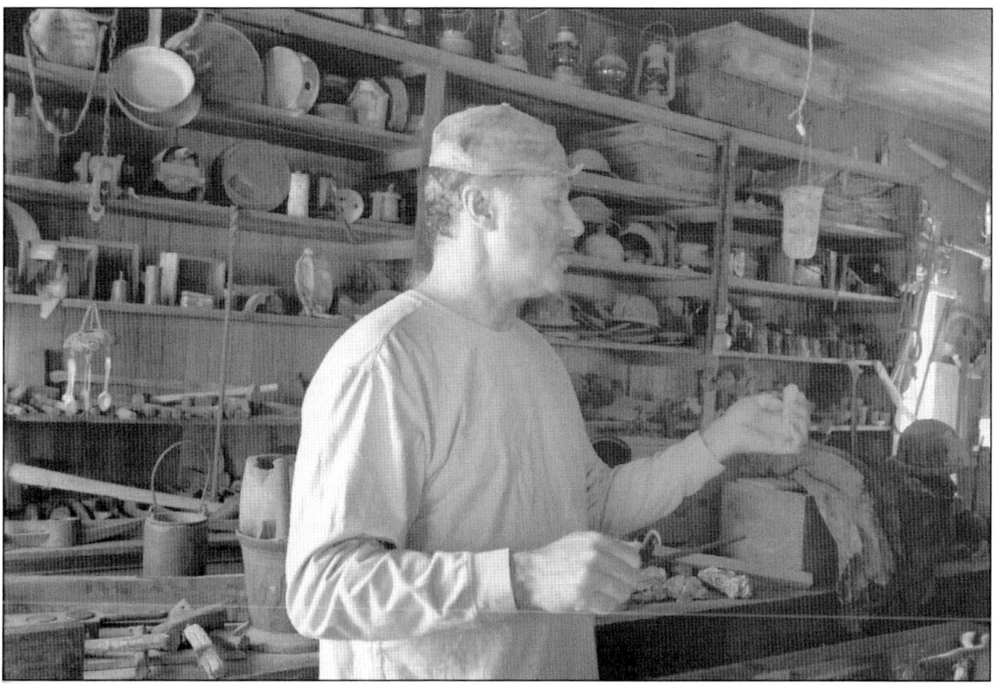

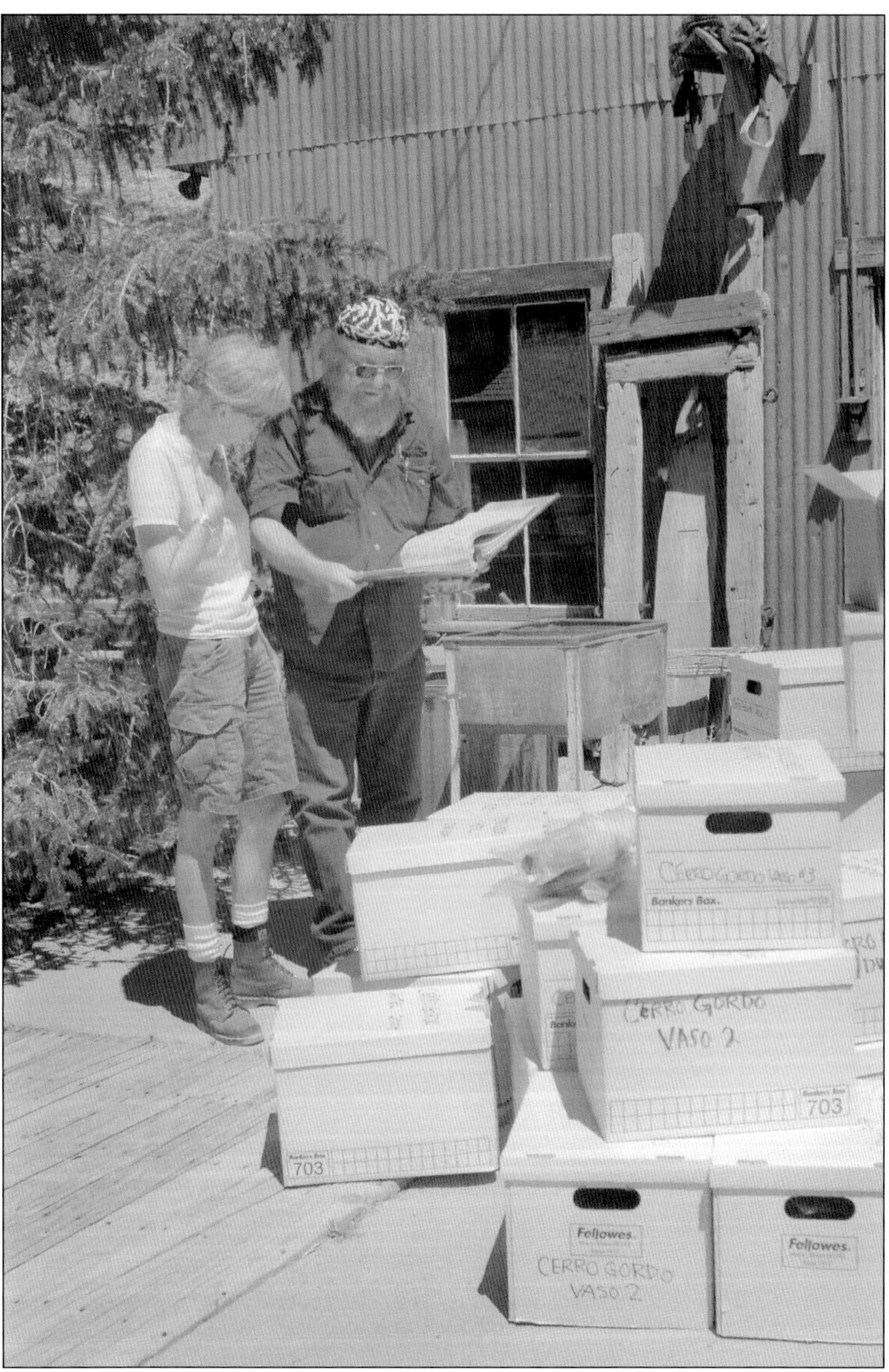

Archaeologists from Antelope Valley College in Lancaster, California, worked with Mike Patterson to catalog and box digs found on his property. Most of the items were from the site of the original Mexican *vasos*, or furnaces, which smelted the silver and lead ore in the early days. (Explore Historic California Collection.)

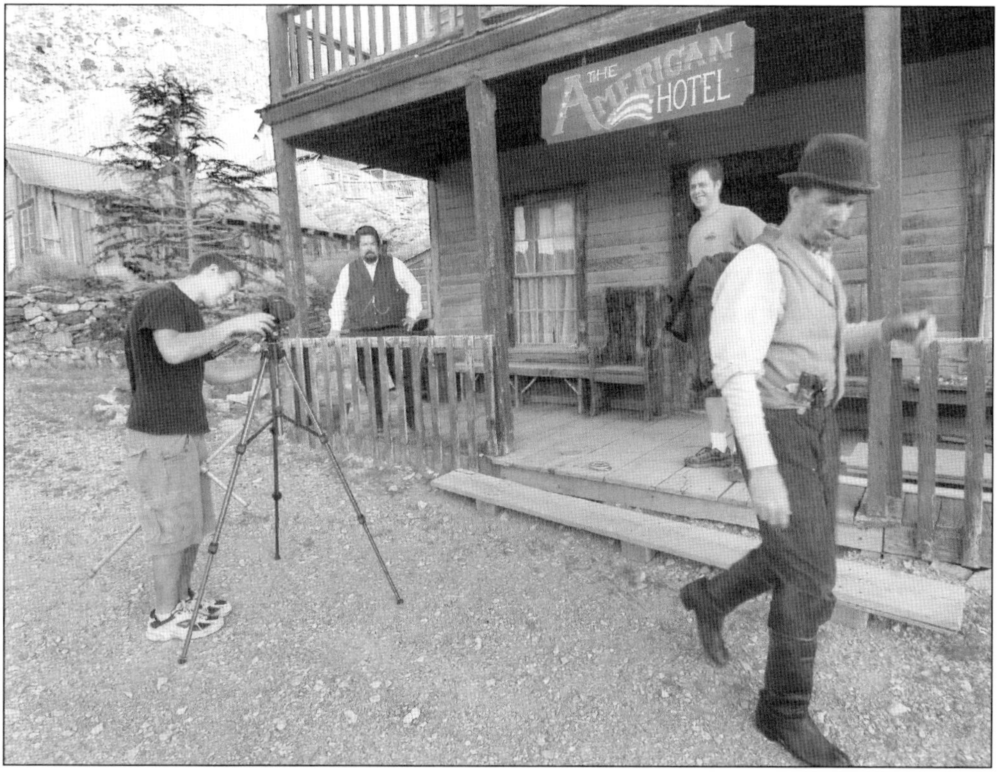

Cerro Gordo has provided background scenes for both noncommercial and commercial film productions. In these two photographs, student filmmaker Seth Castiglione shoots several scenes for his film *Behold the Spirit* with actor Erik Higgins at the American Hotel in 2011. Commercial film credits include the 1966 Henry Hathaway western *Nevada Smith*, staring Steve McQueen, which featured background scenes filmed at Cerro Gordo and the nearby Estelle Mine. Hathaway also used other Owens Valley locations, including the ghost town of Dolomite. Exteriors of the al Qaeda cave where Robert Downey Jr.'s Tony Stark was held captive in 2008's *Iron Man* were filmed below Cerro Gordo on the Yellow Grade Road, which was closed intermittently during the filming. Special effects blasts used at the conclusion of the filming created a significant shockwave and fireball. The 2004 Brian Zor film *Resurrection* used the town for interior and exterior scenes. (Both, Explore Historic California Collection.)

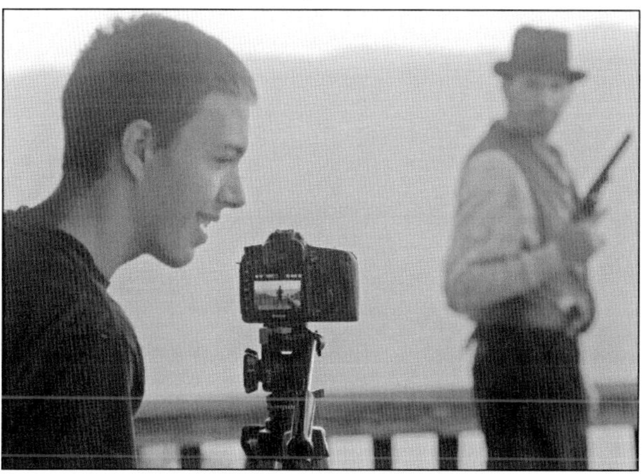

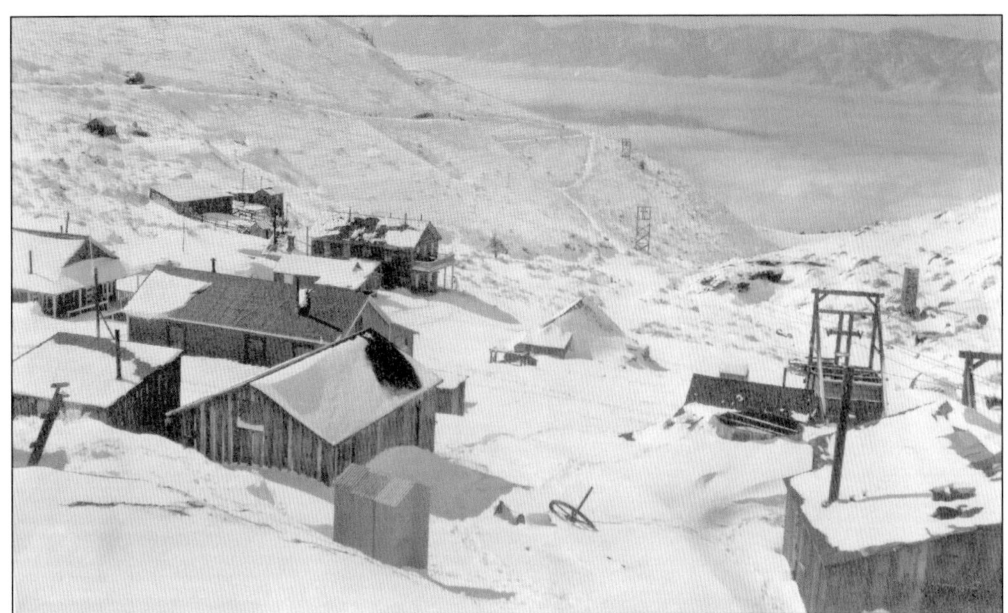

This view of Cerro Gordo from around 1914 shows a snow-covered town during the zinc era looking west to Owens Lake, which is obscured by heavy cloud cover. In the early 20th century, the town had a population of around 100, a far cry from the thousands who lived there 40 years earlier. (L.D. Gordon Collection.)

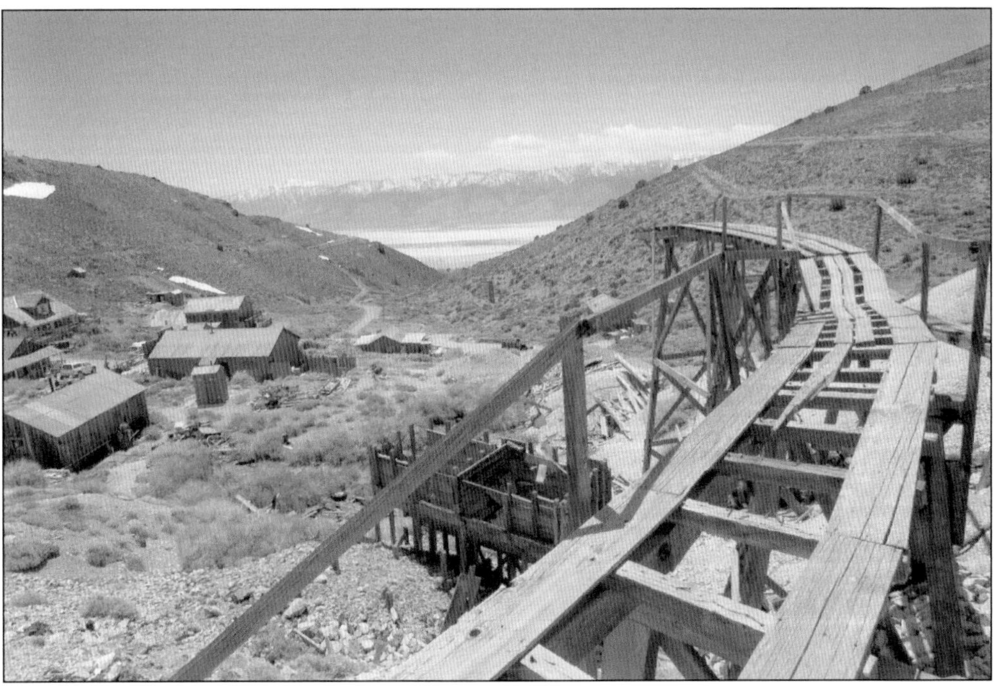

A similar angle from current-day Cerro Gordo shows the remaining structures and Owens Lake drained of its brackish waters. Today, Cerro Gordo's population consists of caretakers and volunteers. (Explore Historic California Collection.)

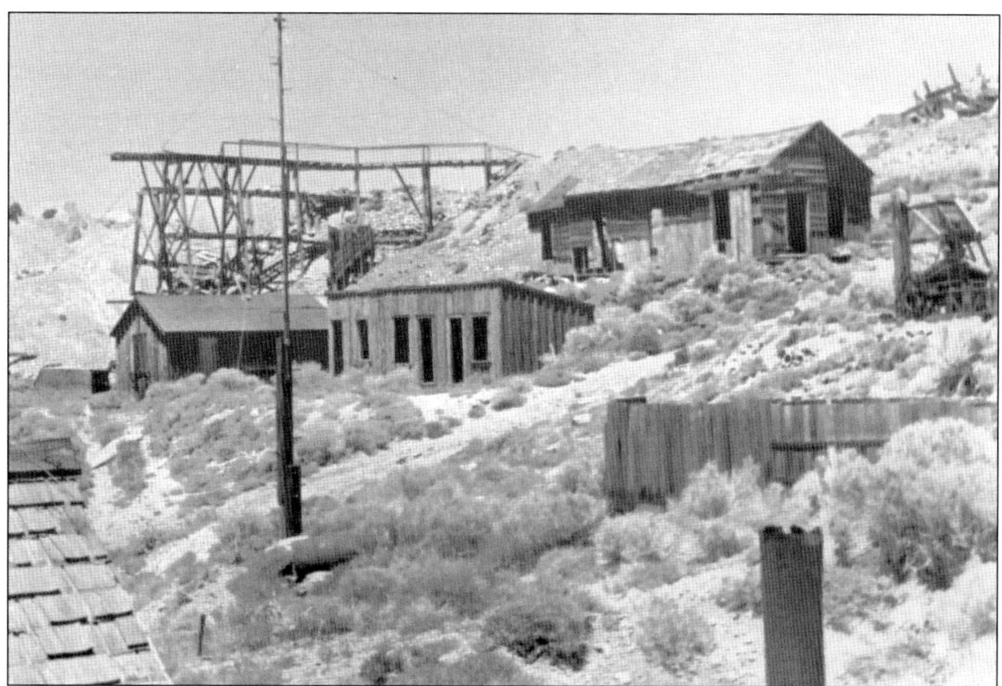

The photograph above, taken by Robert C. Likes in the late 1960s or early 1970s, shows the skeleton of the tram terminal and assorted buildings. A similar scene below from approximately 40 years later shows the gradual disappearance of the historic structures. The ghost town's buildings were damaged by winds and snow. Some were demolished for later reconstruction or because they became unstable and were ready to collapse. (Above, Robert C. Likes Collection; below, Explore Historic California Collection.)

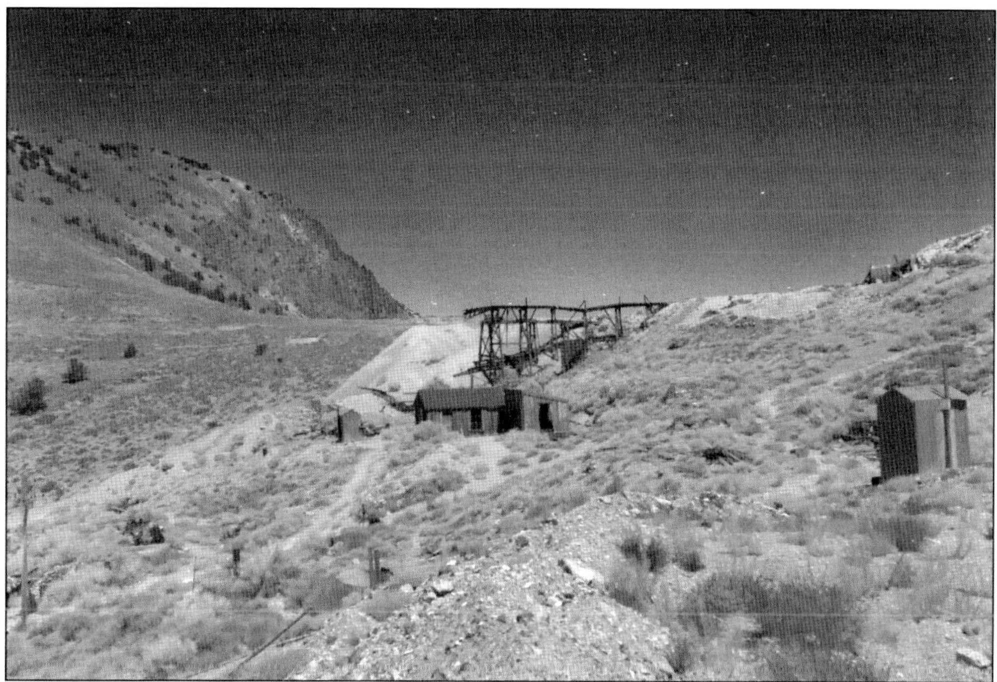

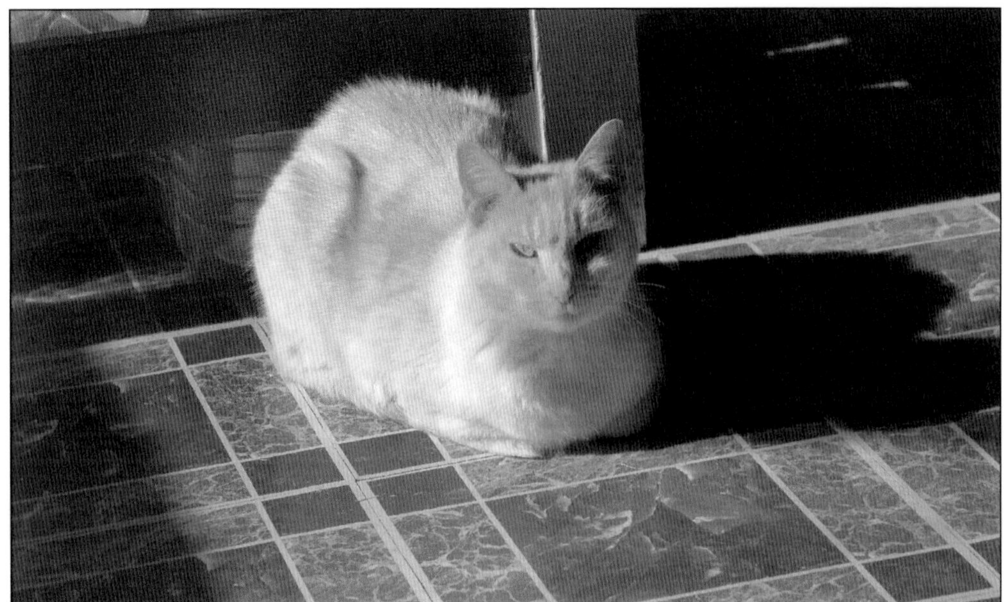

Cats were important in modern Cerro Gordo both as companions and effective rodent killers. Miss Priss, the last of Cerro Gordo's cats, lived in the American Hotel for many years and was a friendly sight for visitors and a terror for the rodents who crossed her path. She would lay out her night's bounty on the floor near the main doorway for whoever opened the hotel in the morning. (Explore Historic California Collection.)

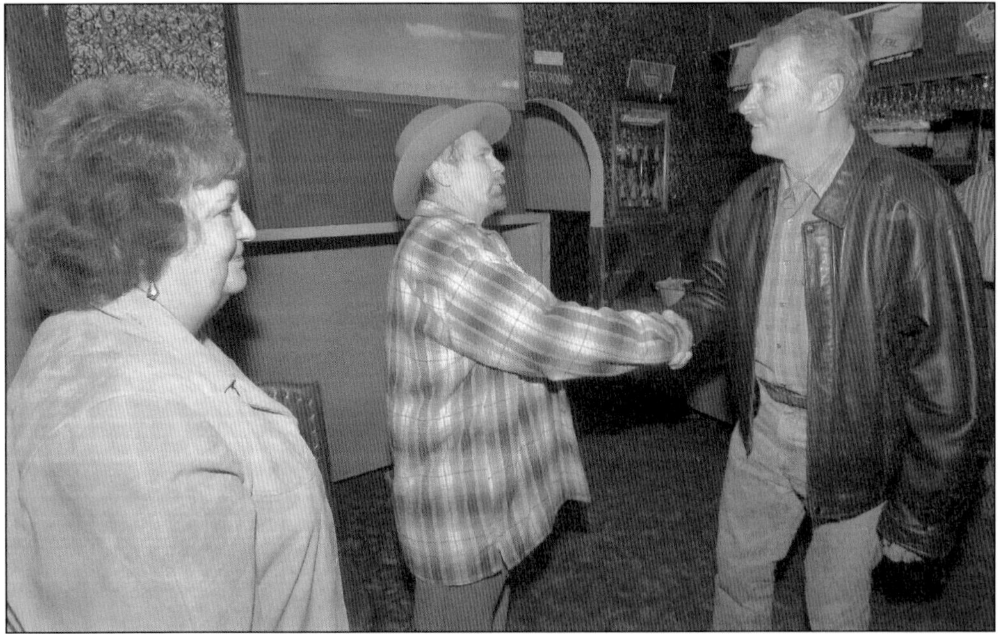

Mike Patterson (right) shakes hands with Robert Desmarais while Robert's wife, Sandy, looks on. Friends and family gathered in a Ridgecrest restaurant for a surprise 60th birthday party for Patterson in 2007. When this photograph was taken, no one knew it showed the future of Cerro Gordo, but when Mike Patterson died in 2009, Robert Desmarais became the resident manager at Cerro Gordo. (Explore Historic California Collection.)

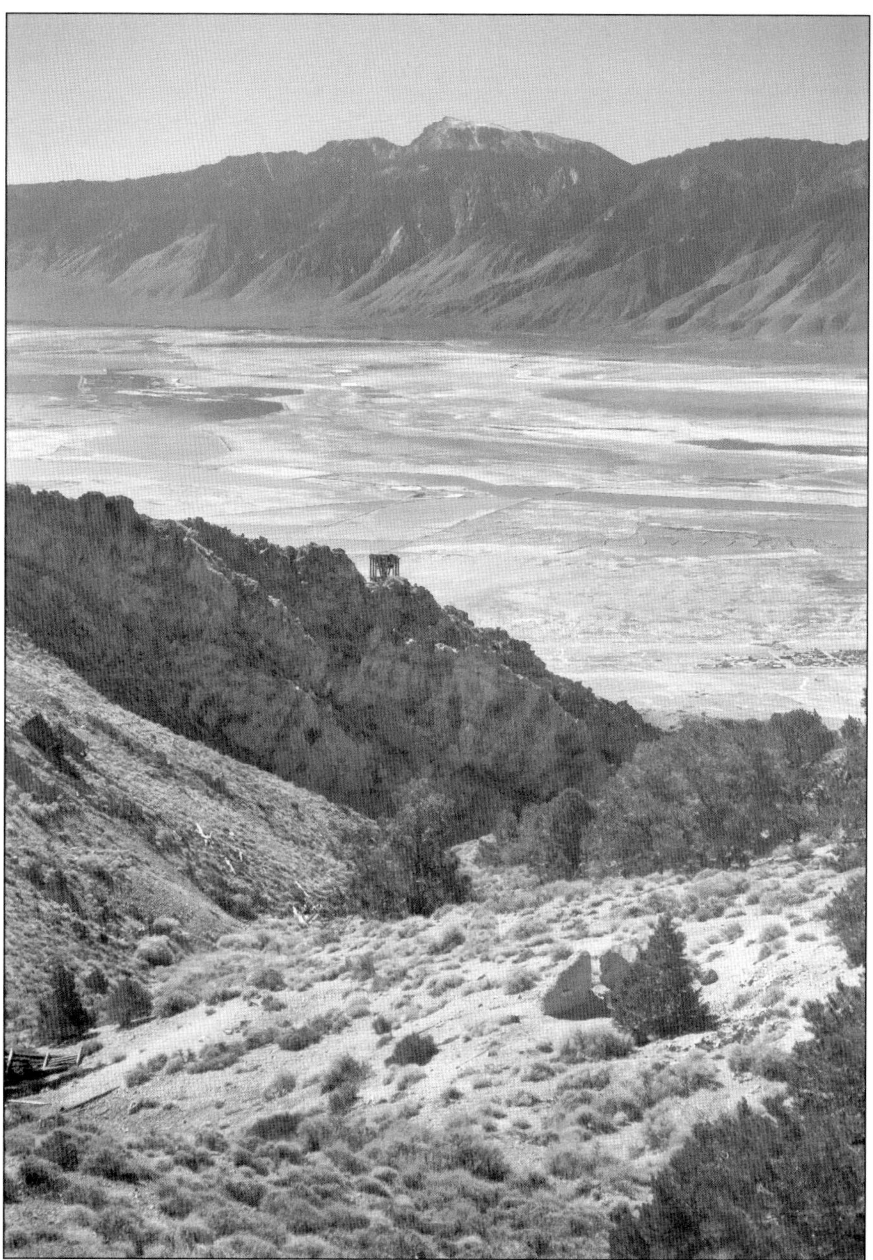

Olancha Peak in the Sierra Nevadas keeps watch over a rewatered Owens Lake and the evidence of mining operations spanning two centuries. Remnants of a Mexican furnace (near the pinion pine at lower right) are from the late 1860s or early 1870s. The silhouetted tram tower on the ridge is from the early 1900s. Owens Lake still reflected the Sierras when the furnace and tram were operational, but began to dry up after water was diverted into the Los Angeles aqueduct. The dry lakebed became a major source of dust pollution and since November 2001, the Los Angeles Department of Water and Power (LADWP) has been flooding sections of the lake in an attempt to control the alkali dust kicked up by frequent winds. After a contentious battle with valley residents and environmentalists, the LADWP was ordered by the courts to take dust mitigation measures. (Explore Historic California Collection.)

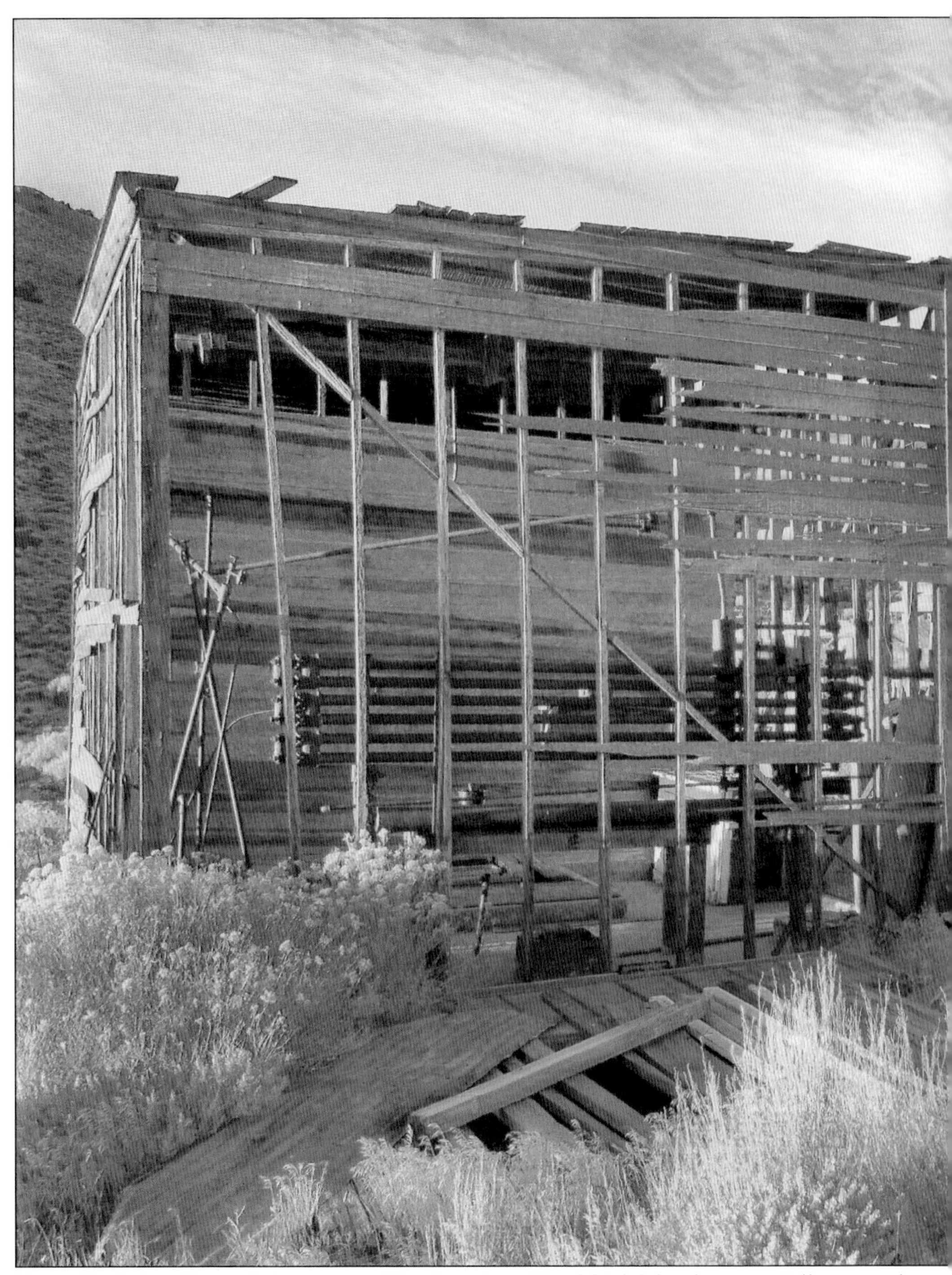

Cerro Gordo is still a work in progress. The American Hotel (right) has been partially restored and reroofed, but the foundation needs additional stabilization. The icehouse (left) deteriorates a little more each year under the constant attack of wind. Volunteers do their best to perpetuate the vision of Jody Stewart and Mike Patterson and keep Cerro Gordo from vanishing into sagebrush, remembered only by books and stories. Cerro Gordo is open to visitors during daylight hours, road

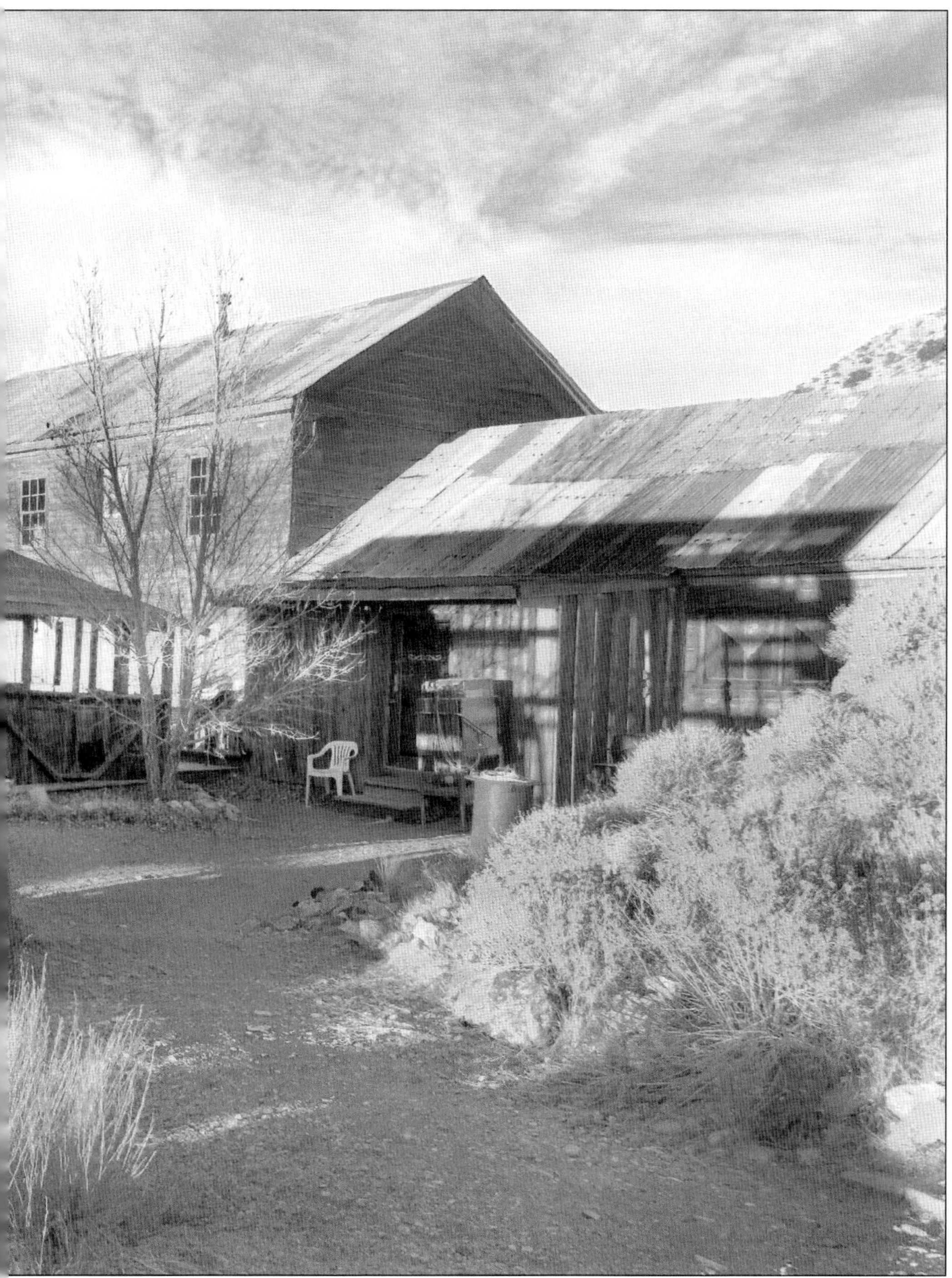

and weather conditions permitting, but there are no amenities (except for outhouses) or overnight accommodations available. The main road is the same today as it was more than a century ago, a poor dirt road that gains 5,000 feet in eight miles from Keeler. The town site is still under private ownership and caretakers live there at all times. The best time to visit is from late spring to early fall. (Explore Historic California Collection.)

Bibliography

Cragen, Dorothy Clara. *The Boys In the Sky Blue Pants*. Fresno, CA: Pioneer Publishing Company, 1975.

DeMarco, Gordon. *A Short History of Los Angeles*. San Francisco: Lexikos, 1988.

Flinchum, Robin. *The Death Valley Red Light Chronicles No. 1: The Life and Times of Cerro Gordo's Lola Travis – Noted Conductress of a Bawdy Dance House*. Tecopa, CA: Half World Books, 2006.

Likes, Robert C. and Glenn R. Day. *From This Mountain Cerro Gordo*. Bishop, CA: Chalfant Press, 1975.

———. *Looking Back at Cerro Gordo*. Pittsburgh, PA: RoseDog Books, 2010.

Nadeau, Remi. *The City Makers – The Story of Southern California's First Boom, 1868–76*. Corona Del Mar, CA: Trans-Anglo Books, 1977.

———. *Ghost Towns and Mining Camps of California – A History and Guide*. Santa Barbara, CA: Crest Publishers, 1990.

———. *The Silver Seekers: They Tamed California's Last Frontier*. Santa Barbara, CA: Crest Publishers, 1977.

Vargo, Cecile Page. *Cerro Gordo: A Ghost Town Caught Between Two Centuries*. Ridgecrest, CA: Historical Society of the Upper Mojave Desert, 2012.

———. *Louis D. Gordon: The Man Behind Cerro Gordo's Zinc Era*. Proceedings of the Eighth Death Valley Conference on History and Prehistory, January 31 to February 3, 2008. Death Valley, CA: Death Valley '49ers Publication Committee, 2008.

———. *The Reinvention of Cerro Gordo*. Boom Town History Centennial Celebration of Nye County, Nevada, and Death Valley–Area Mining Camps. Amargosa, Nevada: Nevada Boomtown History Event, 2006.

Walton, John. *Western Times and Water Wars: State, Culture and Rebellion in California*. Berkeley, CA: University of California Press, 1993.

Weight, Harold O. *Lost Mines of Death Valley*. Twentynine Palms, CA: Calico Press. 1970.

IMAGES

The Cerro Gordo Collection, courtesy Mike Patterson.
The Explore Historic California Collection, courtesy Roger W. Vargo and Cecile Page Vargo.
The Jack Freer Collection, courtesy Jack Freer.
The L.D. Gordon Collection, courtesy of Douglas Gordon.
The Mary Grimsley Collection, courtesy Mary Grimsley.
The Robert C. Likes Collection, courtesy Robert C. Likes, Phyllis Likes Fludine.
Inyo Independent newspaper archives courtesy Barbara Moss and the Laws Railroad Museum and the Bishop Museum and Historical Society, Bishop, CA.

Consistent with our mission to preserve history on a local level, this book was printed in South Carolina on American-made paper and manufactured entirely in the United States. Products carrying the accredited Forest Stewardship Council (FSC) label are printed on 100 percent FSC-certified paper.

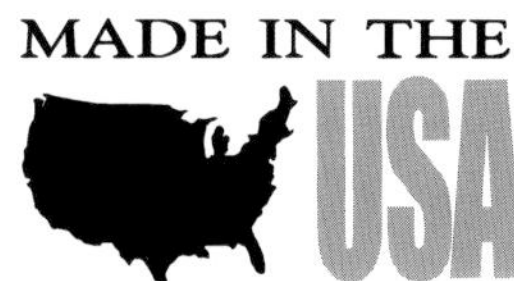